THE
CONFEDERATE
COOKBOOK

*Family Favorites from
the Sons of Confederate Veterans*

THE
CONFEDERATE
COOKBOOK

Family Favorites from the Sons of Confederate Veterans

Edited by Lynda Moreau

Foreword by Patrick J. Griffin III

PELICAN PUBLISHING COMPANY
Gretna 2000

First printing, July 2000
Second printing, October 2000

*The word "Pelican" and the depiction of a pelican are trademarks
of Pelican Publishing Company, Inc., and are registered in the
U.S. Patent and Trademark Office.*

Cover illustration by:
Henry E. Kidd
Kidd Historic Gallery
1-800-423-2237

Back photo: *Historic Elm Springs, International Headquarters of the Sons of
Confederate Veterans and Military Order of the Stars and Bars, Columbia,
Tennessee. Built in 1837.*

Library of Congress Cataloging-in-Publication Data

Moreau, Lynda
  The confederate cookbook: family favorites from the Sons of Confederate Veterans /
edited by Lynda Moreau ; foreword by Patrick J. Griffin III.
    p. cm.
  Includes index.
  ISBN 1-56554-686-5 (alk. paper)
  1. Cookery, American. I. Sons of Confederate Veterans (Organization) II. Title.

TX715 .M8357 2000
641.5973—dc21

00-035979

Printed in the United States of America
Published by Pelican Publishing Company, Inc.
1000 Burmaster Street, Gretna, Louisiana 70053

"Food! Food! Why did the stomach have a longer memory than the mind? . . . There were apples, yams, peanuts, and milk on the table at Tara but never enough of even this primitive fare. At the sight of them, three times a day, her memory would rush back to the old days, the meals of the old days, the candle-lit table and the food perfuming the air."

Margaret Mitchell's *Gone With the Wind,* 1936

"The winter of 63-64 was a terrible winter on us . . . Sometimes, as I had nothing else to employ or interest me, I could indulge in day dreams, sitting by the window looking out—suppose, O suppose, I should see a wagon drive up to the kitchen door, filled—loaded with all sorts of good things, so much of this, and so much of that, and the other, things that I imagined would taste so delightfully."

From *The Civil War Diary of Anne S. Frobel,*
© by Friends of Fort Ward, Fort Ward Museum, 1992,
EPM Publications, Inc., Delaplane, VA 20144.

Contents

Foreword

FROM FLORIDA TO ALASKA, from California to Maine and beyond, you'll find the homes of descendants of Confederate veterans who have migrated to all fifty states, the District of Columbia, and some twenty countries. Each household is historically intertwined with the bond of a proud family heritage and the remembrance of a noble ancestral struggle for Southern independence.

This cookbook presents an interesting array of time-honored family recipes handed down from one generation to the next, as well as a variety of contemporary local and regional specialties. For generations, descendants of Confederate soldiers have represented the very essence of the fabric of society, and our kitchens continue to inspire the gracious concept of "dining in" and sharing good times with family and friends.

We trust that you will find *The Confederate Cookbook: Family Favorites from the Sons of Confederate Veterans* to be one of the most interesting and diversified cookbooks available today. Fascinating anecdotes and some previously unpublished images of identified Confederate soldiers are here for your enjoyment, along with easy-to-use instructions on how to make some of the most delicious dishes ever to grace your sideboard.

We hope that the selection of recipes herein may provide hours of pleasure to those interested in good food and fine dining, and that the individual stories of courage and sacrifice included with the recipes may encourage and inspire others to explore the history of their own families.

PATRICK J. GRIFFIN III, COMMANDER IN CHIEF
SONS OF CONFEDERATE VETERANS
1998-2000

Opposite—Patrick J. Griffin III

Acknowledgments

FELLOW COMPATRIOT AND CO-AUTHOR of *The South Was Right!* Donny Kennedy of Louisiana just knew that an SCV cookbook was a good idea, and fortunately many of us agreed with him when he introduced the concept to the Sons of Confederate Veterans.

The inspiration for this project came from Lynda Moreau, publicist and cheerleader for Pelican Publishing Company in Gretna, Louisiana. Lynda championed the project and provided an excellent presentation before the SCV General Executive Council that culminated in approval and an abundance of interesting work for all parties involved with the undertaking. She is indefatigable and volunteered to contact compatriots, organize recipes, write the manuscript, promote the cookbook, and answer all questions. Lynda's volunteer involvement with this project is the reason that the cookbook will be published and become a success.

The management of Pelican Publishing Company is commended for its professional products, for promotion of our Southern heritage, and for believing in the commercial viability of a Sons of Confederate Veterans cookbook.

SCV Chief of Protocol Bruce Hillis of Missouri, chairman of the SCV cookbook committee, was instrumental in keeping all facets of this endeavor moving forward within the SCV. Bruce contacted many compatriots and organized the flow of information.

Compatriot Henry Kidd of Virginia, a member of the SCV cookbook committee, provided original color artwork for the front cover. Henry's patience with all of us is appreciated, and, as usual, he has produced another stylish rendering.

SCV Historian in Chief Gregg S. Clemmer of Maryland provided text on the history of the SCV, our headquarters at Elm Springs (located in Columbia, Tennessee), and contemporary views of the organization.

Compatriot and artist Ray Driver of Maryland provided original artwork for some line drawings used in the book.

SCV Chief of Staff Patrick J. Hardy, M.D., of Missouri assisted early in the project with recipes and promotion in many states. Dr. Hardy has steadfastly supported this undertaking and has walked the extra mile to ensure its success.

SCV Executive Director Maitland O. Westbrook III of Tennessee was instrumental in researching information and contacting compatriots.

SCV Editor in Chief James N. Vogler, Jr., made room for cookbook promotion and advertising space in *Confederate Veteran* magazine.

Army of Trans-Mississippi Department Commander Edwin L. Deason led the way in promoting the work in the Western region.

Past Commander in Chief Peter W. Orlebeke supplied recipes in a timely fashion and championed the work in Texas.

Compatriot Peter M. Griffin of Maryland coordinated recipes from that state and provided research.

The SCV staff at Elm Springs constantly promoted the venture to our compatriots during business hours. A hearty thanks is given to office manager Patricia Scribner and secretaries Daphne Sullivan, Connie Morris, Cindy Jackson, Wendi Harvey, and Nikki Baggert.

The Colonel John Washington Inzer House Museum, Ashville, Alabama, is recognized for early assistance, support, and promotion.

Compatriot Darrell Glover of Alabama is noted for his enthusiasm, first submission of a Confederate image, and early promotion of the project.

Missouri Division Commander Darrell Maples solicited early responses in his state, prompting other divisions to sign on to the project in a timely fashion.

A hearty Confederate thank you is extended to all of our volunteer compatriots who supplied recipes and lent their personal time to ensure the success of this work.

Deo Vindice!

Sons of Confederate Veterans: A Century of Service, Heritage, and Honor

THE GREETINGS HAD BEEN SAID; the welcomes had been extended. And, in every circumstance, hearty applause had hailed each speaker at the podium.

But when the old man rose to address the 16th convention of the United Confederate Veterans, a great quiet settled on the meeting hall. There in New Orleans, everyone recognized him, the Commander in Chief. Many called him friend, but a precious few actually remembered.

That was what concerned Lt. Gen. Stephen Dill Lee most that April day in 1906.

There was good news, he reported, opening his remarks with thanks to the good citizens of New Orleans. "Again and again we have returned to taste of the inexhaustible bounty of your hospitality, to be refreshed by the patriotism and enthusiasm of this generous and beautiful city."

Where there had been grief for the captured and humiliated people of New Orleans, men now boasted of pride in the city, "standing second only to New York among American ports of export," he said, a reference that brought good-natured grins and murmurs to the audience. Yet, even in flush times, he reminded them, there was still much to do.

"Comrades, there is one thing committed to our care as a peculiar trust—the memory of the Confederate soldier." Men in the audience who had worn the gray nodded, but they were old soldiers whose numbers daily dwindled. Lee recognized the inevitable, and they knew it, too. Yet, to these surviving veterans, he hammered home a challenge. "We must not overtask posterity by expecting those who come after us to build monuments to heroes whom their own generation were unwilling to commemorate."

Lee directed his remarks to the veterans, citing first the recent death of Gen. Joe Wheeler, then reminding all Confederates there that day of their own mortality. Younger men watched and heard his words. They represented a growing number in the sea of faces at the convention hall. They had no firsthand knowledge of the carnage and sacrifice that had so scarred Lee's generation. But to honor their fathers, they had formed their own heritage society—the United Sons of Confederate Veterans—a decade earlier.

"To you, Sons of Confederate Veterans, we will commit the vindication of the cause for which we fought," he declared. "To your strength will be given the defense of the Confederate soldier's good name, the guardianship of his history, the emulation of his virtues, the perpetuation of those principles which he loved and which you love also, and those ideals which made him glorious and which you also cherish."

Stephen Dill looked into the faces of the young men there and, as he had done before on a score of fields a generation before, pressed forward. "Are you also ready to die for your country? Is your life worthy to be remembered along with theirs? Do you choose for yourself this greatness of soul?"

Nearly a hundred years have passed since Lt. Gen. Stephen D. Lee's address to the next generation of his time. The veterans, of course, are long gone, and the "Real Sons" number only a few hundred. But the mission of the Sons of Confederate Veterans (SCV) thrives! With over 700 camps, and more than 27,000 members, the memory and sacrifice of the Confederate soldier and sailor as well as the heritage, history, and record of the Confederate States of America endures.

Today, as the oldest patriotic and hereditary organization for male descendants of Confederate soldiers and sailors, the SCV continues to preserve, defend, and perpetuate the history and principles of the Old South. Non-political by charter and unaffiliated with any organization other than the Military Order of the Stars and Bars, the SCV enters the 21st century with a bright future.

At the 1912 convention held at Macon, Georgia, the United Sons of Confederate Veterans shortened the organizational name to Sons of Confederate Veterans. In the years that followed, membership rose and fell with the times. Efforts directed at battlefield preservation, monument and cemetery upkeep, and record documentation were always foremost.

The civil rights movement of the 1950s and 1960s inadvertently affected the SCV in several peculiar ways. After a half century's record as a commemorative, historical, and preservation organization, agitators on both sides of growing civil rights unrest appropriated such revered Southern symbols as the Confederate Battle Flag and *Dixie* for their own self-serving, intolerant designs.

For over thirty years, the SCV has worked to reverse this damage and theft of Southern icons. The struggle remains a passionate one, yet compatriots across the confederation continue with resolve and dedication to focus their energies on a variety of programs, including

- Record and document preservation
- Genealogical research and assistance
- Confederate grave registration and preservation
- Academic research
- Scholarships—both undergraduate and post-doctoral
- Classroom instruction, from elementary through high school
- Living history presentations
- Defense of Southern and Confederate symbols
- Erection of Confederate monuments
- Maintenance of Confederate monuments and sites
- Cooperation with other hereditary and military groups

In 1992, the SCV, in an effort to establish an international headquarters and broaden its outreach, purchased historic Elm Springs in Columbia, Tennessee, an antebellum Greek Revival mansion built in 1837. Facing the Mooresville Pike (the old stage road from Pulaski to Franklin), Elm Springs witnessed some stirring scenes during the war, including the Confederate march north to Franklin in November 1864.

Today, Elm Springs is international headquarters to the SCV and headquarters of the Military Order of the Stars and Bars. With more than a century of service to the memory and honor of the men who wore the butternut and gray, the SCV stands poised for an exciting entry into the next century.

GREGG CLEMMER
HISTORIAN IN CHIEF
SONS OF CONFEDERATE VETERANS

Why Join the Sons of Confederate Veterans?

TODAY THERE ARE MORE than 27,000 members of the Sons of Confederate Veterans. Each compatriot has a genealogical link to soldiers who sought to preserve constitutional freedom by fighting for Southern independence.

Membership in the SCV is a rewarding experience, offering a continuous common bond—a bond once shared by the veterans themselves and preserved today by their descendants. Fellow compatriots enjoy many benefits, such as the right to attend local meetings in any of some 700 camps, a subscription to the bimonthly *Confederate Veteran* magazine and newsletters, access to the Confederate grave registration and Confederate monument databases, the opportunity to meet and learn from fellow compatriots at division and national conventions, and the chance to learn more about our heritage through historical and genealogical research.

The SCV is non-political and non-sectarian.

Membership is open to all male descendants of any veteran who served honorably in the Confederate armed forces. The minimum age for membership is 12, and an applicant must be able to establish his kinship to a veteran through genealogical records. Both lineal and collateral kinship is acceptable.

A team of regional genealogists will be delighted to assist potential members in proving their heritage by documenting an individual's relationship to his ancestor in the Confederate forces. In most cases, this process is not difficult. Give it a try, and establish a link to your past that will provide a valuable understanding of your American heritage for your family and future generations to contemplate and enjoy. It's fun, it's patriotic, and your posterity will be proud of the contributions your ancestor made to ensure American prosperity and the foundation upon which the nation was built.

Membership information: call 800-MY-DIXIE or 800-MY-SOUTH

SCV International Headquarters
P.O. Box 59, Elm Springs
Columbia, Tennessee 38402-0059

Learn more about the SCV by visiting our website at www.scv.org.

THE CONFEDERATE COOKBOOK

Family Favorites from
the Sons of Confederate Veterans

Appetizers
and
Libations

Shadow Hill Shrimp Paste
Easy Seven Layer Dip
Texas Mucho Torpedoes
Ham Balls
Mint Tea
Hot Curried Cheese Dip
Yvonne's Barbecued Meatballs
Cheesy Rice Salsa
Blue Crab Dip
Cheese-Covered Chicken Gizzards
Vidalia Onion Dip
Cucumber Spread
Hot Spinach Dip
Cindy's Strawberry Cheese Ball
Broccoli Bread
Charleston Cheese
Hot Creamy Sausage Dip
May Hall's Baked Crab Spread
Beef Dip Spread

Liver Nips
Sausage Balls
Mexican Dip
Frances Haley's Favorite
   Barbecued Shrimp
Charlie's Savannah Onion Soup
17th Virginia Beef Jerky
Bourbon Slush
Carolina Plantation Punch
Mom's Clam Dip
Aunt Joh's Summer Veranda
   Cheese Puffs
Confederate Chewing Gum
Hot Broccoli Dip
Spinach Artichoke Casserole
Steel Magnolia Cheese Ball
Azalea Punch
Famous Feaster Family Punch
Caviar Crown

Shadow Hill Shrimp Paste

A classic appetizer from the Shadow Hill Tea Room in Hernando, Mississippi

1 pound cooked shrimp,
   cut up
1 green pepper, cut up
1 cup mayonnaise
2 packages cream cheese

1 stalk celery, cut up
$\frac{1}{2}$ teaspoon mace
Tabasco to taste
Worcestershire sauce to taste
Salt to taste

*M*ix all ingredients and serve in bowl surrounded by fancy crackers.

This recipe was used by my great aunt Mrs. Mae Talbot Holmes, when she ran a tearoom in her home in Hernando, Mississippi. Her establishment was in business from the 1920s through the 1950s and was well known among patrons all around the mid-South.

★
John T. Fargason
Frontier Guard Camp #996
Junction, Texas
★

Great-grandson
Pvt. Lawrence Ewel Talbot
Co. D, McDonald's Battalion

Pvt. Talbot was born in Jackson, Tennessee. He enlisted at the age of 16 and rode with Nathan Bedford Forrest from 1863 to 1865. He was paroled in Selma, Alabama, and died in 1919.

Easy Seven Layer Dip

A real favorite at parties!

1 pound ground beef
1 packet taco seasoning mix
1 can refried beans
1½ cups Mozzarella cheese
1 medium size jar of salsa (hot
    or mild, as you prefer)

1½ cups cheddar cheese
1 cup sour cream
Pickled jalapeño pepper slices

*B*rown ground beef and drain. Add taco seasoning mix to ground beef. In a 2-quart casserole dish, layer the refried beans, ground beef, and mozzarella cheese. Put in a 350-degree oven until cheese melts. Remove from oven and layer the salsa and cheddar cheese. Put back in the oven and bake at 350 degrees for about 15 minutes. Finally, layer the sour cream and sliced jalapeño peppers, and it's ready to eat. Serve with large tortilla chips. Dip is best if kept warm.

★

**Phillip B. Isaacs
Col. Samuel H. Walkup
Camp #1375
Union County, North Carolina**

★

**Great-great-grandson
Pvt. Godfrey Isaacs
Co. A, 28th Regiment, North
Carolina Troops**

Pvt. Isaacs was wounded at Petersburg and surrendered with Lee at Appomattox. His great-great-grandfather was a patriot colonel in the American Revolution. Godfrey and his wife, Pharabe Willey Issacs, both lived to a ripe old age. The chimney from their fireplace can still be seen on what used to be their homeplace.

*Opposite—Godfrey Isaacs
Private, Company A, 28th Regiment
North Carolina Troops*

Texas Mucho Torpedoes

A delicious appetizer that disappears fast

1 (10-ounce) can large, whole, pickled jalapeños, drained
1 (6-ounce) can tuna or crab-meat, drained
¼ cup all-purpose flour
2 tablespoons of corn meal
¼ teaspoon salt
¼ teaspoon pepper
1 cup buttermilk
½ cup flour
¼ cup corn meal
Vegetable oil

Note: You may wish to wear disposable plastic gloves while stuffing peppers.

Cut stems from jalapeños and scoop out seeds with a small, sharp knife (do not cut peppers). Stuff each pepper with meat and set aside. Combine ¼ cup all-purpose flour with next four ingredients to make a batter. Stir until smooth, and set aside. Dip stuffed peppers into the batter and then dredge in ½ cup flour and ¼ cup corn meal. Pour oil to depth of 2-3 inches in a large Dutch oven or a Fry Daddy. Fry jalapeños a few at a time, 1-2 minutes on each side until golden brown. Drain on paper towels. Yields 30 appetizers.

★
Bob G. Davis
Col. George R. Reeves
Camp #349
Sherman, Texas
★
Great-great-grandson
Pvt. Robert R. Bogle
Co. F., 7th Tennessee Infantry

Ham Balls

The tastiest tidbit at the party

1½ pounds sausage
1½ pounds smoked ground
   ham

2 cups crackers, crushed
1 cup milk
2 eggs

*R*oll into 1½-inch balls and bake at 350 degrees for 45 minutes, turning once.

Glaze
½ cup vinegar
2 teaspoons horseradish

1 teaspoon prepared mustard
½ cup water
1 cup brown sugar

*M*ix above ingredients and bring to a boil. Pour over the ham balls and bake another 45 minutes.

★
Roger Hatcher Waring
Fincastle Rifles Camp #1326
Roanoke, Virginia
★
Great-grandson
Pvt. John Ellis Hatcher
Co. D, 4th Virginia Cavalry

When Pvt. Hatcher returned home, months after the war, he arrived in the middle of the night. Rather than wake the family before breakfast, he slept in the yard. He was born and buried in Bedford, Virginia.

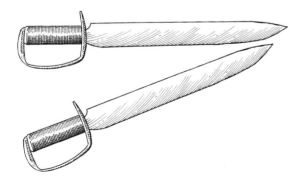

Mint Tea

A refreshing non-alcoholic alternative to the mint julep

5 family-size tea bags	2 small cans orange juice
12 sprigs mint	2 lemons
1 quart boiling water	1 cup pineapple juice
2 cups sugar	1 quart ginger ale

*P*our water over tea bags and mint. Steep for 15 minutes. Pour over sugar. Chill tea before adding juice. Mix orange juice, lemon juice, and pineapple juice. Add to mixture. Add ginger ale when ready to serve. Serve over ice and enjoy. Serves 8-10.

For those Southern belles who would rather leave the mint juleps to the Southern gentlemen, here is a very refreshing brew. It's wonderful for an afternoon tea party on the lawn.

★

Peter W. Orlebeke
Gaston-Gregg Camp #1384
Dallas, Texas

★

Great-grandson
5th Sgt. Wilborn Curry
Co. A, 37th Arkansas Infantry

Wilborn Curry was a farmer living in Arkansas with his wife and children when the war broke out. He enlisted as the Federals were advancing on Arkansas, and was captured at the Battle of Helena. He and his brother-in-law spent eight months at Alton Military Prison. They were later transferred to Fort Delaware. Wilborn survived prison, but his brother-in-law did not. When Wilborn was paroled, he walked back home to Arkansas. Wilborn had jet-black hair when he left to join the army. When he returned home, his hair was snow white. His family did not know who he was until he spoke and they recognized his voice. After the war, he moved to Texas and became active in the United Confederate Veterans. He lived a long life and died in 1912.

Hot Curried Cheese Dip

Serve with crackers and raw vegetables

1 package cream cheese
2 tablespoons milk
¹/₂ cup sour cream
1 (2¹/₂-ounce) package dried
   beef, chopped
2 tablespoons onions,
   chopped

¹/₈ teaspoon black pepper
1 tablespoon green peppers,
   chopped
1¹/₂ teaspoons curry powder
¹/₃ cup chopped nuts

*B*lend cream cheese and milk until smooth. Add sour cream. Add other ingredients except nuts and blend with mixer at low speed. Spoon in baking dish and sprinkle with nuts. Cover and chill. Before serving, heat in preheated 350-degree oven for 20 minutes.

★

**Samuel Terrell ("Terry")
Rowell
Jasper County Grays
Camp #1349
Heidelberg, Mississippi**

★

**Great-great-grandnephew
Lt. Col. James Stephens Terral
7th Mississippi Battalion**

On October 4, 1862, Lt. Col. James Terral was mortally wounded at Shiloh. An eyewitness reported that he was "shot all to pieces." When he was shot from his horse, both legs and arms were broken and he had taken 4-5 bullets through the body. His last words were "Knock them off of their guns, boys, for I can't do it anymore." He succumbed shortly thereafter.

Yvonne's Barbecued Meatballs

A hearty party appetizer that freezes well

Meatballs

3 pounds ground round
1 (12-ounce) can evaporated
  milk
1 cup oatmeal
1 cup cracker crumbs

2 eggs
$\frac{1}{2}$ cup chopped onion
1 teaspoon garlic powder
2 teaspoons salt
1 teaspoon pepper
3-4 teaspoons chili powder

**Steven W. McFarlane
Matthew Fontaine Maury
Camp #1722
Fredericksburg, Virginia**
★
**Great-great-grandson
Pvt. Augustus McFarlane
Co. I, 34th Battalion,
Virginia Cavalry**

To make meatballs, combine all ingredients (mixture will be soft) and shape into walnut-sized balls. If you want to make in advance to use later, place meatballs in a single layer on wax-paper-lined cookie sheets and freeze until solid. Store frozen meatballs in freezer bags until ready to use. To make sauce, combine all sauce ingredients and stir until sugar is dissolved. When ready to cook frozen meatballs, place them in a 13-inch by 9-inch by 2-inch baking pan and pour on the sauce. Bake at 350 degrees for 1 hour.

Sauce

3-4 cups catsup
1 pound brown sugar
1 teaspoon Liquid Smoke

1 teaspoon garlic powder
$\frac{1}{2}$ cup chopped onion
1 (16-ounce) can tomato
  sauce

Recipe can also be made fresh and baked immediately. To do this, place fresh meatballs in single layers in a 12-inch by 17-inch by 2-inch light-colored aluminum pan. Pour on sauce and bake at least 1 hour and 15 minutes. For optimum flavor, meatballs should be cooked until well done. If using a dark-coated pan, you may not need to cook them as long. Serve hot. Yield is 80 meatballs.

Cheesy Rice Salsa

Works well as an appetizer or an entrée

2 cups water
2 chicken bouillon cubes
1 cup long grain rice
1 pound chicken or turkey, ground
1 (14½-ounce) can tomatoes, diced
1 (15-ounce) can tomato sauce

3 teaspoons sugar
½ teaspoon garlic powder
¼ teaspoon onion powder
¼ cup fresh basil, chopped
4 ounces Velveeta loaf cheese
Salt and pepper to taste
White tortilla chips

*P*repare rice according to package directions, dissolving bouillon in the boiling water just before adding the rice. Set aside. Brown ground chicken. Add next 6 ingredients and simmer over low heat for 15 minutes. Combine rice and sauce. Add cheese, stirring until smooth. Season with salt and pepper. Serve with white corn tortilla chips.

★

Kenneth Smith
Chattahoochee Guards
Camp #1639
Mableton, Georgia

★

Great-great-grandson
Color Sgt. Thomas Hines Kennon
Co. H (Young Guards),
3rd Georgia Infantry

Thomas Kennon enlisted in the Confederate forces in 1861 and was present at the surrender at Appomattox. He was the color bearer for his regiment, and was one of the few that survived the war. He died in 1922. The regimental flag he proudly carried is now on display at the Georgia State Capitol, complete with bullet holes.

Blue Crab Dip

The hit of the party!

3 cups blue crab meat
3 (8-ounce) packages cream
  cheese
½ cup Miracle Whip
2 teaspoons powdered sugar

2 teaspoons powdered mustard
¼ cup sherry
Dash of garlic juice
Salt to taste
Onion salt to taste

*B*lend all ingredients. Heat in a double boiler and turn into a casserole dish. Bake for 20 minutes in a 375-degree oven. Serve with chips or crackers.

I have no idea how long my family has been using this prized recipe. Naturally, it has been modified over the years to take advantage of modern ingredients.

★
**William D. Hogan
CSS *Florida* Camp #102
Orlando, Florida**
★
**Great-grandson
Pvt. William Hogan
Co. G, 4th Georgia Infantry**

William Hogan was a miller by trade. During the war, he and his regiment served as guards at Andersonville Prison.

Cheese-Covered Chicken Gizzards

Believe it or not, kids love them!

2 packages chicken gizzards
Salt and pepper to taste
2 eggs
⅓ cup milk
2 cups flour

Tony Chachere's seasoning to
　taste
Oil for frying
Grated cheese

★
Roger White
Brig. Gen. Thomas M. Scott
Camp #1604
Minden, Louisiana
★
Descendant of
Pvt. Edward Eugene Pratt
Co. G., 8th Louisiana Infantry

Season gizzards and pressure-cook for 15 minutes, or boil for 30 minutes. Drain and let cool. Mix eggs with milk and seasonings in one bowl. Mix flour and seasonings in another bowl. Dip gizzards in egg wash and then dredge in flour. Fry in hot oil until crispy, and drain. Quickly sprinkle generously with grated cheese and cover with foil to keep hot and melt the cheese.

This one will fool you! The first time I made this recipe, my wife thought I was crazy, but now we are hooked!

Vidalia Onion Dip

Fast and easy

1 (8-ounce) package cream
    cheese
1 (8-ounce) package Swiss
    cheese, shredded

1 Vidalia onion, chopped
1 cup mayonnaise

*M*ix together and bake for 20 minutes at 350 degrees. Serve warm with potato chips or crackers.

★
Philip Bickerstaff
James R. Chalmers
Camp #1312
Memphis, Tennessee
★
Great-great-grandson
Pvt. William N. Harris
Co. A, 24th Tennessee Infantry

William N. Harris died in 1872 when he was shot by an unknown assailant.

Cucumber Spread

Use for delicious, dainty sandwiches

1 large cucumber
3 tablespoons vinegar
1 tablespoon lemon juice
1 tablespoon sugar
$\frac{1}{4}$ teaspoon salt

Dash of pepper
1 teaspoon grated onion
12 ounces cream cheese
1-2 drops green food color
Fresh parsley

*P*eel cucumber, remove seed, and grate coarsely. Soak pulp for 15 minutes in vinegar, lemon juice, sugar, salt, and pepper. Drain. Blend onion with cream cheese. Add drained cucumber and food coloring. Mix well. Garnish sandwiches with fresh parsley.

★
Samuel Terrell ("Terry")Rowell
Jasper County Grays
Camp #1349
Heidelberg, Mississippi
★
Great-great-grandnephew
Lt. Col. James Stephens Terral
7th Mississippi Battalion

Hot Spinach Dip

Easy to prepare and a hit at parties

1 large onion, chopped
1 rib of celery, chopped
1 (10-ounce) can cream of
   mushroom soup
1 (4-ounce) can chopped or
   sliced mushrooms

2 boxes frozen, chopped
   spinach (thaw, cook, and
   drain well)
½-¾ pound jalepeño cheese,
   cubed

*S*auté onion and celery. Add soup, mushrooms, spinach, and cheese. Heat until thoroughly mixed and cheese is melted. Serve in a chafing dish with corn chips or French bread cubes on the side.

This recipe tastes great and has been a favorite at our parties for the past twenty-five years.

★
**Patrick J. Griffin III
Col. William Norris
Camp #1398
Darnestown, Maryland**
★
**Great-great-grandson
Pvt. James Andrew
Jackson Coker
Co. H., 39th Georgia Infantry**

Cindy's Strawberry Cheese Ball

A tasty party treat

1 cup premium mayonnaise
   (Hellmann's preferred)
1 cup pecans, chopped
1 cup cheddar cheese, grated

1 cup green onions, chopped
1 large jar strawberry
   preserves

*M*ix all ingredients together except preserves. Form into a ball. Pour preserves over the top and chill. Serve with party crackers, or spread a very thin layer on sliced ham and roll into pinwheels.

★
**Aubrey Hayden
Lt. Col. William Walker
Camp #1738
Winnfield, Louisiana**
★
**Great-great-grandson
Sgt. James Madison Rogers
Co. H, 15th
Mississippi Infantry**

Broccoli Bread

A very nice hot hors d'oeuvre

6 ounces cottage cheese
4 eggs, beaten
1 stick margarine, melted
1 small onion, chopped
1 package Jiffy cornbread mix

½ cup flour
2 teaspoons baking powder
1 (10-ounce) box chopped
   broccoli

---

*M*ix first 7 ingredients together, then add broccoli. Place into greased 10-inch by 10-inch pan and bake at 450 degrees for 25-30 minutes. Cut into small squares and serve.

★
Scott L. Peeler, Jr.
John T. Lesley Camp #1282
Tampa, Florida
★

Great-grandson
Pvt. John Wesley Garren
Co. G, 2nd Ashby's Regiment,
Tennessee Cavalry

John Wesley Garren was born in 1841 in Monroe County, Tennessee. He participated in the Battle of Murfreesboro and spent 18 months in prison—9 months at Camp Chase and 9 months at Fort Delaware. He was later exchanged and sent to Richmond, Virginia. After the war, he returned to his trade of blacksmithing, and was appointed Postmaster at Echo, Indian Territory. He died at age 86 in April 1927.

Opposite—John Wesley Garren
Co. G, 2nd Ashby's Regiment
Tennessee Cavalry

Charleston Cheese

Has a nice bacon flavor

½ cup mayonnaise
1 (8-ounce) package cream
    cheese, softened
1 cup sharp cheddar cheese,
    grated

2 green onions, chopped
6 round, buttery crackers,
    crushed
8 slices bacon, fried and
    crumbled

★
Chip Bragg
W. D. Mitchell Camp #163
Thomasville, Georgia
★
Descendant of
Pvt. M. J. Barkley
Co. A., South Carolina
Volunteers

*M*ix mayonnaise, cream cheese, cheddar cheese, and onions in a bowl. Smooth mixture into a shallow greased dish. Top with crushed crackers. Bake at 350 degrees for 15 minutes. Remove from oven and top with crumbled bacon. Serve with crackers.

Hot Creamy Sausage Dip

A hearty appetizer that always disappears quickly

1 pound mild or zesty roll sausage (Bob Evans sausage preferred)

5 green onions, chopped and divided

1 cup sour cream

$^1/_2$ cup mayonnaise

$^1/_4$ cup grated Parmesan cheese

1 (2-ounce) jar chopped pimientos, drained

★

Darrell L. Maples
Mosby Monroe Parsons
Camp #718
Jefferson City, Missouri

★

Descendant of
Pvt. William Maples
Co. C., 29th Tennessee
Infantry

*P*reheat oven to 350 degrees. In large skillet over medium heat, brown and crumble sausage until no longer pink. Remove from heat, drain off drippings, and add all remaining ingredients except 1 green onion. Pour into 1-quart baking dish. Bake 20-25 minutes until bubbly. Garnish with remaining chopped green onion. Keep warm and serve with Melba toast, and sesame or wheat crackers. Can be prepared without baking and refrigerated, then baked just before serving. Serves 8-10.

*It is a good idea to double this recipe and divide into two baking dishes, heating one for the beginning of your party and starting the second a little later.
The green onion and red pimiento colors make this perfect for serving at holiday parties.*

May Hall's Baked Crab Spread

Don't expect leftovers—there won't be any!

¼ pound butter
Salt to taste
1 teaspoon Coleman's dry
    mustard (no substitutions)
Red and black pepper to taste

1 pound backfin crab meat
Cream
Bread crumbs

*H*eat butter, salt, dry mustard, and peppers. Fold in crab meat. Stir in enough cream to moisten, sprinkle with bread crumbs, and bake in 400-degree oven for 15-20 minutes until brown, or brown under broiler. Serve on Ritz crackers. Serves 4-5.

★
A. C. Magruder, Sr.
R. E. Lee Camp #726
Alexandria, Virginia
★
Great-grandnephew
Capt. Henry A. Bowling
(Chambliss' Brigade)
4th Virginia Cavalry

Beef Dip Spread

Has a nice smoky flavor

1 (8-ounce) package cream
    cheese, softened
1 teaspoon onion, minced
1 tablespoon cooking sherry

1 (2½-ounce) package smoked
    Buddig Beef, chopped fine
¼ cup stuffed olives, chopped
2 tablespoons mayonnaise

*C*ream the cream cheese and onion together. Add cooking sherry and mix well. Add chopped beef and mix well. Add olives and mix well. Add mayonnaise. Place in bowl. Serve with crackers. Better if prepared a day ahead so flavors can mix.

★
Lawrence L. Limpus
Sterling Price Camp #145
St. Louis, Missouri
★
Great-grandnephew
Pvt. Benjamine Chance
Co. A, 60th Tennessee
Mounted Infantry

Ben Chance enlisted in 1862 in Wayne County, Kentucky. He served until the end of the war.

Liver Nips

An unusual way to serve liver

2-3 soup bones with some
   meat on them
8 cups water
1 pound liver (beef or pork)—
   must be skinned
2 medium onions, chopped fine
1 teaspoon basil
1 teaspoon oregano

½ teaspoon coriander
½ teaspoon baking powder
2½ teaspoons salt
2 teaspoons red pepper,
   crushed (use a little less if it
   is too much for children)
5 eggs
Flour

*A*dd soup bones to water, bring to a boil, reduce heat to a high simmer, and cook until meat is almost done (about 30 minutes). Add liver and simmer 1 hour. Add water as needed to keep about 8 cups in the pot. Remove liver and soup bones with meat. Remove meat and discard bones. Finely chop meat. Cool liver and grate it. Set aside in a cup of broth to cool.

To the chopped meat and grated liver add the chopped onions, basil, oregano, coriander, baking powder, salt, and red pepper. Mix well and set aside.

Beat the eggs well and add all the flour you can stir in. Add the cup of cooled broth a little at a time, adding more flour as needed to make it very stiff. Add the liver, onion, and seasoning mixture, making it as stiff as you can. Drop mixture (amount that you can hold on the end of a knife, or by the spoonful) into the boiling broth. Reduce heat and simmer about 30 minutes. Makes 6 generous servings.

★

Nick Ulmen
Gen. C.J. de Polignac
Camp #1648
Arlington, Texas

★

3rd great-grandfather
Pvt. Isaiah Price
Co. K, 20th South Carolina
Infantry

Pvt. Price died in December 1864 outside Petersburg, Virginia.

Sausage Balls

These don't last long!

1 pound Jimmy Dean sausage
2 cups Martha White self-
   rising flour

12 ounces extra-sharp cheese,
   coarsely grated (you can
   add more if you like)

*L*et sausage warm to room temperature for about 30 minutes. Mix flour and cheese, then mix in sausage, forming a large ball. Wrap ball in aluminum foil and refrigerate overnight. When ready to cook, preheat oven to 375 degrees. Pinch off a piece of the mixture (a little larger than a quarter). Roll into a ball and place on a cookie sheet. After the sheet is full, place in oven and cook for 15-20 minutes. They are done when the cheese is lightly brown. Makes about 50-60 sausage balls.

★
**James G. Patterson
Murfreesboro Camp #33
Murfreesboro, Tennessee**
★
**Great-great-grandson
Pvt. Archibald James
Patterson
Co. I, 18th Tennessee Infantry**

Archibald Patterson was captured at Fort Donelson and sent to Fort Butler. He escaped and rejoined his unit in time for the Battle of Murfreesboro. He was wounded at Chickamauga, recaptured at the Battle of Missionary Ridge, and sent to Rock Island Prison, where he spent the rest of the war.

Mexican Dip

Serve with your favorite taco chips

1-pound can refried beans
1/2-1 package taco seasoning
   mix
1 1/2 cups sour cream
1 bunch green onions, sliced
1 (4-ounce) can chopped
   black olives
1 small green pepper, chopped

1 small jar pimiento, chopped
1 (4-ounce) jar green olives,
   sliced
Picante or salsa sauce
1 1/2 cups cheddar cheese,
   grated
Quartered cherry tomatoes
Taco chips

*M*ix refried beans and taco seasoning mix. Spread into flat dish. Spread sour cream over bean mixture. Layer green onions, black olives, green pepper, pimiento, and green olives over sour cream. Spread picante or salsa sauce to taste. Add cheese. Arrange tomatoes over cheese. Dip with your favorite taco chips. Serves large number when used as an appetizer.

★

Rex A. Eargle
Wade Hampton Camp #273
Columbia, South Carolina

★

Descendant of
Pvt. John Henry Eargle
Co. D, 15th Regiment, South
Carolina Militia

Pvt. Eargle was 51 years old when he was wounded in battle. He died as a prisoner of war near Lynches Creek, South Carolina. His gravesite remains unknown.

Frances Haley's Favorite Barbecued Shrimp

A longtime family favorite

8-10 pounds medium-sized
   shrimp (about 20 shrimp
   per pound)

Sauce
1 pound butter
1 pound margarine
6 ounces Worcestershire sauce

6 tablespoons black pepper,
   finely ground
1 teaspoon rosemary, ground
4 juicy lemons (may need 6 if
   dry)
1 teaspoon Tabasco
4 teaspoons salt
4 cloves garlic

★

J. Evetts Haley, Jr.
Dunn-Holt-Midkiff
Camp #1441
Midland, Texas

★

Great-grandson
1st Lt. James H. Haley
Assistant Regimental Surgeon,
1st Mississippi Light Artillery

Melt butter and margarine in a 4-quart saucepan. Add Worcestershire, pepper, rosemary, lemon slices, Tabasco, salt, and garlic, and mix thoroughly. Divide shrimp between 2 large shallow pans and pour heated sauce over each. Stir well. Cook in a 400-degree oven for about 15-20 minutes, turning once. Shells should be pink. The meat should be white and not translucent.

Charlie's Savannah Onion Soup

The best onion soup ever

2 large yellow onions
¼ cup butter or oleo
2 tablespoons vegetable oil
2 (14½-ounce) cans beef broth
1 teaspoon sugar

Dash ground nutmeg
3/4 cup dry sherry
4 slices French bread, toasted
3/4 cup mozzarella cheese,
   shredded

Sauté onions in butter and oil in Dutch oven over medium heat until thinly sliced onions are tender, stirring frequently. Add broth, sugar, and nutmeg and bring to a boil. Cover, reduce heat, and simmer 10 minutes. Add sherry, stirring well. Ladle soup into individual dishes on top of French bread slices. Add 2 tablespoons cheese and bake at 300 degrees for 10 minutes or until cheese melts. Serves 4.

Several years ago, my close friend Joseph B. Mitchell and I were dining at a hotel in Savannah. As part of the dinner, I ordered the onion soup, and it was the finest ever to cross a palate. When I arrived home, several attempts were made to recreate this wonder dish. Finally, it was achieved.

★
**Charles H. Smith
Brig. Gen. Stand Watie
Camp #1313
Oklahoma City, Oklahoma**
★
**Great-grandnephew
Capt. John Knight
Co. H, Crescent Regiment,
Louisiana Infantry**

Capt. Knight was wounded in the wrist at Shiloh and died as a result on April 23, 1862.

17th Virginia Beef Jerky

Beef jerky can be quite delicious, as this commemorative recipe illustrates

1 pound flank steak
1 tablespoon salt
1 teaspoon red pepper
1 teaspoon black pepper

1 teaspoon garlic powder
Dash of Liquid Smoke
½-1 cup water, to cover

*T*rim all fat from steak and cut into thin strips. Combine remaining ingredients and use to marinate steak overnight. The next day, smoke 6 hours in a covered grill (a Weber kettle is best). Use 12 pieces of charcoal and choke the kettle down.

On the march, the occasional comforts of camp life were left behind; no more peach pies and sweet tea. "Pocket" food like beef jerky took the place of chicken and dumplings.

★
Samuel L. Riggs
Col. John S. Mosby
Camp #1237
Front Royal, Virginia
★
Great-grandson
Pvt. Reuben Riggs
Co. A, 1st Maryland Cavalry

The 1st Maryland Cavalry fought with distinction at Brandy Station, Gettysburg, and many other battles and skirmishes. Reuben took the oath on May 3, 1865, in Winchester, Virginia. He was a member of the Ridgley Brown Camp, United Confederate Veterans. He died in August 1910 and is buried in St. John's Cemetery in Laytonsville, Maryland.

Bourbon Slush

An adult beverage that is most popular from Thanksgiving through New Year

1 cup sugar
6½ cups water
1 (6-ounce) can frozen lemon-ade concentrate
1 (6-ounce) can frozen orange juice concentrate

1½ cups bourbon or Southern Comfort (can substitute 1 cup bourbon and ½ cup Amaretto)
1 cup brewed tea

*M*ix ingredients together in a large Tupperware-type container and freeze overnight, stirring occasionally to blend flavors. Remove 1 hour before serving. Serves 6-8.

This drink is ideally served in sterling silver goblets, but I have used Mason jars, styrofoam, and Dixie Cups more than a few times!

★
Robert W. Crook
Henry Watkins Allen
Camp #133
Baton Rouge, Louisiana
★

Great-great-grandson
2nd Lt. Benjamin Franklin Crook
Co. C, 8th Mississippi Volunteer Infantry

B.F. Crook became a cotton broker and merchant following the war. His first wife died in 1880, ten days after giving birth to their eighth child. He remarried and fathered five more children. His widow was killed in 1940 when a U.S. Army truck ran over her as she tried to cross the street in Forest, Mississippi.

Carolina Plantation Punch

A drink born for the second-floor porch

Crushed ice
Juice of ½ lime
1 ounce pineapple juice
1 ounce orange juice

½ ounce banana rum
½ ounce coconut rum
2 ounces brown rum
Nutmeg, grated

*M*ix all ingredients in a shaker with 1 scoop crushed ice, and strain into a highball glass with fresh crushed ice. Top with grated nutmeg.

When the summer settles gently in the Low Country and the heat hangs heavy in the air, this drink moves as silently as a Mosby ranger while it influences your conversation and colours your stories. Enjoy it while holding your friends close and your enemies closer.

★

Gene & Michael Givens
Gen. Richard H. Anderson
Camp #47
Beaufort, South Carolina

★

Great-grandson and
great-great-grandson
Pvt. Young Harrington E. Hitch
Co. I, 16th South Carolina
Infantry

Pvt. Hitch died on June 19, 1864, while on picket duty at Kennesaw Mountain, Georgia.

Opposite—Pvt. Young Hitch
Co. I, 16th South Carolina Infantry

Mom's Clam Dip

A tasty addition to any gathering

4 (8-ounce) packages cream cheese, softened
2 tablespoons mayonnaise
1 teaspoon Worcestershire sauce

1½ dozen fresh clams, minced or chopped (can use 3-4 cans clams)
Milk or canned clam liquid
Garlic powder to taste
Salt and black pepper to taste

*B*lend cream cheese, mayonnaise, and Worcestershire sauce until smooth. Stir in clams. Add about 2 tablespoons milk or clam liquid to soften. Season with garlic powder and salt and pepper. Serve immediately, or chill for up to an hour to firm.

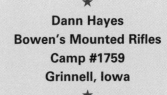

★
Dann Hayes
Bowen's Mounted Rifles
Camp #1759
Grinnell, Iowa
★
Great-great-grandson
Capt. Mace Andrew
Augustus Mayes
Co. C, 9th Battery, Georgia
Cavalry (Georgia State Guard)

Capt. Mayes died in Cobb County, Georgia, on February 16, 1906. He is buried in the Mayes Family Cemetery.

Aunt Joh's Summer Veranda Cheese Puffs

Serve warm from the oven

1 (8-ounce) brick cream
   cheese
¼ cup onions, finely diced
1 egg yolk

¼ teaspoon salt (kosher tastes
   best)
1 small loaf French bread, cut
   into ¼-inch slices

*B*lend cream cheese, onions, egg yolk, and salt until smooth. Spread onto slices of French bread or pipe onto bread with pastry bag and medium tip. Bake on a non-greased baking sheet for 10-15 minutes at 375 degrees until bread turns golden brown and cheese mixture is puffed and browned. Makes about 2 dozen slices.

*This noted delight is from the kitchen of the
Massachusetts Rebel, Johanna Griffin, who states
in her best Yankee twang, "This is my most requested recipe."
Southerners will find it hard to believe that such a tasty
treat comes from so far up north!*

★
Gregg Clemmer
Col. William Norris
Camp #1398
Gaithersburg, Maryland
★
Great-great-grandson
1st Lt. Mathew Bolling Clay
Co. C, 9th Virginia Infantry

Confederate Chewing Gum

A cheap appetizer for a gathering of good ole boys

5 pounds packaged chicken gizzards
1 bottle hot sauce (your choice)
1 bottle Worcestershire sauce
1 can beer (your favorite)
3 ounces prepared mustard
Cold water
Barbecue sauce (your choice)

★

James M. Mills
The Thomasville Rifles
Camp #172
Thomasville, North Carolina

★

Descendant of
Capt. Winnfield Scott
Lineberrry
Co. F., 70th Regiment,
North Carolina Troops

Wash gizzards after taking them out of package. Prepare marinade of hot sauce, Worcestershire sauce, and beer by mixing them together in a gallon jug (an old milk jug works well). Add mustard to jug and then fill with cold water (2 inches from top) and mix by shaking. Spear about 5-6 gizzards on shish-kabob sticks and place in a deep pan. Pour marinade mixture over the gizzards, cover and refrigerate for 24 hours.

The next day, remove and drain marinade. Place gizzards on an outdoor grill when coals are white and hot and cover, checking on them every few minutes. Cooking tip: start off by placing the meat directly over the coals to brown the gizzards, turning them over after about 5 minutes to brown the other side, then move the meat to the other end of the grill so that gizzards are not directly over the coals. Use barbecue sauce of your choice and brush on. Cover with lid and cook for 30 minutes or until done. Do not over cook, as they will become tough. Remove from grill and serve. Eat off the stick.

Men seem to like this served with a cold beverage. For some strange reason, most ladies don't care for this dish.

Hot Broccoli Dip

May be frozen and reheated

1 package frozen chopped
   broccoli
3 stalks celery, chopped fine
1 small onion, chopped fine
1 small can mushrooms,
   chopped

1 tablespoon butter
1 roll garlic cheese
¾ can cream of mushroom
   soup

*C*ook broccoli and drain well. Sauté celery, onion, and mushrooms in butter. Melt cheese in double boiler. Mix all ingredients with cream of mushroom soup and serve in a chafing dish to keep warm. Serve with crackers or chips.

★

Allen M. Trapp, Jr.
McDaniel-Curtis Camp #165
Carrollton, Georgia

★

Great-great-grandnephew
Capt. Edwin Allen
Co. C, 26th
Tennessee Infantry

Spinach Artichoke Casserole

Can also be used as a dip

½ cup onions, finely
   chopped
1 (10-ounce) package frozen
   chopped spinach
1 stick butter
1 pint sour cream

1 large can artichoke hearts,
   drained and cut in half
¾ cup Parmesan cheese
Salt and pepper
Bread crumbs, fresh and
   buttered

*P*repare spinach according to box directions; drain. Sauté onions in butter. Mix all ingredients and put in buttered casserole. Sprinkle a little extra cheese on top. Cover lightly with buttered bread crumbs. Bake at 350 degrees for 25-30 minutes.

★

The Reverend M. Don Majors
James P. Douglas Camp #124
Tyler, Texas

★

Great-great-grandson
Pvt. Ephraim Majors
Co. B, 19th Texas Cavalry

Steel Magnolia Cheese Ball

There won't be any left!

1 small package Monterey Jack cheese
1 small package Muenster cheese
1 small package Coon brand extra-sharp cheese
1 pound sharp cheddar cheese
1 (8-ounce) package Edam cheese
1 (8-ounce) package pepper cheese
1 large package cream cheese, softened

1 large jar pimiento peppers, mashed
1 carton sour cream
Mayonnaise (if needed)
3 teaspoons garlic powder
3 teaspoons onion powder
Lea & Perrins sauce
Louisiana hot sauce (your choice)
3 cups pecans, finely chopped

★
R. W. P. Patterson
Gen. J. H. McBride
Camp #632
Springfield, Missouri
★
Great-grandnephew
Sgt. W.W. Cupit
Co. E, 7th Mississippi Infantry

*P*lace cheeses in freezer just until firm, then remove and grate. Add softened cream cheese, pimiento peppers, and sour cream. Mix well. If mixture is stiff, add a little mayonnaise to make smooth. Add onion and garlic powder to mixture, then Lea & Perrins to taste. If still not hot enough for your taste, add some hot sauce. Place mixture into an empty Cool Whip bowl and freeze. Take out of freezer about 2 hours before serving and roll in pecans. Serves up to 20.

Azalea Punch

Perfect for a wedding or shower

4 cups cranberry juice
4 cups pineapple juice
1 tablespoon almond extract

1½ cups sugar
Large bottle ginger ale

*I*n a large jar, blend cranberry and pineapple juices with extract and sugar. Chill thoroughly. Just before serving, add chilled ginger ale. Makes about 3 quarts.

★
**Conwill Randolph Casey
Old Free State Camp #1746
Victoria, Virginia**
★
**Great-grandson
Pvt. Barzilla Harris Mixson
Co. H, 53rd Alabama
Mounted Infantry**

Famous Feaster Family Punch

Serves 100

2 quarts sugar
2½ gallons water
½ cup mint leaves, if desired
2 quarts strong tea

1 quart can pineapple juice
1 quart lemon juice
1 quart orange juice
1 quart grape juice

*M*ake a syrup of sugar and water, mixing thoroughly with balance. Chopped fruits or fruit cocktail may be added. Serve with colored ice made from orange Kool-Aid or cake coloring.

★
**Walter L. Eaton
Kirby Smith Camp #1209
Jacksonville, Florida**
★
**Great-grandnephew
Pvt. John Luther Eubanks
63rd Regiment, Georgia
Volunteer Infantry**

Caviar Crown

Fit for a king!

2 (8-ounce) packages cream
  cheese
2 tablespoons green onion
  tops, chopped

8 hard boiled eggs, chopped
1 (8-ounce) carton sour cream
Red Romanov lumpfish caviar

*B*eat cream cheese. Add eggs and onion tops and mix until smooth. Spray an 8-inch ring mold with non-stick cooking spray and spoon in cheese mixture. Refrigerate overnight. To serve, unmold ring and ice with sour cream. Scoop out a trench around the top of the crown and fill with caviar. Serve with Melba toast.

★
Calvin R. Crane
Fincastle Rifles Camp #1326
Roanoke, Virginia
★
Son
Pvt. James Antony Crane
13th Virginia Light Artillery
(Ringold Battery)

James, the son of a tobacco plantation owner, was 17 when he enlisted in the Confederate Army. He was the father of 21 children and died in 1918.

Salads, Sauces, and Breads

The Major's Rolled Herb Biscuits
Macaroni-Cheddar Salad
Angel Biscuits
Ritz Cracker Slaw
Mediterranean Rice Salad
Aunt Eleanor's Sour Cream Corn Bread
Bumper Crop Zucchini Bread
Mexican Corn Bread
Cabbage-Parsley Slaw
Watermelon Rind Pickles
Rebel Temper Hot Sauce
Southern Chicken Pasta Salad
Baked Potato Salad
Holiday Sweet Potato Biscuits
Southern Hush Puppies
Banana Bread
Traditional Potato Salad
Easy Three-Bean Salad
Batter Bread
Spinach and Rice Salad
So Sweet Corn Bread
Baron de Bastrop Mandarin Salad
Grandpa Smith's Cast-Iron
   Skillet Corn Bread
Wilted Lettuce
1-2-3 Beer Rolls
Aunt Rosa Lee's
   Confederado Biscuits
Cracker's Salad
Black-Eyed Pea Corn Bread
Sweet Potato Biscuits
Great-Aunt Alese's Easy Cole Slaw
Dirt Farm Corn Bread

Johnny Cakes
Grandma Bethard's Yeast Rolls
Aunt Sadie's Sweet Garlic Dills
Old-Fashioned Banana Nut Bread
Easy Applesauce Nut Bread
Grandma's Potato Salad
Aunt Ottis' Strawberry Salad
Hot Macaroni Salad
Grandma's Grit Corn Bread
Broccoli Delight Salad
Iced Green Tomato Pickles
Southern Spoon Bread
Spoon Bread
Layered Salad
North Carolina Corn Bread
Stonegate Confederate
   Barbecue Sauce
Lynchburg Layered Salad
Two-Hour Yeast Rolls
Mama's Chicken Salad
Corn Bread Salad
Zesty Black-Eyed Pea Salad
Mexican Corn Bread
Bob's Potato Salad
Amy Huss's Cranberry Salad
Grandma Coleman's Hoe-Cake
Grandpa's No Frills Corn Bread
Hot Slaw
Grandma Wright's Mashed
   Potato Salad
Buck Bread
Fish Fry Cole Slaw
Corn Meal Mush

The Major's Rolled Herb Biscuits

A sure crowd pleaser when matched up with beans, stew, or a thick soup

2 cups biscuit mix
1 tablespoon Parmesan
   cheese, grated
¼ teaspoon dried dill

¾ cup milk
2 teaspoons parsley flakes
1 teaspoon dried minced
   onion

*P*reheat oven to 450 degrees. Mix all ingredients until a soft dough forms (it may be lumpy). If too sticky, gradually mix in enough additional biscuit mix to make the dough easier to handle. Dust a flat surface with biscuit mix. Place the dough on the flat surface. Roll the dough in the baking mix and shape into a ball. Knead the dough for about 30 seconds. Roll the dough out until it is ½-inch thick. Cut the dough into 2-inch round biscuits. Place on a lightly greased baking pan. Bake for 7-9 minutes, or until golden brown. Makes about 8 biscuits.

This recipe won a ribbon at the Monroe County, New York, fair.

★

**William S. Poulton, Jr.
A. P. Hill Camp #167
Petersburg, Virginia**

★

**Great-great-grandson
Sgt. William Franklin Poulton
Co. H, 8th Virginia Infantry**

William Poulton fought with the "Bloody Eighth" from Ball's Bluff to Sayler's Creek. He was captured during Pickett's Charge at Gettysburg and was a "guest" of the Federal Government at Point Lookout from 1863 to 1865. After the war, he became a gentleman farmer and founded the Leesburg, Virginia, Camp of the United Confederate Veterans. He died in 1911.

Macaroni-Cheddar Salad

Very nice for a special luncheon

3 cups medium shell maca-
   roni (about 10 ounces)
1 cup sour cream
1 cup mayonnaise
¼ cup milk
½ cup sweet pickle relish
2 tablespoons vinegar

2 teaspoons prepared mustard
¾ teaspoon salt
2 cups cubed cheddar cheese
   (8 ounces)
1 cup chopped celery
½ cup chopped green pepper
¼ cup chopped onion

★

Phillip B. Isaacs
Col. Samuel H. Walkup
Camp #1375
Monroe, North Carolina

★

Pvt. Godfrey Isaacs
Co. A, 28th North Carolina
Regiment
Lane's Brigade,
Wilcox's Division

*C*ook macaroni according to package directions; drain.
Rinse with cold water and set aside. Combine sour
cream, mayonnaise, and milk. Stir in pickle relish, vinegar,
mustard, and salt. In another large bowl, toss together
cooked macaroni, cheese, celery, green pepper, and onion.
Pour sour cream mixture over all; toss lightly. Chill several
hours or overnight before serving. Serves 12.

Angel Biscuits

A sure way to get everyone to the table in a hurry

5 cups plain flour
1/2 cup sugar
3 teaspoons baking powder
1 teaspoon soda
1 teaspoon salt

1 cup shortening
1 package dry yeast
2 tablespoons warm water
2 cups buttermilk

★
Connie M. Morris
International Headquarters
Staff, Elm Springs
Sons of Confederate Veterans

*S*ift dry ingredients together; cut in shortening. Dissolve yeast in water. Add yeast water and buttermilk to other ingredients. Cover with cheesecloth, set in a warm place, and let it rise about 1 1/2 hours. Knead down and roll out 1/4-inch thick. You can dip in oil if desired, or brush tops with butter. Bake for 15 minutes at 350 degrees. Makes 2 dozen or more.

Ritz Cracker Slaw

Stuff into tomatoes for a delicious salad

1 medium cabbage, grated
1 medium onion, chopped
   finely
2/3 cup celery, chopped
2/3 cup bell pepper, chopped
2 cellophane packages Ritz
   crackers, crushed

2 tablespoons pickle relish
2 cups mayonnaise
4 tablespoons mustard
Salt and pepper to taste
1 cup sharp cheese, grated

Gary C. Walker
Fincastle Rifles Camp #1326
Roanoke, Virginia
★
Great-grandson
1st Lt. Thomas Fowler Walker
Co. G, 36th Virginia Infantry

Lt. Walker was captured at
the third Battle of Winchester
and sent as a prisoner of war
to Point Lookout, Maryland.
He was paroled in June 1864.

*M*ix all ingredients together except the cheese. Sprinkle grated cheese on top of slaw. Chill. Serves 12-15.

Mediterranean Rice Salad

A pretty salad that tastes great

1 cup long grain rice
1 teaspoon salt
3 tablespoons olive oil
3 tablespoons tarragon
   vinegar
3 large ribs celery (cut into
   bite-sized pieces)
1 small can sliced black olives,
   drained

1 can artichoke hearts (not
   marinated), drained and
   quartered
1 peeled tomato, chopped
1 small can pimientos,
   drained and chopped
Fresh basil leaves, chopped
Freshly grated nutmeg

*B*oil the rice in 2 cups of water with 1 teaspoon salt. When the rice comes to a boil, turn it down to the lowest heat for 20 minutes, with the lid on the pot. At the end of 20 minutes, the rice should have absorbed all the water. Place in a salad bowl and while still hot pour on the oil and vinegar and mix. Let cool. When cool, add the celery, olives, artichoke hearts, tomato, pimientos, and at least 6 basil leaves. Mix well and sprinkle with a good pinch of nutmeg. Chill and serve. Serves 6-8.

**Father Alister Anderson
Jefferson Davis Camp #305
Washington, D.C.**

**1st cousin, 3 times removed
Capt. Aristides Doggett
Co. A, 3rd Florida Infantry**

Aristides Doggett was a lawyer who studied under his father in Jacksonville, Florida. He served as a volunteer in the Mexican War under the command of Gen. Winfield Scott. In the War Between the States, he saw action at Shiloh and Franklin. He died in Jacksonville, Florida, in 1890.

Aunt Eleanor's Sour Cream Corn Bread

The white cornmeal makes the difference

1 cup self-rising white corn meal (personally, I think only Yankees use yellow meal)

1 cup sour cream

2 eggs

½ cup cooking oil

1 can of cream-style corn (I use ½ can to keep it from turning out too moist)

---

*P*reheat oven to 425 degrees. Mix all ingredients. Bake in a 9-inch cast-iron skillet for 35 minutes or more. Green peppers, onions, cheese, or any other ingredient can be added, if you prefer.

★

James D. Kegley
Wise Partisan Rangers
Camp #1756
Norton, Virginia

★

Great-great-grandson
Pvt. Thomas Jefferson Kegley
Co. A, 8th Virginia Cavalry

Thomas enlisted with his brother Daniel. After the war, he returned to farming in Smyth County, Virginia, where he reared a large family. He died in 1911.

Bumper Crop Zucchini Bread

Tastes like banana nut bread

3 cups flour
2 teaspoons baking soda
1 teaspoon salt
½ teaspoon baking powder
1½ teaspoons baking powder
1½ teaspoons cinnamon
¾ cup chopped nuts (walnuts are best)

3 eggs
2 cups sugar
1 cup cooking oil
2 teaspoons vanilla
1 (8-ounce) can crushed pineapple
2 cups zucchini, shredded

*M*ix all ingredients together well, and put into a loaf or bread pan. Bake for 1 hour at 350 degrees. If you use a standard-size loaf pan, recipe is enough for 2 loaves.

My wife, Sherri, used to help her parents on their farm, and one year they had a "bumper crop" of zucchini. After trying all kinds of recipes in an attempt to get rid of it all, she and her father decided to try making some bread with it. They came up with this tasty variation. Each and every summer since, my wife turns our kitchen into a bakery for about a week and "goes to town" making zucchini bread for family members. You can wrap the loaves in aluminum foil and they freeze just fine.

★
**Robert T. Millikin III
Lee-Jackson Camp #1
Richmond, Virginia**
★
**Great-grandnephew
Pvt. John Thomas Dutton
Co. B, 26th Virginia Infantry**

John T. Dutton of Gloucester, Virginia, was one of four brothers who fought for the Confederacy. He was wounded at Petersburg, and present at last muster at Appomattox Courthouse. He died in the early 1900s from acute rheumatism, and his remains were carried back to Gloucester aboard the steamer *Mobjack*.

Mexican Corn Bread

Serve with a cold glass of buttermilk

½ cup corn meal
1 #2 can cream-style corn
2 eggs
2 tablespoons bell pepper (any color) chopped
3 jalapeño peppers, finely chopped (best if you can't see them)

1 teaspoon salt (use garlic salt if you prefer)
3 teaspoons baking powder
1 cup sour cream
⅔ cup cooking oil (old Rebels can use the low cholesterol kind)
1 cup sharp cheese, grated

★
Lawrence Smith
General Albert Pike
Camp #1439
Wichita, Kansas
★
Descendant of
Pvt. James Smith
Co. H, 1st Alabama Cavalry

*M*ake a batter of all ingredients except the cheese. Pour half the batter into a greased iron skillet. Sprinkle with ½ cup grated cheese. Repeat process. Bake at 425 degrees for 45 minutes. Serves 8.

Cabbage–Parsley Slaw

A family favorite that goes with anything

½ head of small, compact cabbage, sliced thin
1 bunch curly parsley, chopped (discard stems)
Juice of 1 lemon

½ teaspoon lemon pepper seasoning
2 tablespoons olive oil
Salt to taste
Pepper to taste

★
Patrick J. Griffin III
Col. William Norris
Camp #1398
Darnestown, Maryland
★
Great-great-grandson
Pvt. James Andrew
Jackson Coker
Co. H, 39th Georgia Infantry

*M*ix ingredients in a large salad bowl, chill, and serve. Serves 8-10.

A family recipe handed down through four generations and used at festive occasions and regular meals. It has always been a favorite of our children.

65

Watermelon Rind Pickles

An unusual pickle that's absolutely delicious!

¼ cup pickling lime or non-iodized salt
8 cups cold water
4 quarts 1-inch cubed, pared watermelon rind
1 piece ginger root

3 sticks cinnamon, broken into pieces
2 tablespoons whole cloves
8 cups cider vinegar
9 cups sugar

---

*D*issolve salt in cold water. Heat to boiling. Cook rind, uncovered, just until tender (10-15 minutes) and drain. Tie spices into a cheesecloth bag. Heat spice bag, vinegar, and sugar to boiling and boil uncovered for 5 minutes. Add rind and simmer uncovered for 1 hour. Remove spice bag. Immediately pack mixture in hot jars, leaving a ¼-inch head space. Wipe jar rims. Seal and process in boiling water bath for 10 minutes. Makes 7-8 pints.

★
John Reynolds
Thomas Goode Jones
Camp #259
Montgomery, Alabama
★
Great-grandson
1st Lt. Dozier Thornton
Co. D, 15th Alabama Infantry

Dozier Thornton enlisted in 1861 at the age of 21. He was wounded several times, and fought at Chancellorsville, Gettysburg, Winchester, and the Wilderness. After the war, he became a cotton broker in Kentucky. He died in 1919.

Opposite—Elam Dozier Mills Thornton
1st Lt., Co. D, 15th Alabama Regiment.
Probably taken just prior to enlistment.

Rebel Temper Hot Sauce

The name says it all

3-4 tablespoons McCormick
  pickling spice
1 gallon fresh tomatoes,
  peeled
1 quart onions, chopped
1½ cups hot peppers (can use
  more, if desired)

1 cup sweet peppers, chopped
5 teaspoons salt
5 teaspoons sugar
2 teaspoons black pepper
1 large can tomato sauce
1 bottle catsup
1 quart vinegar

*P*ut the pickling spice in a clean stocking and tie off a knot at the end. Boil all ingredients except vinegar for 1 hour. Add vinegar and boil until sauce reaches desired consistency. Pour into sterilized pint or quart canning jars, heat the seals, and screw them down tightly on the jars. Refrigerate after opening. Good on anything from beans and peas to chips.

★
**Michael Passons
Maj. Gen. William T. Martin
Camp #590
Natchez, Mississippi**
★
**Great-great-grandson
Pvt. James M. Ray
Co. D, 30th Mississippi
Infantry**

James Ray was captured at the Battle above the Clouds and sent to prison at Rock Island, Illinois. He was one of the few men to escape, and he rejoined his regiment and fought until the end of the war. He is buried in Attala County, Mississippi.

Southern Chicken Pasta Salad

Perfect for a bridge party or ladies' lunch

3 whole chicken breasts
1 (8-ounce) box seashell pasta
½ cup olive oil Italian dressing
½ cup mayonnaise
2 (6-ounce) cans sliced, pitted
    black olives

★
Randy Young
W. D. Mitchell Camp #163
Thomasville, Georgia

*B*oil chicken breasts. Cool and remove bones from meat. Chop into large chunks. Cook pasta until almost done (but firm), about 2 minutes less than suggested cooking time. Drain pasta, cool, and place in large bowl with cooked chicken. In another bowl, mix mayonnaise and Italian dressing. Place olives on top of pasta and chicken, add mayonnaise/dressing mixture, and combine well. Flavor improves if salad is refrigerated several hours or overnight before serving. Serve on lettuce or with crackers. Serves 4-6.

Baked Potato Salad

Serve warm

5 pounds red potatoes (cubed,
    cooked, and drained)
1 pound Velveeta cheese,
    cubed
1 onion, chopped
1 cup mayonnaise
1 tablespoon bacon grease

★
Joseph W. Halsey
Col. Harry W. Gilmore
Camp #1388
Baltimore, Maryland
★
Great-grandson
Cpl. William Halsey
Co. I, 51st Virginia Infantry

*G*rease a 9-inch by 13-inch baking dish. Combine all these ingredients in it and cook at 300 degrees for 50 minutes.

Holiday Sweet Potato Biscuits

Really dresses up your serving table with their bright yellow color

1 egg, slightly beaten
$\frac{1}{2}$-$\frac{3}{4}$ cup cooked sweet pota-
    toes, mashed
2 tablespoons margarine,
    softened

$\frac{1}{4}$-$\frac{1}{2}$ cup sugar
3 tablespoons shortening
2 cups self-rising flour

*M*ix egg, sweet potatoes, margarine, sugar, and short-ening in a bowl and beat until smooth. Stir in enough flour to make a soft dough (will be softer than regular biscuit dough). If stiff enough, turn out on a floured surface and knead a few times. Roll out $\frac{1}{4}$-inch thick, cut with a biscuit cutter, and bake on an ungreased baking sheet at 350 degrees for about 15 minutes. Makes about 1$\frac{1}{2}$ dozen small biscuits.

Note: If potatoes are juicy, $\frac{1}{2}$ cup will probably be enough. If they are very sweet, only use about $\frac{1}{4}$ cup of sugar. If the dough is too soft to roll, flour your hands and pinch off pieces about the size of a walnut, then roll and flatten in your hands.

This recipe has been used by my family for over one hundred years, and it is a big hit during the holiday season.

★
Albert Bennett Mewborn
47th Regiment
North Carolina Troops
Camp #166
Wake Forest, North Carolina
★
Great-grandson
Capt. Lemuel Joshua Mewborn
20th North Carolina Infantry

Capt. Mewborn fought and served honorably for four years. He was a farmer, banker, and deacon in the Primitive Baptist Church. He had a large family, and lived to a ripe old age.

Southern Hush Puppies

No fish fry is complete without these

2 cups corn meal
1 cup buttermilk
1½ teaspoons baking soda
2 teaspoons baking powder

1 teaspoon salt
1 egg
½ cup onion, finely chopped

Thoroughly mix all ingredients. Drop a tablespoon of the batter for each hush puppy into hot, deep fat (360 degrees). Using fat or grease in which fish has been fried adds flavor. Fry a few at a time until golden brown. Serve hot. Makes about 40 hushpuppies.

★
Donald Smart
Dick Bowling Camp #1863
Beaumont, Texas
★
Great-grandson
Pvt. Francis M. Drake
Spaight's Battalion, 11th
Texas Volunteers

Francis Drake enlisted at the age of 19. His service was spent mostly in Texas, where he participated in the Battle of Sterling Plantation. He died in 1906.

Banana Bread

One of the best recipes ever

1¾ cups all-purpose flour
1½ cups sugar
½ teaspoon baking soda
½ teaspoon salt
2 eggs
2 ripe bananas, mashed

½ cup vegetable oil
½ cup plus 1 tablespoon buttermilk or Half and Half
1 teaspoon vanilla
1 cup nuts, chopped (your choice)

Sift together flour, sugar, baking soda, and salt. Combine eggs, mashed bananas, oil, buttermilk, and vanilla. Add sifted ingredients to liquid ingredients, stirring until combined. Fold in nuts. Pour into a greased and floured 9-inch by 5-inch by 3-inch loaf pan. Bake for approximately 1 hour and 20 minutes.

Note: this recipe does not double well.

★
Allen M. Trapp, Jr.
McDaniel-Curtis Camp #165
Carrollton, Georgia
★
Great-great-grandnephew
Capt. Edwin Allen
Co. C, 26th Tennessee Infantry

Traditional Potato Salad

No family gathering is complete without it

6 cups cubed, cooked potatoes
1/3 cup celery, diced
3/4 cup sweet pickles, chopped
2 tablespoons minced onion
4 hardboiled eggs, chopped
1 1/4 teaspoons salt

1/4 teaspoon yellow mustard
1 tablespoon white vinegar
1 cup mayonnaise
Paprika

*P*lace all ingredients, except the mayonnaise and paprika, in a large mixing bowl. Stir, then add mayonnaise and mix well, but lightly. Sprinkle with paprika after pouring into a serving dish.

★
Jim Moore
CSS *Florida* Camp #102
Orlando, Florida
★
Great-great-grandson
Pvt. John Moore, Jr.
Co. G, 26th Georgia Infantry

John Moore died in the hospital at Lynchburg, Virginia, and is buried there in the Confederate cemetery.

Easy Three-Bean Salad

A vegetarian treat

1 can cut green beans, drained
1 can yellow wax beans, drained
1 can kidney beans, drained
1 large onion, cut julienne style

1 cup vinegar
1 cup sugar
2 tablespoons oil

*M*ix beans and onion together. Bring vinegar, sugar, and oil to a boil. Pour mixture over beans and onion and marinate overnight in refrigerator before serving.

★
Mathew and Jeffrey Wilson
McDaniel-Curtis Camp #165
Carrollton, Georgia
★
Descendants of
Capt. Edwin Allen
Co. C., 26th Tennessee
Infantry

72

Batter Bread

As light and airy as a soufflé

1 cup white corn meal
1¼ cups boiling water
½ teaspoon salt
1 tablespoon butter

2 eggs, well beaten
1 cup buttermilk
½ teaspoon baking soda

Edwin L. Kennedy, Jr.
Brig. Gen. William Steele
Camp #1857
Leavenworth, Kansas

*P*our meal into a bowl without sifting. Scald meal by pouring boiling water over it and stirring to prevent lumps. Add water slowly, stirring all the while. If batter is lumpy, it must be strained. Add salt and butter, and let butter melt. Mix well and set aside to cool slightly. Add eggs beaten with buttermilk and baking soda. Beat well. Pour into a greased baking dish or casserole (it is served in the same dish it is baked in). Set in a hot (450-degree) oven and leave for 30-40 minutes or until batter no longer shakes in the middle. If done correctly, it is light and airy. Serve at once.

Spinach and Rice Salad

A very pretty dish

1 cup Uncle Ben's Converted
    Rice
½ cup Italian salad dressing
1 tablespoon soy sauce
½ cup sugar
2 cups fresh spinach, cut in
    thin strips

½ cup celery, chopped
½ cup green onion, chopped
⅓ cup crisp bacon, crumbled
½ cup mushrooms
½ cup black olives, pitted

Cook rice according to package directions. Transfer to a large bowl and cool. Combine dressing, soy sauce, and sugar. Stir mixture into warm rice. Cover and chill. Fold in remaining ingredients before serving. You can double the recipe for a large crowd. Serves 6.

★
Ed Moody
River's Bridge Camp #842
Bamberg County,
South Carolina
★
Great-grandson
Pvt. John Andrew Moody
Co. D, 2nd South Carolina
Artillery

John Moody had three brothers and four first cousins who fought for the Confederacy. All returned after the war.

So Sweet Corn Bread

Another variation of a Southern staple

2 cups yellow corn meal, stone ground
1 cup all-purpose flour
1½ teaspoons baking powder
2 eggs

½ teaspoon salt
3 tablespoons sugar
½ cup honey
1¼ cups milk
2 tablespoons vegetable oil

*P*reheat oven to 350 degrees, and heat a greased 9-inch pan or iron skillet. Combine all dry ingredients in a mixing bowl. Add all other ingredients, then mix. Small lumps are okay. Pour batter into heated pan and bake approximately 20 minutes or until inserted toothpick comes out clean.

★
Joseph S. Estes
Gen. Lewis Armistead
Camp #1847
Wamego, Kansas
★
Grandson
Lt. Joseph Pruett Estes
Co. C, 26th North Carolina
Home Guard

Joseph Estes was a black-smith by trade. His family fled North Carolina during Reconstruction (1867) and moved to Kansas. Because he had been a Confederate officer, he was refused home-stead land and was not allowed to vote until 1870.

Baron de Bastrop Mandarin Salad

Serve this salad and get ready for rave reviews!

1 head romaine lettuce
1 cup celery, chopped
2 whole green onions,
  chopped
1 head iceberg lettuce
1 (11-ounce) can mandarin
  oranges, drained

Almond Candy Topping
6 tablespoons sugar
1 cup sliced almonds

Dressing
1 teaspoon salt
Dash pepper
1 cup vegetable oil
1 tablespoon parsley
1 tablespoon sugar
2 tablespoons vinegar
Dash Tabasco

★
Peter Orlebeke
Gaston-Gregg Camp, #1384
Dallas, Texas
★
Great-grandson
5th Sgt. Wilborn Curry
Co. A, 37th Arkansas Infantry

To prepare the topping, sprinkle almonds over tin foil that has been put on a cookie sheet. Melt sugar in a small pan over medium heat. Stir constantly, as it will burn. Drizzle melted sugar over almonds. Let them cool and dry. Store in an airtight container in refrigerator. Mix all dressing ingredients and chill. Mix lettuce, celery, and onions. Just before serving, toss in dressing and oranges and sprinkle almond candy mixture on top.

This wonderful recipe comes from the Baron de Bastrop Chapter, Daughters of the Republic of Texas, in Bastrop, Texas.

Grandpa Smith's Cast-Iron Skillet Corn Bread

Serve with sorghum syrup—heavenly!

2 tablespoons vegetable oil
1 cup yellow corn meal
3 heaping teaspoons baking
   powder

1 cup flour
1⅓ cups milk
1 teaspoon salt
2 eggs

Heat oven to broil; pour 2 tablespoons oil in cast-iron skillet and place skillet in oven for 10-12 minutes until oil starts to smoke and pan is sizzling hot. Meanwhile, combine other ingredients in a mixing bowl, adding milk until mixture has the consistency of pancake batter (thick but still runny). Turn down oven to 425 degrees; remove skillet with heavy oven mitt and immediately pour in mixture. Return skillet to oven and bake for 18-20 minutes. Let cook for awhile in skillet before removing. Serve with chili, butter, or (the Reverend J. T.'s favorite) sorghum syrup. Enjoy!

This recipe has been passed down from the Reverend James T. Smith. He carried a small skillet on his later travels so he could always have his hosts bake him some corn bread. It was first written down in 1994 by his granddaughter (my grandmother), who still has "Rev. J. T.'s" individual-portion skillet (well oiled, of course)!

★
Randolph W. Baxter
James Iredell Waddell
Camp #1770
Orange County, California
★
Great-great-grandson
Pvt. James T. Smith, Sr.
12th Texas Cavalry

Wilted Lettuce

Prepare this in the spring when leaf lettuce and onions are young and tender

16 ounces of leaf lettuce (I
   prefer fresh from garden)
5-6 small spring green onions,
   including tops

¼ cup vegetable oil
¼ cup white vinegar
2 tablespoons water
Salt and pepper to taste

Shred or cut lettuce into medium-sized pieces. Slice onion into thin slices, including green tops. Place in heat-proof bowl. Boil oil, vinegar, water, salt, and pepper together in a quart pan. Pour hot oil-vinegar-water mixture over lettuce and onions. Serves 4-5.

Serve this dish with corn bread, boiled potatoes, country ham, and sweet tea for a mouth-watering meal.

★

**Danny Casstevens
Yadkin Gray Eagles
Camp #1765
Yadkinville, North Carolina**

★

**Great-grandnephew
Sgt. Samuel Speer Harding
Co. I, 28th Regiment North
Carolina Troops**

Sgt. Harding was killed at the Battle of Reams Station, near Petersburg, Virginia, on August 25, 1864. A fellow soldier and friend Thomas G. Scott wrote home to Sam's father, William Harding, about his death. William and his youngest son, Thomas (my great-grandfather), drove a wagon to Virginia and brought the body back to Yadkin County for burial in the family cemetery near Yadkinville.

1-2-3 Beer Rolls

So simple, yet so good!

1 can warm, stale beer   3 cups Bisquick
2 tablespoons sugar

Mix ingredients. Lightly grease a muffin tin and fill each muffin cup ²/₃ full. Bake 25-30 minutes at 350 degrees. Makes 10-12 yeast-like rolls.

★

**Jerry Brimberry
Eli P. Landers Camp #1724
Lilburn, Georgia**

★

**Great-great-grandson
Pvt. George Anderson
Brimberry
Co. L, 28th Texas Cavalry**

George Brimberry was born in 1843 in Claiborne Parish, Louisiana. He was the youngest of five brothers who fought for the Confederacy, and one of thirty-three cousins who fought for the South. He saw action in Arkansas and Louisiana, most notably at the Battle of Mansfield and Pleasant Hill. After the war, he became a farmer. He was very active in the United Confederate Veterans. His progeny included seven children and thirty-three grandchildren. He died in 1923.

Aunt Rosa Lee's Confederado Biscuits

The best biscuits in Brazil

2 cups flour
1 teaspoon salty water
4 teaspoons baking powder

2 full tablespoons vegetable lard
1 cup milk (may use slightly
    less)

Sift the dry items. Add lard and mix well with your hands. Add milk slowly, until homogeneous dough is obtained, with no lumps. Knead dough only until consistent, roll out and cut in round discs. Bake as needed, according to biscuit thickness. Serve with butter, hickory syrup, or sugar cane syrup.

This is a traditional Southern recipe carried by Confederate immigrants to Brazil, and is frequently offered at the Camp Cemetery Meetings in Santa Barbara D'Oeste, State of Sao Paulo, Brazil.

★
Daniel Carr De Muzio
C. S. Confederados
Camp #1653
Americana, Brazil
★
Descendant of
Pvt. Albert Gallelon Carr
Co. A, 56th Alabama Infantry

Cracker's Salad

Hearty and unique

1 skillet corn bread (cold)
2 eggs, hardboiled
2-3 slices of fried bacon,
  crumbled

1 tomato, sliced and drained
1 bunch of green onions, diced
1 jalepeño pepper, diced

---

*M*ix all ingredients together and let chill.

*This recipe came from my grandmother Zelma Mangrum,
who is descended from several hardy Confederate
soldiers. I remember eating Granny's special
recipe many times as a child when working on my
grandparent's farm near Franklin, Tennessee.*

★

**Ronny Mangrum
Tod Carter Camp #854
Franklin, Tennessee**

★

**Great-great-grandson
Vacheal Isaih Barnhill
Capt. Baxter's Tennessee Light
Artillery**

Vacheal was born in March 1841 in Hickman County, Tennessee. He enlisted in 1862, along with his brother James. They served together until James was captured during the Atlanta Campaign. James froze to death on a train while being taken to Camp Douglas, where he is buried. Family legend says that Vacheal Barnhill went to war with a double-barreled shotgun named "Old Boxley." When he returned in 1865, he is reported to have said, "Me and Old Boxley has been a long ways and seen many things."

Black-Eyed Pea Corn Bread

Makes a great one-dish meal

1 pound pork sausage
1 onion, chopped
½ cup bell pepper, chopped
3 packages corn bread mix
¾ cup creamed corn

8 ounces grated cheese
1 (15-ounce) can or 2 cups of
  black-eyed peas (drain
  most of the juice)

*B*rown sausage, onion, and bell pepper. Drain. Make corn bread mix according to package directions. Add sausage mixture, corn, cheese, and peas to corn bread. Bake in 9-inch by 13-inch dish at 350 degrees for 50-55 minutes.

★
Ben Head
General Richard Taylor
Camp #1308
Shreveport, Louisiana
★
Great-great-grandson
Pvt. Levi Marion Head
Co. H, 20th Texas Calvary

Levi was wounded in the left leg at Honey Springs, Oklahoma (Indian Territory). The leg had to be amputated at the knee. Unfortunately, gangrene set in and he endured another amputation farther up the leg. Surviving both operations, he returned to his home west of Alvarado, Johnson County, Texas. He had a large family and was a prosperous farmer. Later he became the tax assessor for Johnson County and lived a long and successful life.

Opposite—Levi Marion Head
Private, Co. H, 20th Texas Cavalry

Sweet Potato Biscuits

A new twist on a Southern favorite

2 cups of sifted all-purpose
  flour
3 teaspoons baking powder
½ teaspoon baking soda
¾ teaspoon salt
¾ tablespoon brown sugar

Dash of cinnamon
½ cup of melted butter
1 cup boiled, peeled, mashed
  sweet potatoes (use 15-
  ounce can if desired)
⅔ cup buttermilk

*P*reheat oven to 450 degrees. Sift flour, baking powder, baking soda, salt, brown sugar, and cinnamon and set aside. Using a medium bowl, beat melted butter into the sweet potatoes. Add dry ingredients, stirring in a little at a time, alternating with buttermilk. Mix well enough to moisten all ingredients. Form into a ball and turn out onto lightly floured board. Lightly pat top side with flour as well, since it is a rather sticky batter. Roll out to ½- to ¾-inch thickness with floured rolling pin. Cut with a floured biscuit cutter. Bake for 20-25 minutes. Makes 12 to 14 biscuits.

★
Bob G. Davis
Col. George R. Reeves
Camp #349
Sherman, Texas
★
Great-great-grandson
Pvt. Robert R. Bogle
Co. F., 7th Tennessee Infantry

Great-Aunt Alese's Easy Cole Slaw

A nice cool treat on a hot summer day

4 cups cabbage, shredded
3-4 tablespoons Miracle Whip
    (sweeter in taste, so no sub-
    stitutions!)
½ teaspoon salt

½ teaspoon onion powder
¼ teaspoon celery seed
1½ teaspoons vinegar
2 tablespoons sugar

Soak cabbage in iced water for 1 hour before shredding. Mix the remaining ingredients together and toss with the cabbage.

★

Gerald Bayer
Pvt. E. Scott Dance
Camp #1751
Monkton, Maryland

★

Great-great-grandnephew
Pvt. Richard Thomas Bledsoe
Co. A, 13th Virginia Infantry

Richard T. Bledsoe was one of three brothers who served the Confederacy. He was killed at the Battle of Spotsylvania in May 1864. After learning of his death, his mother and a servant retrieved his body from the battlefield and buried him in the family cemetery. Richard Bledsoe's name appears on the Confederate monument in front of the Orange County Courthouse in Orange County, Virginia.

Dirt Farm Corn Bread

A family staple when times were hard

2 (6-ounce) packages corn
   bread mix
2 eggs
1¼-1½ cup milk
½ cup celery, finely diced
½ cup green onions, finely
   diced

½ cup green bell peppers, finely diced
½-¾ pound seasoned pork
   sausage
Sugar to taste (optional)
Salt and pepper to taste

★
Dave Easterling
Lt. Gen. Nathan B. Forrest
Camp #513
Norman, Oklahoma
★
Descendant of
Lt. Col. William Kennon
Easterling
46th Mississippi Infantry

*E*mpty mix into bowl and add eggs and milk. Stir to make a free-pouring batter. Mix in vegetables and spices. Fold in sausage. Add more milk if required to maintain a smooth batter. Grease large (10- to 12-inch) iron skillet or corn stick mold, pour in batter, and bake about 20 minutes or until golden brown. These may also be cooked like pancakes on a stovetop griddle. Brown on one side and then flip over like pancakes. Serve hot with lots of butter and a big glass of chilled buttermilk.

This corn bread recipe has been floating around my family for several generations. It has been variously known as "Poor Folk Corn Bread," "Land Run Corn Bread," "Make Do Corn Bread," and several other names I don't remember. Over the years, it became a Southern staple to help stretch out what little the folks had. As a young'un, I remember many nights when times were hard that this corn bread in a big bowl of chilled buttermilk or a large bowl of beans with ham hocks might be all we had for supper after a long day of tending livestock or hoeing cotton. I have taken the liberty to modernize it a little by using pre-packaged corn bread mix, but you diehard cooks go right ahead and make your own.

86

Johnny Cakes

A traditional breakfast treat

1 cup white corn meal
1 teaspoon salt
1 tablespoon butter
1 cup boiling water

1 tablespoon sugar
¼-½ cup milk
Bacon drippings

Combine the corn meal, salt, butter, boiling water, and sugar into a small bowl. Add the milk and mix well. Batter should be a little thicker than pancake batter. Drop the batter by tablespoons onto a hot griddle that has been well greased with bacon drippings. Press the batter to about ½-inch thickness, using a greased pancake turner. Cook a few at a time over moderate heat until brown and crisp (about 5-10 minutes). Turn and brown both sides. Serves 4.

★
Wm. Darrell Glover
Lt. W.W. Pettus Camp #1762
Lexington, Alabama
★
Great-grandson
Pvt. Daniel McDougal Killen
Co. E, 27th Alabama Infantry

Grandma Bethard's Yeast Rolls

From the piney woods of LaSalle Parish, Louisiana

1 package yeast
1½ cups lukewarm water
½ cup shortening
½ cup sugar

1 egg, unbeaten
½ teaspoon salt
2 cups lukewarm water
8 cups flour

Dissolve yeast in ½ cup water. Cream shortening and sugar in ½ cup water. Add egg, salt, and yeast, and then the flour. Mix well and put in a large bowl. Refrigerate until needed. When you are ready to prepare, make out in rolls, let rise until double in size, and bake until nicely browned on top.

★
Alvin Y. Bethard
Gen. Franklin Gardner
Camp #1421
Lafayette, Louisiana

Aunt Sadie's Sweet Garlic Dills

These are fantastic!

1 quart sliced hamburger dill pickles	1 medium bulb garlic
	2 cups sugar

---

*D*rain pickles in colander for 2-3 hours. Discard liquid. Peel and slice 6 cloves garlic. Put garlic in bottom of sterilized jar and add pickles. Pour sugar over pickles, cap, and let sit at room temperature for a week or until sugar has dissolved completely. The pickles will be covered with liquid made by the sugar. Store in refrigerator.

My aunts offered these on the sideboard at every meal. I don't know where the recipe came from, but these are the best pickles in the South!

★
James L. Dean
William C. Oates Camp #809
Dothan, Alabama
★
Great-great-grandson
Pvt. William Harris
33rd Alabama Infantry

Pvt. Harris died at Chickamauga during the charge of log breastworks on Snodgrass Hill. According to the Official Records, he was cited for heroism after the battle.

Old Fashioned Banana Nut Bread

Kids love this!

1 stick oleo
1 cup sugar
2 eggs
3 ripe bananas, mashed

1 cup nuts
2 cups flour
½ teaspoon baking soda
1 teaspoon baking powder

*C*ream sugar and butter, and add eggs (one at a time). Beat well. Mix bananas and nuts and add to mixture. Add flour, sifted with baking powder and soda. Bake in loaf tin at 350 degrees for 45 minutes to 1 hour, or until straw through center comes out clean.

★
John T. Fargason
Frontier Guard Camp #996
Junction, Texas
★
Great-grandson
Pvt. Lawrence Ewel Talbot
Co. D, (McDonald's Battalion),
Tennessee Cavalry

Easy Applesauce Nut Bread

Moist and delicious

2 cups flour
1 cup chopped nuts
¾ cup sugar
1 tablespoon baking powder
1 teaspoon salt

½ teaspoon baking soda
½ teaspoon nutmeg
1 large egg, lightly beaten
1 cup applesauce
¼ cup oil

*M*ix flour through nuts well. Stir in remainder just until all ingredients are moistened and egg disappears. Pour into oiled 5-inch by 9-inch bread pan. Bake in 350-degree oven for 50 minutes or until toothpick inserted in center comes out clean.

★
William Nelms
Hood's Texas Brigade
Camp #153
San Antonio, Texas
★
Descendant of
Pvt. Martin Ransom Gwyn
Co. D., 16th Tennessee
Infantry

Grandma's Potato Salad

For those who like it a little on the sweet side

4-5 pounds white potatoes
  (any waxy potato will do)
³/₄ cup onions, chopped
½ cup sweet pickles,
  chopped
½ cup celery, chopped
2 hard-boiled eggs, cooled and
  chopped

Dressing
1³/₄ cups regular mayonnaise
  (do not substitute)
1½ teaspoons prepared yellow
  mustard
2 tablespoons cider vinegar
¼ teaspoon sugar
½ teaspoon salt
⅛ teaspoon black pepper

Peel and chop potatoes into 1-inch cubes. Boil in salted water until tender. Pour into colander and drain well. Empty into large bowl. Into a small bowl mix the dressing in the order given. Seasonings may be adjusted to taste. While the potatoes are still slightly warm, add onions, pickles, celery, and boiled eggs. Pour dressing over salad and fold in until well mixed. Taste again for seasonings. Serves 10-12.

★
Stephen Lucas
Gen. W. L. Cabell
Camp #1313
Dallas, Texas
★
Great-great-grandson
Pvt. Henry B. Iddings
Co. I, 54th Virginia Infantry

Henry Iddings was born in 1839 in Montgomery County, Virginia. He enlisted in Confederate service and served actively until he was sent home sick from Dalton, Georgia, in 1863. He married and raised a large family. During his marriage Henry built his wife, Martha, a fine new house on a hill overlooking their old place. After spending one night there, Martha decided it was too "drafty," and they moved back into the old house. That old house is long gone, but the "new" house still stands adjacent to the Iddings family cemetery, where Henry and Martha now rest.

Aunt Ottis' Strawberry Salad

Cool and tasty

1½ cups miniature marshmallows

2 (3-ounce) packages strawberry Jell-O

2 cups boiling water

1 (10-ounce) package frozen strawberries and juice

1 small can crushed pineapple

1 (8-ounce) carton Cool Whip

1 cup pecans, chopped

---

*A*dd marshmallows and Jell-O to boiling water, then add frozen strawberries and pineapple. Let thicken, then add Cool Whip and pecans.

★

**Billy Ed Bowden
Maj. James Morgan Utz
Camp #1815
Florissant, Missouri**

★

**Great-grandson
1st Sgt. William Jordan Bowden
2nd Co. K, 10th Regiment
Tennessee Cavalry**

Sgt. Bowden's regiment fought in more than 100 battles and skirmishes and suffered a 25 percent casualty rate. Bowden was wounded in the leg in east Tennessee and later surrendered with Nathan Bedford Forrest in Alabama.

Hot Macaroni Salad

Can be frozen and cooked later

1 (8-ounce) package of
   macaroni
1 cup mayonnaise
1 can mushroom soup
1 small jar pimiento

1 small jar mushrooms
½ pound sharp cheese, grated
½ cup onion
¼ cup bell pepper
Crushed crackers

*C*ook macaroni according to package directions and drain. Add remaining ingredients. Pour into a casserole dish and top with crushed crackers. Cook at 350 degrees for 30-45 minutes.

★
Jerry Hicks
W. C. Oates Camp #809
Dothan, Alabama
★

Great-great-grandson
Pvt. Daniel Brooks Story
Co. K, 34th Alabama Infantry

Daniel Story was captured at Missionary Ridge and sent to Rock Island Prison. After his release, he returned to farming in Alabama. He died in 1906.

Grandma's Grit Corn Bread

Another variation of a Southern favorite

⅓-½ cup cooked grits
½ cup flour
½ cup lard

1 cup House Autry brand corn
   meal
Milk to consistency

*M*ix ingredients in a greased cake pan. Put butter or fatback grease on top to brown. Bake in a 350-degree oven for about 45 minutes.

Thomas L. Myers
North Carolina Divison, SCV
Fayetteville, North Carolina
★
Great-great-grandson
Pvt. William Holly Thigpen
Co. A, 38th
North Carolina Troops

Broccoli Delight Salad

Has a hearty, crunchy texture

1 large broccoli bunch, cut
    into pieces
10 strips bacon, cooked and
    crumbled
2 cups raisins
$\frac{1}{4}$ cup red onions, diced
1 cup sunflower seeds

Dressing
3-4 tablespoons sugar
1 tablespoon vinegar
$\frac{1}{2}$ cup mayonnaise

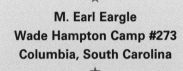

★

M. Earl Eargle
Wade Hampton Camp #273
Columbia, South Carolina

★

Descendant of
Pvt. Simion Loyd Addy
Co. C, 15th South Carolina
Infantry

Pvt. Addy was wounded at
the Battle of The Wilderness
in 1864. He died of typhoid
fever on June 6, 1864, at
General Hospital No. 3 at
Lynchburg, Virginia. He is
buried in the Confederate
Cemetery.

*P*ut washed, well-drained broccoli pieces into a large
bowl. Add bacon, raisins, onions, and sunflower seeds.
Mix dressing ingredients and pour over salad. Makes 6
servings.

Iced Green Tomato Pickles

A wonderful pickle that's worth the trouble

7 pounds green tomatoes
   (small, immature), sliced
2 gallons water
3 cups Mrs. Wages pickling
   lime

5 pounds sugar
3 pints vinegar
1 teaspoon each: cloves,
   ginger, allspice, celery seed,
   mace, cinnamon

*W*ash and slice tomatoes. Soak for 24 hours in lime water, making sure that all tomatoes are covered by using a weighted plate to hold them under the surface of the water. Drain and soak in fresh, cold water for 4 hours, changing water every hour. Drain after last soak. In a large kettle, place sugar, vinegar, and spices. Bring this syrup to a boil, and remove from heat. Add the drained tomatoes. Allow to stand overnight. In the morning, bring to a boil, and simmer for 1 hour. Place tomatoes into hot, clean glass jars, cover with syrup, wipe jar tops, and seal with hot lids with ring bands. Makes 4-5 pints. Wait at least 3 weeks before serving. Refrigerate the night before serving and afterward to assure crispness.

The lime makes the tomatoes crisp. My wife, Judy,
usually makes these pickles in the fall, when it is time for
first frost and my tomato vines have lots of small
green tomatoes left on them. This recipe has been passed
through several generations of my wife's family,
and it is a real treat.

★
Miles Jackson
Confederate Memorial
Camp #1432
Stone Mountain, Georgia
★
Descendant of
Allen Stephens Alford
Co. B, Blount's Battalion,
Georgia Militia

Allen Alford enlisted as a courier when he was 15 years of age. He and his father were the youngest, and the oldest, to join the Confederate forces from Putnam County, Georgia. He survived the war and lived a long life.

Southern Spoon Bread

Served regularly at Sunday dinner

1 cup corn meal	1 teaspoon salt
3 cups milk	3 teaspoons baking powder
3 eggs, well beaten	1 tablespoon butter, melted

Stir meal into 2 cups milk. Let it come to a boil, making a mush. Add remainder of milk, eggs, salt, baking powder, and melted butter. Bake in moderate oven 30 minutes or until done.

★

David R. Hereford
Col. Andrew Jackson May
Camp #1897
Prestonsburg, Kentucky

★

Great-grandson
1st Cpl. James Henry
Hereford, Jr.
10th Kentucky Infantry

James H. Hereford, Jr., was captured at the Battle of Ivy Mountain near Prestonsburg, Kentucky. A family member managed to get him paroled near Pikesville, with the proviso that he would return home and no longer support the Confederate cause. After he was safely away from his Federal captors, he promptly reenlisted. After the war, he became a noted attorney and wrote a widely circulated pamphlet advocating that the government compensate former slaveholders for their freed slaves. He reared a family of six children and lies buried in the family cemetery in Prestonsburg.

95

Spoon Bread

Delicious even when reheated

2 cups milk	2 teaspoons baking powder
³/₄ cup yellow corn meal	2 tablespoons sugar
2 eggs	2 tablespoons butter, melted
³/₄ teaspoon salt	

Scald milk. Add corn meal and stir mixture until thick. Remove from heat. Add eggs, one at a time, stirring well after each addition. Add salt, baking powder, sugar, and melted butter. Pour into a greased baking dish and bake for 25 minutes at 400 degrees.

Note: This recipe doubles nicely.

★

J. E. B. Stuart IV
Col. U.S. Army (Ret.)
Lee-Jackson Camp #1
Richmond, Virginia

★

Great-grandson
Major General J. E. B. Stuart
Commander—Cavalry Corps
Army of Northern Virginia

The experiences of J. E. B. Stuart's Cavalry Corps can be summed up in their trademark song:

"If you want to have a good time,
  Jine the Cavalry!
If you want to catch the devil,
If you want to have some fun,
If you want to smell Hell,
  Jine the Cavalry!"

Major General Stuart was killed at the Battle of Yellow Tavern in 1864. His unusual (and illustrious) name has been passed down through his direct descendants to J. E. B. Stuart VI, who is now nine years old.

Layered Salad

All ages like it

Torn lettuce
½ cup celery, chopped
¼ cup green onion, finely
    chopped
⅓ cup bell pepper, chopped
1 small can Le Seur English
    peas, drained
2 cups premium mayonnaise
    (I like Hellmann's)

2 tablespoons sugar
1½ cups cheddar cheese,
    grated
½ cup bacon, cooked and
    crumbled (or use bacon
    substitute)

★
Tad D. Shelfer
John B. Hood Camp #50
Houston, Texas
★
3rd great-grandson
Pvt. Levi Shelfer
Co. G, 2nd Florida Cavalry

*I*n a large, rectangular glass casserole dish, arrange enough torn lettuce to reach ⅔ of the way to the top. Layer the next 4 ingredients, in order, on top of the lettuce. Spread mayonnaise over the top, sealing well all around. Sprinkle sugar over mayonnaise. Top with cheese and bacon. Chill. Serves 10-12.

North Carolina Corn Bread

Perfect with black-eyed peas and greens

3 cups fine ground corn meal
   (do not use self-rising)
½ teaspoon salt
½ cup flour

1 cup milk or ¼ cup powdered
   milk
Enough hot water to make a
   thick batter (not boiling)

*M*ix ingredients well and pour in hot pan that has oil (or grease) running smoothly over the bottom—for best results, use a well-seasoned (no aluminum or glass) pan. An iron skillet is strongly preferred. Spoon oil from edges over bread mixture. Bake in hot oven 45-60 minutes at 425 degrees on the lower shelf. This will produce a pan of thin corn bread, North Carolina style!

★

William McGrath
William M. Burdine
Camp #1775
Coconut Beach, Florida

★

Great-grandson
Pvt. Josiah J. Hughes
Co. E, 61st North Carolina
Troops

After the war, Josiah Hughes returned to farming and reared a family of five children. He was very active in the United Confederate Veterans, and attended many conventions and reunions. He lived a long life, and is buried in Snow Hill, Maryland. His home is still standing along Highway 258 near Lizzie, North Carolina.

Stonegate Confederate Barbecue Sauce

Delicious on chicken or steak

½ cup cooking oil
¾ chopped onion
Juice of 1 lemon
¾ cup ketchup
¾ cup water
3 tablespoons sugar

3 tablespoons Worcestershire
   sauce
2 tablespoons French's
   prepared mustard
2 teaspoons pepper

*C*ook onion until soft in hot oil (not too hot). Add remaining ingredients. Simmer 15 minutes.

This recipe has been used in our family for nearly half a century and was developed by my mother, a longtime member of the United Daughters of the Confederacy. Sadly, this delight was not available to our ancestors during the late (but still lively) hostilities.

★

John P. Zebelean III, Lt. Col., USAF (Ret.)
Maj. Gen. Isaac Ridgeway Trimble Camp #1836
Catonsville, Maryland

★

Descendant of
Pvt. Matthew Jordan Hane Co. I, 35th Infantry, North Carolina Troops

Lynchburg Layered Salad

Feeds 12 Yankees or 6 Confederates

1 head iceberg lettuce, torn into bite-sized pieces
$\frac{1}{2}$ cup onion, chopped
$\frac{1}{2}$ cup celery, diced
1-2 carrots, thinly sliced
1 (5-ounce) can water chestnuts, drained and sliced
1 (10-ounce) package frozen peas (don't thaw them out!)
1 teaspoon sugar
2 cups Miracle Whip salad dressing

1 clove garlic, crushed
2 medium tomatoes, thinly sliced
4 hard-boiled eggs, sliced
6 slices bacon, cooked crisp, crumbled (use more if desired)
Cheddar cheese, grated (enough to create a $\frac{1}{2}$-inch layer)

---

*I*n a large glass bowl, start with a base layer of the lettuce. Mix onion and celery for next layer. Layer carrots and water chestnuts. Add a layer of unthawed peas and sprinkle with sugar. Combine Miracle Whip and garlic cloves to create next layer. Refrigerate.

Just before eating, add layers of sliced tomatoes, sliced hard-boiled eggs, bacon bits, and grated cheese. Each portion should include every layer, so "dig deep" when serving.

★

The Reverend Louis V. Carlson, Jr., O.S.T.
Capt. James Iredell Waddell
Camp #1770
Orange County, California

★

Great-grandson
Col. Granville Revere Lewis
Assistant Surgeon,
Headquarters Company
Army of Northern Virginia

Dr. Lewis was paroled in Hampton, Virginia, in 1865. After the war, he headed an orphanage in Lynchburg for more than 30 years. He rarely talked about his war service, but a small portrait of Robert E. Lee hung in the parlor until his death. The portrait remains in the family.

Two-Hour Yeast Rolls

A tried and true family favorite

2 cups milk
2 tablespoons sugar
1½ teaspoons salt
2 packages yeast

5-6 cups flour
4 tablespoons shortening or
   butter, melted

Scald milk. Add sugar and salt. Cool to lukewarm. Stir in yeast and dissolve. Add 3 cups flour and beat until smooth. Add melted butter and remaining flour (or enough to make an easily handled dough). Knead well. Place dough in greased bowl. Cover. Set in warm place free from draft. Let rise until doubled in bulk (about 1 hour). Shape into rolls and place in well-greased pan. Cover and let rise until double (about 45 minutes). Bake in hot oven (400 degrees) for about 20 minutes or until done.

★
Mason Sickel
Col. Robert G. Shaver
Camp #1655
Jonesboro, Arkansas
★
Great-great-grandson
Pvt. Daniel E. (J. D.) Ellis
Co. K, Freeman's Missouri
Cavalry

Pvt. Ellis was born in Surry County, North Carolina. In 1908, while closing his mercantile business, he was brutally murdered. His killer was never apprehended. He is buried in an unmarked grave in St. Francis County, Arkansas.

Mama's Chicken Salad

Perfect for a ladies' brunch

3½-4 pounds split chicken
 breast with bones in and
 skin on
Salt
Black pepper

1 bunch celery
3 bunches green spring onions
2 cups premium mayonnaise
 (Hellmann's is best)

Wash chicken breasts and place in a 6-quart sauce pan. Add enough water to cover. Add 1 tablespoon each of salt and pepper. Bring to a hard boil and turn heat down. Simmer on medium heat for 1 hour. Turn off heat and let cool. Remove chicken from broth and remove skin and bones. Save broth. Tear each breast into 4-5 pieces, following the grain of the meat. Chop across the grain into ½-inch pieces. Place in a 10-quart bowl. Sprinkle about ½ cup of broth over cut-up chicken and mix well.

Wash celery and onions. Remove onion roots and chop into ½-inch pieces using green tops also. Split each stalk of celery lengthwise into 4 slices, then chop sections into ½-inch pieces. Add chopped celery and onions to chicken. Mix well. Add mayonnaise and ½ teaspoon black pepper and mix well. Taste and add additional salt/pepper to your taste. Refrigerate until ready to serve on bread, crackers, or just lettuce. Yields approximately 12 cups.

★

**David Lamon
Col. Edmund N. Atkinson
Camp #680
Valdosta, Georgia**

★

**Great-grandson
Pvt. William James Lamon
Co. D, 2nd Battalion Florida
Infantry**

William Lamon was a small farmer. After the war, he was married and fathered ten children. He died in 1906, and is buried in Dixie, Georgia, a fitting resting place for a man who loved the South as he did.

Corn Bread Salad

A new way to enjoy corn bread

4 tomatoes, peeled and
    chopped
1 onion, chopped
½ cup sweet pickles,
    chopped

9 slices bacon, cooked and
    crumbled
1 cup mayonnaise
1 (8-inch) skillet of corn
    bread, crumbled

Combine tomatoes, onion, pickles, and bacon. Drain off excess juice and mix in mayonnaise. Crumble corn bread and vegetable mixture. Toss gently. Put mayonnaise on top of salad, cover, and chill overnight.

★
Wayne Culver
Simonton-Wilcox Camp #257
Covington, Tennessee
★
Descendant of
Ely Frederic Broughton
Co. A., 15th Alabama Infantry

Zesty Black-Eyed Pea Salad

Very good summer salad

2 (15-ounce) cans black-eyed
    peas, drained
1 cup celery, chopped
1 bell pepper, chopped
1 large tomato, chopped
1 clove garlic, minced
2 green onions, chopped

1 (4-ounce) jar sliced mush-
    rooms, drained
1 (4-ounce) jar pimientos,
    diced and drained
1 (8-ounce) bottle Italian
    dressing

Mix all ingredients (except dressing) gently in a large bowl. Pour dressing over all and mix again. Cover and chill for at least 8 hours.

★
Buddy Kirtland
Col. Jacob B. Biffle
Camp #1603
Lawrenceville, Tennessee
★
Descendant of
Cpl. John A. McGill
Co. K, 17th Tennessee Infantry

Mexican Corn Bread

Created in the scorching heat of the Texas border country

1 can cream-style corn
1 cup yellow corn meal
1 cup milk
2 eggs, well beaten
½ cup fried bacon grease
½ teaspoon baking soda

1 teaspoon salt
1 pound ground meat
1 medium onion, chopped
4 jalapeño peppers, chopped
Sharp cheddar cheese (8-ounce block), grated

*I*n a large mixing bowl, combine the cream-style corn, corn meal, milk, eggs, bacon grease, baking soda, and salt. Stir and set aside. Brown the ground meat with the onions mixed in. Drain the mixture and add jalapeño peppers. Mix well. Add cheese and stir it in. Set mixture aside. Pour half the batter into an iron skillet. On top of this, add the meat mixture. Pour remaining batter mixture over the meat mixture. Put into oven and bake at 350 degrees for 50-60 minutes.

This corn bread is so good I have to be driven away from the table with a buggy whip and run off the premises with dogs just so my wife and kids can have a little. My wife's daddy has eaten tons of it during his lifetime, as did his daddy before him. I have eaten so much of it that I've grown thin from toting it around!

Warning: It is a well known fact that Pancho Villa will come out of the grave and ride for miles to get a pone of this corn bread, so don't cook it up when the wind is blowing from the South.

★
Nathaniel Gibbs
States Rights Guards
Camp #1551
Rochelle, Georgia
★
Great-grandson
Pvt. Nathaniel Gibbs
Co. E, 49th Georgia Volunteer Infantry

Nathaniel Gibbs was a farmer from Wilcox County, Georgia. He was detailed as a male nurse at Chimborazo Hospital in Richmond. During the course of his duties, he contracted pneumonia and died there on April 21, 1863, never having seen his new son, Nathaniel, Jr., who was born the month before. He is buried in the Confederate Cemetery in Richmond, Virginia.

Bob's Potato Salad

No picnic is complete without it

5 medium red potatoes
2 eggs, hard boiled
¾ cup mayonnaise
1 teaspoon prepared mustard
1 teaspoon Worcestershire
   sauce
Salt to taste

3 ribs celery, chopped
5 green onions (whites only),
   chopped
3-4 medium-sized green
   peppers, chopped
1 dill pickle, chopped

★
**Charles H. Smith
Brig. Gen. Stand Watie
Camp #1303
Oklahoma City, Oklahoma**
★
**Great-grandnephew
Capt. John Knight
Co. H, Crescent Regiment,
Louisiana Infantry**

*B*oil potatoes in salted water. Peel potatoes and shell eggs. Dice potatoes into small cubes. Mash eggs fine with fork. Mix mayonnaise, mustard, and Worcestershire sauce with eggs. Add salt to taste. Mix with remaining ingredients and refrigerate immediately. Serves 6-8.

My sister was a great hand at preparing potato salad. She passed on her recipe to me, and I once prepared it for our camp's annual Commander's Picnic. My late friend Robert Henson loved it, and at every picnic thereafter he would insist that I bring his favorite potato salad. It is appropriate that the dish should bear his name.

Amy Huss's Cranberry Salad

A big hit at holiday time

2 cups cranberries
3 cups apples, chopped
1½ cups sugar

Topping
½ stick margarine, softened
½ cup brown sugar
⅓ cup plain flour
⅓ cup pecans, chopped

---

*P*ut cranberries in the bottom of a casserole dish. Layer the apples over the cranberries and cover with sugar. Mix topping together and spread over sugar. Bake at 350 degrees for 45 minutes to 1 hour.

★
John E. Huss
47th Regiment, North Carolina
Troops Camp #166
Raleigh, North Carolina
★
Great-grandson
Pvt. Henry Huss
Co. G, 57th North Carolina
Troops

Henry Huss was a farmer from Lincoln County, North Carolina. He fought with his unit at Gettysburg and Fredericksburg, and was captured at Rappahannock Bridge on November 7, 1865. Henry was sent to Point Lookout Prison and remained there until March 1865. Years after the war, he was knocked into a creek and suffered some broken ribs while cutting a tree on his property. He succumbed to pneumonia a few days later at the age of 92.

Grandma Coleman's Hoe-Cake

Especially good with Georgia cane syrup

4 cups self-rising flour　　　1 cup buttermilk
4 tablespoons Crisco
　shortening

★
**Gerald L. Engle
1st Lt. Daniel Sloan
Camp #1709
Geneva, Florida**
★
**Great-grandson
Pvt. Charles Matthew Coleman
Co. H, 48th Georgia Infantry**

*P*our flour into a deep bowl. Make a hole in the center of the mound of flour. Add Crisco and buttermilk into the hole and mix all ingredients together with your hand. It will be thin and sticky, but keep incorporating the flour with each motion until you form a ball of dough. If it is too sticky, add a little more flour.

Heat a 9-inch flat griddle or cast-iron frying pan and grease with Crisco. Mash the dough flat into the skillet and cook over medium heat until dough begins to brown on one side. Flip the dough over and allow it to begin browning on the opposite side. At this point, the dough should be cooked through. Remove the finished cake and break into servings. Serve with butter, jelly, or syrup.

*This recipe was my favorite breakfast when I stayed on
Grandma Coleman's farm in rural Emanuel County,
Georgia. It helped my family outlast the deprivations
of Reconstruction, and it was a staple during
the Great Depression. My grandma made this for me on a
wood-burning stove. I can still smell the wood fire, the
sausage, and the hoe-cake reaching across the years.*

Grandpa's No Frills Corn Bread

About as close to Confederate "corn pone" as you can get

2 cups corn meal, white or yellow (no mixes or leavening)
1 tablespoon salt
¼ cup cooking oil, vegetable shortening, bacon fat, or pure lard

¾ cup liquid (may be water, milk, or buttermilk—buttermilk is best)

P lace meal in mixing bowl and add salt. Mix well. Add your choice of oil and mix until batter looks like large crumbs. Add ½ cup of liquid. Mix and allow time to set (about 5 minutes). The meal will absorb the liquid and the batter will become very stiff. Add the remaining ¼ cup of liquid and mix again. Batter should be somewhat creamy but not flowing.

Grease (no-stick spray is okay) an iron frying pan or skillet (Pyrex baking dish may be used). Place the batter in the pan or dish and spread no thicker than ⅜ inch. Bake in a preheated oven at 450 degrees or until the top of the bread begins to brown slightly. Remove and brush top with butter.

★

**Robert Downing
Fayetteville Arsenal
Camp #168
Fayetteville, North Carolina**

★

**Grandson
Cpl. William Henry Downing
Co. D, 68th North Carolina
Troops**

William Henry Downing enlisted in the Confederate forces at the age of 16. He was a very enterprising young man who became quite successful in business after the war. He purchased great quantities of land outside Fayetteville that had been considered worthless and began to grow corn. He became known as "Corn Downing" because farmers eventually had to go to him to buy corn for their livestock. He became a rich man by the standards of the day, but was scrupulously honest. He abhorred smoking and would allow no tobacco to be grown on his land, nor would he allow anyone to smoke on it. He had a large family and died in 1927.

William Henry Downing
Corporal, Co. D, 68th North Carolina Troops

Hot Slaw

An alternative to cold cole slaw

1 head of cabbage
1 tablespoon bacon drippings
¼ cup salad dressing or
   mayonnaise
Pepper to taste
Salt (optional)
1 tablespoon vinegar

Slice and core cabbage, then rinse in colander. In large saucepan over medium heat, put cabbage and bacon drippings. Steam until tender. Drain excess water in pot. Add salad dressing or mayonnaise, pepper, salt (optional), and vinegar. Mix well. Serve hot.

★
John R. Lumsden
Robert E. Lee Camp #726
Alexandria, Virginia
★
Great-grandson
James Marshall Duncan
CSS *Patrick Henry*,
Confederate Navy

James Duncan was a veteran of the British navy and worked on the docks in Glasgow, Scotland, when he decided to cross the ocean and join the Confederate forces. After the war, he returned to Scotland and brought his family back to settle in Virginia. In later years he was a farmer and deacon in the Methodist Church. He died in 1911.

Grandma Wright's Mashed Potato Salad

Best if served warm

6 white potatoes
1 medium onion, diced
6 eggs, hard boiled

2 tablespoons cider vinegar
Salt and pepper to taste

Cook and mash white potatoes and prepare as for regular mashed potatoes. Add onion, eggs, and cider vinegar. Season to taste with salt and pepper. Mix until nice and fluffy. Slice 1 boiled egg to decorate top of salad. Serves 6-8.

★
David E. Curtis
Dillard-Judd Camp #1828
Cookeville, Tennessee
★
Great-grandson
Pvt. Thomas A. Curtis
Co. I, 25th Tennessee Infantry

Thomas Curtis was a farmer and deputy sheriff in Overton County, Tennessee. He died in 1919.

Buck Bread

Autumn bread baked mainly in the fall and winter months

½ cup margarine
⅔ cup sugar
2 eggs
2 cups self-rising flour
1 cup chunky applesauce

¾ cup sharp cheddar cheese, shredded
½ cup minced cracklings (try the bacon or seasoning meat department at the market)

Cream together margarine and sugar until light and fluffy. Add eggs and beat well. Add flour and stir well. Stir in applesauce, cheese, and cracklings. Turn into a greased 9-inch by 5-inch by 3-inch loaf pan. Bake 50-55 minutes at 350 degrees. Cool 10 minutes in pan. Remove bread from pan and cool on rack. Yields 1 loaf.

★

**Billy K. Buck
Urquhart-Gillette Camp #1471
Franklin, Virginia**

★

**Great-great-grandnephew
Pvt. Frederick W. March
Co. A, 16th Virginia Infantry**

Fred March left home to join the Confederate forces when he was 17 years old, and saw action at Malvern Hill, Chancellorsville, the Wilderness, and Spotsylvania. In October 1864, he was captured at Burgess Mill, Virginia, and sent to Point Lookout Prison. He was released in June 1865. Instead of signing his name on his release papers, he made an "X," although he could read and write. It was his final act of defiance, affirming that he never truly surrendered.

Fish Fry Cole Slaw

The perfect accompaniment to catfish

2 bags grated cabbage
½ Vidalia onion, grated
1 teaspoon lemon juice
1 tablespoon vinegar

1 tablespoon dill pickles,
   chopped
2 tablespoons mayonnaise
Salt and pepper to taste

*M*ix all ingredients in a large bowl. Let sit in refrigerator a couple of hours for flavors to mix. Serve cold. Serves 6-8.

★

Charles Lunsford
Chattahoochee Guards
Camp #1639
Atlanta, Georgia

★

Great-grandson
Pvt. Andrew Jackson Lunsford
36th Georgia Regiment
(Cummings Brigade)

Andrew Lunsford was a farmer from Gwinnett County, Georgia. He entered the service with his brothers-in-law and fought with the Army of Tennessee, beginning with the Vicksburg Campaign. He was captured just before the siege of Vicksburg, sent to Fort Delaware, and later parolod. He rejoined his unit at Chattanooga and fought in the Atlanta Campaign. Pvt. Lunsford was captured again in the Battle of Atlanta and held until after the war. He received a Confederate pension until his death in 1903.

Corn Meal Mush

Serve with fried eggs and bacon

6 cups water
1 tablespoon salt
¼ cup flour

2 cups stone ground corn meal
1 teaspoon sugar (optional)

*B*oil salt in water. Sift in meal and flour, stirring constantly. Cook 15 minutes. Pour into loaf pan. Allow it to cool. When cold, slice and fry to a golden brown. Serves 3.

I cut my teeth on this recipe and find that no breakfast is complete without it.

★
Greg Michael
Garnett Camp #1470
Huntington, West Virginia
★
Great-great-grandson
Pvt. Samuel Farmer
Co. A, 45th Virginia Infantry

Pvt. Farmer was captured at the Battle of Piedmont and sent to prison at Camp Morton, Indiana. He was exchanged in February 1865 and returned to Wayne County, West Virginia. He founded a Masonic lodge there. Samuel died in 1920.

Main Dishes, Soups, and Stews

Sylvia's Southern Lasagna
Georgia's Mexican Casserole
Hearty Buffet Chili
Grandma's Smothered Chicken
Prejean's Championship Chicken and
    Sausage Gumbo
Becky's Beer Brisket
Shrimp Creole
Salisbury Meat Loaf
Chicken Chinnabee
Oyster Bisque
Crab Cakes
Quick Hamburger Stroganoff
Kay's Moonshine Pork Chops
Cornish Pasties
El Dorado Casserole
Shrimp Pie
Chicken and Sour Cream Enchiladas
Escalloped Trout
Mammy's Spaghetti
Commander-in-Chief Crab Cakes
Salmon Patties for Two
Easy Southeastern Kentucky Mountain Chili
Peggy's Famous Meat Loaf
Low Country Boil
Hazel's Famous Beef Bourguignonne
Confederate Chicken Bogg
Crock Pot Barbecue
Dove Breasts in Red Wine Sauce for Two
Patty's Beef Spaghetti Pie
Southern Meat Loaf
White Chili
Ocean Isle à la Fairmont
Bow Tie Pasta with Basil Chicken
Rebel's Favorite Chili
Mom's Shrimp Diablo
Seafood Pie
Miss Betty's Chicken Stew
Jeff Davis Spaghetti
Hearty Crock Pot Clam Chowder
Ham Pie Casserole
Crawfish Jambalaya
Fried Chicken and Gravy
Jesse's Black Bean Soup
Venison Steak Parmesan
Br'er Rabbit Stew
Hot Dog Spaghetti Casserole
Southern Ham and Bean Soup
Cranberry Meatballs

Tennessee Red Beans and Rice
Lauren Haley's Fine Fettuccine
Confederate Clam Chowder
Granny Coleman's Brunswick Stew
My Guy's Smothered Venison
River Road Brisket of Beef
Meat Loaf à la Haley
Prize Winning Stuffed Cornish Hens
Missouri Cabbage Soup
Duck Camp Red Beans and Rice
Sherried Beef
Chicken, Broccoli, and Peaches
Southern Lemon Chicken
Fried Rabbit with Mushroom Sauce
Grilled Peppered Beef
Chicken and Sausage Gumbo
Crowd Chicken Casserole
California Style Pork Barbecue
Southern Pasta
Fort Concho Frijoles
Classic Shrimp Creole
Easy Chicken and Dumplings
Meatball Stew for a Crowd
Sweet and Sour Chicken
Catfish Stew
Low Country Deviled Crab
Southern Maryland Stuffed Ham
Oyster Jambalaya
Shipwreck Casserole
South Georgia Stuffed Quail
Mexican Chicken
Seafood Gumbo
Chicken and Rice Casserole
Louisiana Red Beans and Rice
Hot Texas Chili
Southern Fried Venison & Gravy
Shrimp Sauce Piquante
Poppy Seed Chicken
Oysters Johnny Reb
Viva La Chicken Tortilla Casserole
The Judge's Tex-Mex Bean Soup
King Ranch Casserole
Leftover Turkey Casserole
Skillet Chicken and Gravy
Grandma Curcio's Chicken Cacciatore
Chicken Crunch Casserole
Old Virginia Brunswick Stew
Hungry Soldier Bean Soup

Sylvia's Southern Lasagna

Contains sour cream instead of ricotta cheese for a slightly different taste

1 onion, chopped
1 large bell pepper, chopped
1 clove garlic, chopped
1½ pounds of ground beef
1 (16-ounce) can whole
   tomatoes
1 (8-ounce) can tomato sauce
1 small can tomato paste
1 tablespoon minced parsley
1 tablespoon sugar

1½ teaspoons salt
1 teaspoon basil
1 teaspoon Italian seasoning
1 small box lasagna noodles
1 pound mozzarella cheese,
   grated
1 pound cheddar cheese,
   grated
1 pint sour cream
Parmesan cheese

★

Phillip B. Isaacs
Col. Samuel H. Walkup
Camp #1375
Union County, North Carolina

★

Great-great-grandson
Pvt. Godfrey Isaacs
Co. A, 28th Regiment, North
Carolina Troops

*B*rown onion, garlic, bell pepper, and ground beef. Drain. Add tomatoes, sauce, paste, and spices. Cook over medium-low heat for 1 hour, stirring occasionally. Cook noodles as directed. Place layer of noodles on bottom of a 9-inch by 13-inch pan. Spread half the sour cream over noodles. Spread half the mozzarella cheese and half the cheddar cheese as the next layer. The next layer will be half of the meat sauce. Then generously sprinkle a layer of Parmesan cheese. Repeat. Bake at 350 degrees for 35-45 minutes. Let cool for about 30 minutes before serving. It holds together better as it cools. Serves 8.

This is my mother-in-law's recipe and is the best lasagna I've ever had.

Georgia's Mexican Casserole

Bring this to your next potluck supper!

1½ pounds ground beef
1 large onion, chopped
1 can cream of chicken soup
1 can Ro-Tel tomatoes

1 can ranch style beans
½ pound Velveeta cheese
Flour tortillas
Corn chips, crushed

*B*rown meat and onion. Drain fat and add soup, Ro-Tel, beans, and cheese. Stir until cheese melts. Grease 9-inch by 13-inch casserole dish. Line bottom of dish with tortillas. Spread half meat mixture over tortillas. Make another layer of each. Top with crushed corn chips. Heat in 350-degree oven until bubbly—about 10 minutes. Serves 8-10.

This recipe comes from my wife, Georgia, who is the
3rd great-granddaughter of Pvt. John Wesley Hockersmith,
Co. C, 49th Alabama Infantry. He was wounded and
captured at the Battle of Port Hudson. His daughter,
Nancy Jane Hockersmith, was a young girl when
her father left to join the Confederate forces.
Her mother died of complications from the measles the
invading Federal army brought into town.

★
Ben Head
Gen. Richard Taylor
Camp #1308
Shreveport, Louisiana
★
Great-great-grandson
Levi Marion Head
Co. H, 20th Texas Calvary

Opposite—John Wesley Hockersmith
Private, Co. C, 49th Alabama Infantry

Hearty Buffet Chili

Perfect for a family get-together

1 pound ground beef
½ cup chopped onion
1 clove garlic, minced
1 (16-ounce) can whole tomatoes, cut up
1 (15-ounce) can tomato sauce
2 teaspoons chili powder
1 teaspoon salt
½ teaspoon crushed red pepper
¼ teaspoon black pepper
1 (15-ounce) can of kidney beans in chili sauce

Place in individual bowls:
1 cup shredded jack or cheddar cheese
½ cup chopped onion
½ cup sour cream
1-2 cups cooked rice

*C*ook beef, onion, and garlic in large pan until beef is brown and onion is tender. Drain fat. Stir in undrained tomatoes, tomato sauce, chili powder, salt, red pepper, and black pepper. Bring to a boil. Reduce heat, cover, and simmer for 1 hour. Add beans with chili sauce, cover, and simmer for 30 minutes.

Set out rice, cheese, onion, and sour cream in small individual bowls for guests or family members to serve themselves. For each serving, place some cooked rice in bowl. Top with chili mixture, then cheese, onions, or sour cream if desired.

★
**Charles A. Riffee
John S. Mosby Camp #1237
Front Royal, Virginia**
★
**Grandson
Pvt. Amos D. Riffee
22nd Virginia Infantry**

Amos Riffee was a farmer in western Virginia. He and his two brothers enlisted in the Confederate army early in the war. Amos was 17 years old at the time of his enlistment. He was captured in 1864 and sent to Fort Delaware Prison, where he remained until he was released in 1865. After the war, he was cofounder of the Pleasant Valley Baptist Church in Kenna, West Virginia, and it remains an active church today. Pvt. Riffee died in 1906.

Grandma's Smothered Chicken

A traditional Southern dish that's good any time

1 3-4 pound chicken	2 cups water
3 tablespoons flour	1 small to medium onion,
Salt and pepper to taste	sliced
Shortening or vegetable oil	

*C*ut up chicken. Wash well. Flour, salt, and pepper each piece. Heat shortening or oil in an iron skillet. Cook chicken pieces about 15 minutes on each side at medium-high heat. Make sure each side is browned. Remove from pan. Pour off all but 2-3 tablespoons of oil. Stir in flour. Brown flour a few seconds, stirring constantly. Add water and onions, and salt and pepper to taste. Simmer 30 minutes in uncovered skillet for gravy to cook down and cling to chicken. Stir occasionally to prevent sticking. Serves 6-8 people. Refrigerate any leftovers.

This recipe came down through our family from my wife's grandmother, Mary Elizabeth (Betty) Gooch. This was a popular recipe in her family since they always had a barnyard full of chickens!

★

Keith Thomason
Chief Clinton Camp #366
Abilene, Texas

★

Great-grandson
Jessie James Cotter
3rd Battery, Maryland Artillery

Jessie James Cotter fought in seventeen battles and was captured twice while in Confederate service, first at Vicksburg and again at Nashville. He was a prisoner of war at Camp Douglas. After he returned home to Sullivan County, Tennessee, his first wife and two children tragically burned to death in a house fire. He moved to Texas and later remarried. He died in 1912 in Kimble County, Texas.

Prejean's Championship Chicken and Sausage Gumbo

From Prejean's Restaurant in Lafayette, Louisiana

½ cup corn oil
½ cup flour
2 medium fryers
1¼ gallons water
2 cups onions, diced
2 cups celery, diced
1 cup bell pepper, diced
¼ cup chicken bouillon granules

2 teaspoons Kitchen Bouquet
2 teaspoons cayenne pepper
4 cups smoked sausage, sliced
1 teaspoon black pepper
1½ teaspoons granulated garlic powder
¼ teaspoon Tabasco sauce

*M*ake a roux by heating oil in a skillet until smoking hot (6-7 minutes) over medium heat. Gradually add flour while whisking continuously. Be careful not to let roux stick to bottom and do not splash onto skin. Mixture will brown rapidly. Cook until roux is chocolate brown (like an old penny), whisking vigorously 8-10 minutes, then remove from heat. Continue to stir until cool. Boil chickens in water for 30 minutes. Remove with tongs, cool birds, and pick meat off bones. Set aside. Add onions, celery, and bell pepper to boiling water. Add roux and stir in well until dissolved with a wire whip. Add remaining ingredients (except meat) and boil over medium heat for 45 minutes. Add chicken and sausage and continue to boil for 10 minutes. Remove from heat and let gumbo stand for 10 minutes. Skim oil off the top. Serve over rice in a large bowl. Serves 8-10.

continued on next page

★
Ronald G. Ward
Battle of Massard Prairie
Camp #1830
Fort Smith, Arkansas
★
Great-great-grandson
Cpl. Houston Nelson Ward
Co. H, 4th Arkansas Infantry

Houston Ward enlisted with his father, Granberry Ward. Granberry was later sent home because of his age. Houston had several careers, including a stint taking care of Belle Starr's horses and serving as a lawman. He died in 1911.

THE CONFEDERATE COOKBOOK

This recipe was reprinted with the permission of Chef James Graham (World Champion Gumbo Chef, 1991-1999), Prejean's Restaurant, Lafayette, Louisiana.

Back in 1992, Chef James Graham of Prejean's Restaurant served bowls of his world championship gumbo at Central Mall in Fort Smith, Arkansas, as a "thank you" to the area for aiding Louisianians after the state was threatened by a hurricane. I saw small children eating his gumbo, huffing and trying to cool their mouths, while saying, "Mommy, this is hot, but it sure is good! Can I have some more?"

Becky's Beer Brisket

Really juicy and tender

1 large onion, sliced
1 trimmed brisket
1 (12-ounce) can of beer
¼ cup chili powder

4 or more cloves of garlic, chopped
1 tablespoon flour
½ cup cold water

Place sliced onions in bottom of baking dish. Arrange brisket on top of onions. Mix beer, chili powder, and garlic and pour over brisket. Cover well and bake at 300 degrees for 3 hours. Remove brisket from pan and pour liquid in small saucepan. Thicken the liquid with flour and water. Slice brisket when slightly cooled and pour gravy over it.

Tip: Use a layer of heavy-duty foil on the bottom of the baking dish as well as on top. It makes clean up much easier.

★
Roger White
Brig. Gen. Thomas M. Scott
Camp #1604
Minden, Louisiana
★
Descendant of
Pvt. Edward Eugene Pratt
Co. G, 8th Louisiana Infantry

Shrimp Creole

A savory New Orleans classic

1 medium onion, chopped
1 green pepper, chopped
2½ cups sliced mushrooms
2 to 3 cloves of garlic, minced
2 tablespoons butter or olive oil
16 ounces of stewed tomatoes

16 ounces of tomato sauce
1½ teaspoons sugar
½ teaspoon Creole seasoning
⅛ teaspoon paprika
1½ pounds shrimp, deveined

Sauté the onions, green peppers, mushrooms, and garlic in butter (or olive oil) in a large skillet. Stir in stewed tomatoes, sauce, sugar, Creole seasoning, and paprika. Bring to a boil. Reduce heat and simmer uncovered for 20 minutes. Add shrimp and simmer for another 10-12 minutes or until shrimp is done. Serve over rice or pasta (angel hair or bow tie). Serves 4 to 6.

★
James K. Turner
Sam Davis Camp #1293
Nashville, Tennessee
★
Descendant of
Pvt. Joseph Mitchell
Williamson
Co. K, 17th Tennessee Infantry

Salisbury Meat Loaf

A family dinner staple

2 eggs, beaten lightly
1 cup milk
¼ teaspoon pepper
2 teaspoons salt
2 tablespoons minced onion

1 teaspoon Worcestershire
  sauce
1½ pounds ground beef
¼ pound ground sausage (hot
  sausage best)

Combine all ingredients and mix well. Pack into a greased loaf pan. Bake at 350 degrees for 1¼ hours.

★
Jim Moore
CSS *Florida* Camp #102
Orlando, Florida
★
Descendant of
Jim Moore, Jr.
Co. G, 26th Georgia Infantry

THE CONFEDERATE COOKBOOK

Chicken Chinnabee

From Chinnabee House, on the grounds of The Cedars Plantation

4 cloves fresh garlic, chopped
1/2 cup fresh onion, chopped
4 large, boneless chicken
  breasts
2 chicken bouillon cubes, dissolved in water
Salt
Pepper
2 teaspoons tarragon

Poultry seasoning
1/2 cup red wine
1 cup mushrooms, cut in large
  chunks
2 cups sour cream, regular or
  low fat
1 cup walnuts, chopped
  coarsely
Parsley

★

W. Patrick Reaves
Lt. A. J. Buttram Camp #1818
Munford, Alabama

★

Descendant of
1st Lt. Bryant Pearce
Co. F, 31st Alabama Infantry

*L*ightly sauté the onions and garlic in 3 tablespoons of olive oil until golden brown. About halfway into the sauté, place the 4 chicken breasts into the skillet and brown both sides. Add the bouillon cubes, salt, pepper, tarragon, and poultry seasoning. You may vary the seasoning to your taste. After the breasts are browned several minutes over a medium to medium-high heat, add 1/2 cup of a good red wine (no cooking wine or vinegar). Cook over medium heat for 4-5 minutes, add mushrooms, and cook gently until all the ingredients are cooked in. Add sour cream, mix in well (covering the chicken), and place in a 325-degree to 350-degree preheated oven for about 30-45 minutes or until chicken is done. Do not overcook, as the sour cream will cook down excessively and brown. Place each breast on a plate, spoon sour cream sauce from skillet on top, cover with 1/4 cup of chopped walnuts, sprinkle with parsley, and serve. Serves 4.

The Cedars Plantation originally consisted of over 7,500 acres near Munford, Alabama. The plantation was founded in 1833 by the Reverend Joseph Camp, a friend of Chief Selocta Chinnabee of the Natchez-Creek Confederation.

125

Oyster Bisque

Rich and creamy

1 quart cream	½ cup celery, chopped
1 tablespoon flour	1 tablespoon chopped parsley
1 tablespoon butter	1 quart oysters
Salt and pepper to taste	Worcestershire sauce

Make a soup of cream thickened with flour. Add butter, salt, and pepper to taste, chopped celery, and parsley. Add oysters and keep soup hot. Never let it boil, as it will curdle. Add a dash of Worcestershire sauce just as you serve it.

★
John T. Fargason
Frontier Guard Camp #996
Junction, Texas
★
Great-grandson
Pvt. Lawrence Ewel Talbot
Co. D (McDonald's Battalion),
Tennessee Cavalry

Crab Cakes

These are good!

1 pound crab meat, picked free of shells	1 egg
½ cup crushed Ritz crackers	1-2 teaspoons Worcestershire sauce
3 green onions, chopped fine (include tops)	1 teaspoon yellow mustard
¼ teaspoon garlic powder	1 teaspoon salt
¼ cup mayonnaise	¼ teaspoon cayenne pepper
	Flour

Mix all ingredients except flour. Shape into patties and coat with flour. Preheat oil (peanut or salad) over medium-high heat. Cook one side of patty until golden brown, then flip and cook other side. Serves 4-6.

★
Jim Moore
CSS *Florida* Camp #102
Orlando, Florida
★
Descendant of
Jim Moore, Jr.
Co. G, 26th Georgia Infantry

Quick Hamburger Stroganoff

*A **quick, inexpensive supper***

2 pounds ground beef
1 cup onions, diced
1 can mushrooms, chopped
Salt and pepper to taste

1 can cream of mushroom
  soup
1 small container sour cream
1 package egg noodles

*B*rown meat and onions in skillet. Add mushrooms, salt, and pepper. Stir in cream of mushroom soup. Heat to boiling. Reduce heat and add sour cream during last 15 minutes of cooking. Spoon over noodles and serve hot.

★

James Ronald Moore
Camden Mounted Rifles
Camp #747
Camden County, Georgia

★

Descendant of
Sgt. James E. Timmons
Co. D, 2nd South Carolina
Artillery

Kay's Moonshine Pork Chops

Great pork chops

¼ cup bourbon whiskey
¼ cup soy sauce
½ cup molasses
¼ cup Dijon mustard
½ cup water, boiling

2 cloves garlic, crushed
1 dried red pepper
¼ teaspoon black pepper
6-8 pork chops

*C*ombine all ingredients (except pork chops) and mix well. Marinate pork chops for 24 hours. Place chops in a baking dish and cover with marinade sauce. Bake at 350 degrees for 45 minutes to an hour.

★

Bill Hancock
Cedar Fork Rifles Camp #1827
Chatham County,
North Carolina

★

Great-great-grandson
Pvt. William Henderson
Graham
Co. B, 13th Light Artillery,
North Carolina Troops
(Starr's Battery)

Cornish Pasties

Delicious meat pies that originated in Cornwall

3 cups self-rising flour
¼ cup lard
1 cup suet, ground fine
6-7 tablespoons cold water
2 large potatoes, sliced thin
1 teaspoon salt
Pepper to taste

1 turnip, sliced thin
1 onion, sliced thin
1 pound lean beef, diced or
    cubed
½ pound lean pork, diced or
    cubed

*B*lend lard into flour. Add suet, then cold water. Roll out dough and cut into sections. For each pie, put ½-inch layer of potatoes seasoned with salt and pepper. Next, add layer of turnips, then layer of onions. Cover with a tablespoon of beef and pork mixture. Fold dough over and crimp the edges. Slit top of crust, put on a greased cookie sheet, and bake at 400 degrees for 1 hour.

These tasty meat pies probably originated in Cornwall as a lunch for the miners in the tin mines. These pasties likely found their way to America prior to the War Between the States.

★
Kevin Easterling
Lt. Gen. Nathan B. Forrest
Camp #513
Norman, Oklahoma
★
Descendant of
Col. William Kennon Easterling
Lt. Col., 46th Mississippi
Infantry

William Easterling was born in 1822 in South Carolina. By the beginning of the War Between the States, he had established a large plantation in Rankin County, Mississippi. At the outbreak of war, he raised a company called the Fireside Farmers and was commissioned a captain in the Mississippi State Guard. His unit was transferred to the Confederate army and became part of the 46th Mississippi. After the fall of Vicksburg, he returned to his plantation and was elected to the Mississippi state legislature. In December 1863, he left the legislature and raised the 3rd Mississippi Cavalry. He served until the end of the war.

El Dorado Casserole

An easy casserole with a "South of the Border" taste

1½ pounds ground beef,
  browned and drained
2 (8-ounce) cans tomato sauce
1 package mild taco powder
1 large carton cottage cheese
1 (8-ounce) carton sour cream

2 cans green chili peppers,
  chopped
1 medium bag Doritos
2 packages grated Monterey
  Jack cheese

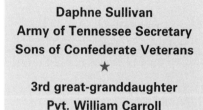

★
Daphne Sullivan
Army of Tennessee Secretary
Sons of Confederate Veterans
★
3rd great-granddaughter
Pvt. William Carroll
North Carolina Troops

Mix beef, tomato sauce, and taco powder. Mix cottage cheese, sour cream, and chili peppers. Crush Doritos. Layer one time in sheet cake pan in following order: ¾ bag Doritos, hamburger, cottage cheese mixture, Monterey Jack cheese, and remaining Doritos. Bake at 350 degrees for 20 minutes until hot. Let set for 10 minutes before serving. Serves 8-10.

Shrimp Pie

Your guests will think you've spent all day in the kitchen

2 pounds shrimp
2 cups bread crumbs
2 cups tomato juice
½ teaspoon salt
2 tablespoons butter

1 tablespoon hot sauce
2 tablespoons Worcestershire
  sauce
1 cup tomato catsup

★
James Ronald Moore
Camden Mounted Rifles
Camp #747
Camden County, Arkansas
★
Descendant of
Sgt. James E. Timmons
Co. D, 2nd South Carolina
Artillery

Cook and peel shrimp. Mix all ingredients together and bake in a casserole dish for 30 minutes. Yields 8 servings.

Chicken and Sour Cream Enchiladas

Gets every dish in the kitchen dirty, but worth the effort

1 pound cooked chicken, chopped (all white meat)
1 cup Ranchero Sauce (recipe follows)
Salt
Cumin
Cooking oil

1 can red enchilada sauce
12 burrito-size tortillas
Sour Cream Sauce (recipe follows)
Jalapeño slices
Paprika

★
Jim Templin
O. M. Roberts Camp #178
Waxahachie, Texas
★
Great-grandson
Pvt. Otto Templin
5th Texas Field Artillery

Otto was a native of Prussia who came to Texas in 1856 from the town of Templin (about 60 miles northeast of Berlin). During his long life he fathered twelve children. He lived and died in High Hill, Texas, and rests in the Old High Hill Cemetery under his newly acquired Confederate grave marker.

*A*dd Ranchero Sauce to chicken. Add salt and cumin to taste. Mix thoroughly. Set aside. Heat oil in one skillet and enchilada sauce in another. With tongs, dip a tortilla into oil and then into enchilada sauce to coat. Place some of the chicken mixture in center of tortilla and roll up. Place in a covered oven-proof dish. Repeat until all chicken mixture is used. Pour sour cream sauce over enchiladas. Top with cheese. Garnish with jalapeño slices and sprinkle with paprika. Cover and bake at 350 degrees until cheese melts and enchiladas are hot throughout.

Ranchero Sauce
2 tablespoons butter
2 medium onions, diced
1 bell pepper, diced (remove seeds)
4 tomatoes, chopped

1 (10-ounce) can tomato sauce
1-2 teaspoons cumin
1 teaspoon garlic powder
Salt to taste

*S*auté onions and bell pepper in butter until onions are clear. Add tomato sauce, chopped tomatoes, and spices. Reduce heat and simmer 15-30 minutes.

continued on next page

Sour Cream Sauce
2 cups water
1 tablespoon chicken bouillon
Juice of half a lemon

$^1/_2$ cup flour
$^1/_4$ cup oil
2 cups sour cream

*B*ring water to boil in a saucepan. Add bouillon and lemon juice. Boil until bouillon is dissolved. Make a roux with the flour and oil by placing the oil in the pan, then heating it, stirring in the flour a bit at a time until it thickens, then add to water. Remove from heat and allow to cool 5-10 minutes. Mix in sour cream.

Escalloped Trout

A wonderful seafood entrée

1 pound of tenderloin of trout,
    broiled and chilled
1 tablespoon olive oil
2 heaping tablespoons butter
1 dozen oysters

$^1/_2$ green pepper
Salt, pepper, parsley
6 strips of bacon
Pinch of cayenne
$^1/_2$ cup toasted bread crumbs

★
John T. Fargason
Frontier Guard Camp #996
Junction, Texas
★
Great-grandson
Pvt. Lawrence Ewel Talbot
Co. D, McDonald's Battalion

*S*hred the trout and put in baking dish. Pour olive oil over the fish and dot with butter. Put a layer of oysters, then a sprinkling of the green pepper, salt, pepper, cayenne, and bread crumbs. Layer again, making sure bread crumbs are on top. Cover with bacon. Cook in moderate oven at 350 degrees for 30 minutes.

Mammy's Spaghetti

A crowd pleaser

1 pound spaghetti
2 tablespoons butter or margarine
1 pound ground chuck
½ cup Vidalia or yellow onion,
  chopped fine

½ teaspoon dried oregano
Salt and pepper to taste
1 small can tomatoes (about
  14 ounces)
1 small can carrots (about 10
  ounces), drained

★
Tad D. Shelfer
John B. Hood Camp #50
Houston, Texas
★
3rd great-grandson
Pvt. Levi Shelfer
Co. G, 2nd Florida Cavalry

*C*ook spaghetti according to package directions. After draining, toss with butter until melted. Meanwhile, in a large skillet, brown ground chuck with onion, oregano, salt, and pepper until done. Stir in tomatoes and carrots, and heat through. Top each serving of spaghetti with some of the skillet mixture. Serve with grated Parmesan cheese. Serves 6.

My wife's great-grandmother fixed this version of spaghetti for her family during the Depression years. We have adapted it somewhat by using canned carrots instead of fresh.

Commander-in-Chief Crab Cakes

A Chesapeake Bay classic

½ teaspoon salt
¼ teaspoon pepper
¼ teaspoon dry mustard
2 teaspoons Worcestershire
sauce
3 tablespoons mayonnaise,
heaping

1 egg
1 tablespoon dry parsley,
chopped
1 pound crab meat
2 slices bread, chopped
Corn flake cereal, crushed

---

*M*ix all ingredients except crab, bread, and corn flakes. Add crab and bread, shape into pancakes, and roll in corn flake crumbs. Place in pan, cover with Saran wrap, and refrigerate for 2 hours. Roll in corn flakes again before frying in butter. Serves 4-6.

*Maryland is known the world over for its crab industry,
and this recipe is sure to delight those who
have a taste for crabs.*

**Patrick J. Griffin III
Col. William Norris
Camp #1398
Gaithersburg, Maryland**
★

**Great-great-grandson
Pvt. James Andrew
Jackson Coker
Co. H, 39th Georgia Infantry**

James Andrew Jackson Coker was born in 1829 in Ringgold, Georgia. At age 32, he kissed his wife goodbye, hugged his four small children, bade them all farewell, and went off to war. Like hundreds of thousands of other Confederate soldiers, he owned no slaves, but left everything behind to remove an aggressor from Southern soil. He was wounded and captured at Baker's Creek, Mississippi, in 1863. After parole and subsequent service, he was recaptured at Lookout Mountain, Georgia, and sent to Camp Morton, Indiana. He died as he lived, a farmer toiling Georgia's soil, in 1874.

133

Salmon Patties for Two

Add salad and a side dish, and you've got a meal!

1 can skinless, boneless
    salmon, drained
1 large egg, beaten
¼ cup finely chopped onion
1 teaspoon dried tarragon or
    dill (your preference)

½ teaspoon each, salt and pepper
3 tablespoons self-rising flour
Vegetable oil

★
Tad D. Shelfer
John B. Hood Camp #50
Houston, Texas
★
3rd great-grandson
Pvt. Levi Shelfer
Co. G, 2nd Florida Cavalry

Combine all ingredients except oil in a large mixing bowl. Heat ½ inch of oil in a large skillet over medium heat. Divide salmon mixture into quarters and carefully drop with a spoon into the hot oil, forming 4 patties. Cook about 7 minutes each side or until golden brown, turning once with a spatula. Serves 2.

THE CONFEDERATE COOKBOOK

Easy Southeastern Kentucky Mountain Chili

Simple to make and very tasty

3 pounds ground chuck
1 (10½-ounce) can tomato
   paste
2 teaspoons garlic salt
1 teaspoon Tabasco sauce

3 teaspoons paprika
6-8 teaspoons chili powder
1 cup corn flakes, crushed
1 can of beer
Salt to taste

*B*rown meat and drain. Add all other ingredients. Simmer for about 45 minutes.

★

Les Williamson
Pvt. E. F. Arthur Camp #1783
Corbin, Kentucky

★

Great-great-grandson
Pvt. Francis Marion Baker
21st Virginia Infantry

Francis M. Baker was born in Sullivan County, Tennessee. He was anti-liquor and very religious. His nickname was "Homepaw." He had three brothers who also served in the Confederacy. During one period they were so hungry they had to eat bark and grass to survive. They also rolled rocks down on the Federal soldiers due to shortage of ammunition. Francis served with his unit until it disbanded in Roanoke at the end of the war. A Confederate stone marks his grave.

Peggy's Famous Meat Loaf

Good any time

1 pound ground chuck
1 can tomato soup, divided
¼ cup onion, finely chopped
1 large egg, beaten
1 teaspoon dried bell pepper
   flakes
3 tablespoons self-rising flour

½ teaspoon each salt and
   pepper
1 teaspoon hearty brown
   mustard
Water
1 cup mild cheddar cheese,
   shredded

★

Tad D. Shelfer
John B. Hood Camp #50
Houston, Texas

★

3rd great-grandson
Pvt. Levi Shelfer
Co. G, 2nd Florida Cavalry

*P*reheat oven to 350 degrees. In a large mixing bowl, mix ground chuck with ⅓ can of soup (reserving remainder in can), onion, egg, pepper flakes, flour, salt, and pepper. Shape into loaf in a square, glass, baking dish. Bake for 1 hour. Stir mustard in can of soup. Top with water to fill can and stir well. Pour over meat loaf. Top with cheese. Bake for an additional 10 minutes or until sauce bubbles and cheese is melted. Serves 4.

My wife inherited this recipe from her mother.
It is economical, delicious, and comforting after
a hard day at work.

Low Country Boil

A South Carolina classic

Water
Salt
McCormick Old Bay
    Seasoning
1/2 pound shrimp (per
    person)

1/4 pound smoked sausage
    (precooked andouille best),
    cut into 2-inch pieces (per
    person)
1-2 ears corn (per person)

---

*B*ring large amount of water to boil. You should have twice the amount of water as you do food. Add 1/4 cup salt per gallon. Put in 1/2 cup Old Bay Seasoning per person. Add sausage and boil about 10 minutes. Add corn and boil for 7 more minutes. Add shrimp and boil for exactly 3 minutes. Drain and serve in large bowl or tub.

This recipe is also known as Frogmore Stew or Beaufort Stew. It is a great way to feed a lot of people with a minimal amount of trouble or clean up. The combination of flavors is awesome. No condiments needed—sometimes simplicity yields the greatest rewards!

★
Richard Pettus
J. E. B. Stuart Camp #1343
Richmond, Virginia
★
Great-grandnephew
Pvt. Wyatt C. Pettus
Staunton Hill (Virginia)
Artillery

Hazel's Famous Beef Bourguignonne

A meal in itself

1 cup sliced fresh mushrooms
3 pounds sirloin (cut into ¾-inch cubes)
3 tablespoons all-purpose flour
½ teaspoon salt
½ teaspoon pepper
½ teaspoon thyme
1 (10 ¾-ounce) can of beef broth
1 cup Burgundy wine
2 large onions, sliced and quartered

★
J. Keith Somerville
Dunn-Holt-Midkiff Camp #1441
Midland, Texas

*P*reheat oven to 325 degrees. Sauté mushrooms in 1 tablespoon butter. Brown meat in shortening. Add flour, salt, pepper, and thyme. Place in a 3-quart baking dish. Add beef broth and wine. Cover and bake 2 hours. Add mushrooms and onions. Bake an additional 1½ hours, covered. Add equal portions of wine and water if meat appears too dry. Serve over noodles or rice.

Confederate Chicken Bogg

A good cold weather dish

1 whole Southern chicken
1 whole Hillshire turkey
   kielbassa sausage

Cajun spice
Garlic
Uncle Ben's converted rice

---

*B*oil whole chicken with Cajun spice for about 45 minutes or until done. Take chicken out of pot to cool off, strain broth, and set aside. After chicken cools enough to handle, tear it into small chunks and throw back into pot. Do not put insides back into pot—let your dog have a treat! Slice entire sausage into small chunks and add to pot. Add Cajun spice and garlic to taste. Do not add salt or pepper while cooking. Put in $6^2/_3$ cups of saved broth. Stir mixture and bring to a boil. When pot begins boiling, add 2 $^1/_2$ cups of rice and stir one more time. When it boils again, reduce heat and cover. Simmer for 20 minutes on medium heat (do not lift lid!). After 20 minutes, check to see if all broth has been absorbed by rice. If not, stir and put lid back on for 5-minute intervals until broth is absorbed. Remove from heat and let cool. Serves 10.

I learned the basic recipe from a fellow Southerner from Easley, South Carolina. Over the years I have refined it to my liking. It can be stored in the refrigerator for a few days, or you can freeze it. I tend to cook it more often during the cold months as it is a great hot, filling dish.

★

Tim Fetner
Gen. Wade Hampton
Camp #273
Mt. Pleasant, South Carolina
★

Great-great-grandson
Pvt. William Earl Nunn
Co. B, 15th South Carolina
Infantry

Pvt. Nunn was wounded at Battery Wagner. He died in the Old Soldier's Home in Columbia, South Carolina, in 1914.

Crock Pot Barbecue

Serve on buns with pickle and onion

3 pounds beef brisket shoulder
½ cup water
3 tablespoons vinegar
2 tablespoons Worcestershire
   sauce

2 teaspoons cumin or chili
   powder (cumin preferred)
1 (18-ounce) bottle of barbecue sauce (your choice)

Trim excess fat from meat. Place meat in crock pot. Mix water, vinegar, Worcestershire sauce, and cumin or chili powder and pour over meat. Set crock pot for 12 hours or overnight on low. When done, shred meat into bowl and mix barbecue sauce into meat until desired consistency attained.

This recipe comes from my wife, Christa, a Northern lady born on Robert E. Lee's birthday. Her grandmother's farm was on the path taken by General Morgan on his famous raid. One of her 3rd great-uncles walked back to their Indiana farm from Andersonville. His arrival caused his sister (who thought he was dead) to faint at the sight of him.

★

**Michael M. Sinclair
John Hunt Morgan
Camp #1342
Louisville, Kentucky**

★

**Great-grandson
Pvt. Robert Raymond Reid
22nd Georgia Infantry**

Pvt. Reid was wounded at Malvern Hill and died of his injuries in November 1862.

Dove Breasts in Red Wine Sauce for Two

Chicken can be substituted

3 dove breasts
1 tablespoon flour
2 ounces butter
1 tablespoon black currant jelly
   (any slightly tart jelly will do)

1 tablespoon red wine
2 tablespoons thick cream
Freshly ground black pepper
   to taste

Cut breasts into thin strips lengthwise. Roll breast strips in flour and sauté in butter (about 1 minute each side). Remove the breasts to a warmed serving dish. Add the jelly, wine, and cream to the sauté pan. Simmer, stir, and allow to bubble for a few minutes. Pour over the cooked breast strips, add pepper to taste, and serve immediately. Works well served over cooked rice. Serves 2.

Dove hunting is a time-honored Southern sport. It is an exhilarating and, for me, often humiliating sport! Still, every so often I bag a few. This recipe is quite simple and very tasty—factors I tend to look for in a dish.

★
D. Keith Baker
Robert E. Lee Camp #726
Alexandria, Virginia
★
Great-grandson
2nd Sgt. Calvin Luther Peek
Co. I, 61st Virginia Infantry

Calvin Peek, along with his brother, volunteered to serve the Confederacy in 1861. He was wounded at the Battle of the Crater and later contracted typhoid fever. He was captured in 1864 near Burgess Mill and sent to Point Lookout Prison, where he spent the remainder of the war. In his later years, he was very active in the United Confederate Veterans. He died in 1917.

Patty's Beef Spaghetti Pie

Great dish for a potluck dinner

1 pound lean ground beef
1 teaspoon garlic powder
½ teaspoon salt
½ teaspoon ground cumin
1 (10-ounce) can diced
   tomatoes with green chilies,
   drained

¾ cup light dairy
   sour cream
1 cup Monterey Jack or cheddar
   cheese, shredded

★
Paul W. Vaughn
Lt. John W. Inzer Camp #308
Riverside, Alabama

*H*eat large skillet over medium heat until hot. Add ground beef and brown 4-5 minutes, breaking up into ¾-inch crumbles. Pour off drippings, then season with garlic powder, salt, and cumin. Stir in tomatoes. Bring to a boil. Cook 3-5 minutes or until liquid is almost evaporated, stirring occasionally. Reserve 2 tablespoons of the beef mixture for garnish. Stir sour cream into remaining beef and spoon into pasta shell. Place 1 cup cheese in center, leaving a 2-inch border around the edge. Spoon the reserved beef mixture onto center of cheese and bake 15 minutes or until heated through. Serves 4.

Pasta Shell
1 (7-ounce) package uncooked
   spaghetti
⅓ cup Monterey Jack or cheddar cheese, shredded

1 egg
½ teaspoon salt
¼ teaspoon garlic powder

*T*o make shell, heat oven to 350 degrees. Cook pasta according to package directions; drain. Whisk together remaining pasta shell ingredients. Add pasta and toss. Arrange in 9-inch pie dish, pressing to form a shell.

142

Southern Meat Loaf

Very good when sliced and served cold

2 pounds ground beef (may also use pork or veal)
1 can tomatoes, drained
2 cups bread crumbs
4 eggs

2 large onions, chopped
1/2 green pepper, chopped
1/4 teaspoon black pepper
1 teaspoon salt

*M*ix everything together. Place in a greased loaf pan (you can use cooking spray) and bake in a 350-degree oven for 1 1/2-2 hours.

★
Gyeral B. May
Stonewall Camp #380
Chesapeake, Virginia
★
Great-great-grandson
Pvt. John Kees
Co. K, 53rd North Carolina
Infantry

White Chili

Makes a large quantity—invite the whole crowd!

3-4 chicken breasts
1 cup chicken broth
2 cans cream of mushroom soup
2 cans white navy beans (do not drain)
2 cans shoe peg corn (do not drain) (regular corn is ok)

1 pound Velveeta cheese (for a spicier chili, use Mexican variety)
1 can Ro-Tel diced tomatoes with green chilies (do not drain)
1 medium onion, chopped

★
Paul W. Vaughn
John W. Inzer Camp #308
Riverside, Alabama

*B*oil chicken breasts until done (about 45 minutes). Reserve 1 cup of the chicken broth. Shred chicken and add both to a 5-quart crock pot. Add all other ingredients to the crock pot (it will fill the pot) and cook on high for about 3-4 hours. Stir when needed.

143

Ocean Isle à la Fairmont

Not to be prepared or consumed by anyone with high blood pressure or heart problems!

4 strips bacon
½ pound Italian sausage
1 large onion, chopped
1 large green pepper, chopped
1 can Italian tomatoes
1 (6-ounce) can tomato paste

Dash salt, pepper,
　Worcestershire sauce
1½ pounds boiled and peeled
　shrimp (small)
1½ pounds rice, raw

Cut bacon and sausage into small pieces. Cook over low heat until brown, then drain off half the grease. Add the onion and pepper to the meat mixture and cook 30 minutes. Add tomatoes, tomato paste, salt, pepper, and Worcestershire sauce and cook an additional 30 minutes. Add the cooked shrimp about 15 minutes before serving. Serve over rice cooked according to package instructions, seasoned to taste. Real Tabasco sauce must be used for seasoning—anything else will render this fine Southern dish inedible.

★
John F. Courtney, Jr.
Maj. Egbert A. Ross
Camp #1423
Charlotte, North Carolina
★
Great-great-grandson
Pvt. Francis Asbury Hardin
6th South Carolina Infantry

Francis Hardin was in his mid-forties when the war started. He died in 1870, leaving a widow and six children.

Bow Tie Pasta with Basil Chicken

An elegant addition to a candlelight dinner

1 (8-ounce) package bow tie pasta
3 chicken bouillon cubes
3 tablespoons olive oil
½ medium onion, finely chopped
1 tablespoon garlic, finely chopped
1 (14½-ounce) can diced tomatoes

1 (15-ounce) can tomato sauce
3 teaspoons sugar
1 teaspoon dried ground marjoram
¼ cup fresh basil, chopped
2 cups roasted chicken breast, cut into 1-inch cubes
1 cup smoked Gouda cheese, finely shredded

★
Kenneth Smith
Chattahoochee Guards
Camp #1639
Mableton, Georgia
★
Great-great-grandson
Color Sgt. Thomas Hines Kennon
Co. H (Young's Guards), 3rd Georgia Infantry

*P*repare pasta according to package directions, dissolving bouillon cubes in boiling water before adding pasta. Drain and set aside. Sauté onion in the olive oil over medium heat until onion is tender. Add garlic and sauté until onion is transparent. Add tomatoes, tomato sauce, and sugar. Simmer on low heat for 10 minutes. Add marjoram and basil and simmer 10 more minutes. Add chicken to the sauce. Toss with the cooked pasta and garnish with cheese. Serves 6-8.

Rebel's Favorite Chili

Serve on Super Bowl Sunday

3- to 4-inch strip of suet
4 pounds ground beef
    (ground-chili style)
2 large onions, chopped
1 green pepper, chopped very
    fine
¼ cup chili powder (or accord-
    ing to taste)
1 (46-ounce) can tomato juice
Dash of Tabasco sauce
2 tablespoons sugar

2 teaspoons salt
1 #2 can Ro-Tel tomatoes with
    peppers
Black pepper to taste
½ teaspoon dry mustard
    (optional)
1 teaspoon garlic powder, or
    fresh garlic, minced
2 teaspoons cumin powder
3 slices lemon, minced
¾ cup cracker meal or bran

*F*ry out suet in deep pot. Add meat, onions, and pepper, and brown thoroughly. Add chili powder, tomato juice, Tabasco, salt, and a bit of boiling water to half fill Dutch oven. Add Ro-Tel with peppers, cover, and simmer 30 minutes. Add remaining ingredients and cracker meal or bran to thicken to desired consistency. Heat 10 more minutes. Serves 12-15.

★
Edwin L. Deason
Capt. Clem Vann Rogers
Camp #481
Oklahoma City, Oklahoma
★
Great-great-grandson
Pvt. John. J. Deason
Co. B, 33rd Arkansas Infantry

John Deason enlisted in the Confederate forces at the age of 34. He saw action in the Red River Campaign and was wounded at the Battle of Pleasant Hill in Louisiana. After he was paroled in Marshall, Texas, in 1865, he moved with his family to Vernon Parish, Louisiana, and lived out his life as a farmer. He died in 1895.

THE CONFEDERATE COOKBOOK

Mom's Shrimp Diablo

Serve with linguine or rice, salad, and hot bread

¼ cup olive oil
4 cloves garlic, minced
¼ cup butter
1 pound large or jumbo
   shrimp, cleaned and
   de-veined

1 small can chopped tomatoes
   (can use fresh)
¼ cup parsley
4-5 dried red chilies
Salt and pepper to taste
White wine (optional)

*I*n a large skillet, heat oil and butter. Add garlic and brown. Add shrimp and cook until they become pink. Add remaining ingredients and simmer for 15-20 minutes.

★
Gene and Michael Givens
Gen. Richard H. Anderson
Camp #47
Beaufort, South Carolina
★
Great-grandson and great-great-grandson
Pvt. Young Harrington E. Hitch
Co. I, 16th South Carolina
Infantry

Seafood Pie

Makes two scrumptious pies

¾ pound crab meat
½ pound shrimp, cooked and
   chopped
½ pound Swiss cheese, grated
½ cup celery, minced

½ cup scallions, minced
1 cup mayonnaise
2 tablespoons flour
1 cup dry white wine
4 eggs, slightly beaten

*C*ombine crab, shrimp, cheese, celery, and scallions and put mixture into 2 baked pie shells. Combine the rest of the ingredients and pour over the seafood. Bake at 350 degrees for 35-40 minutes.

★
Jerry Wayne Harris
Fincastle Rifles Camp #1326
Roanoke, Virginia
★
Grandson
Pvt. Charles Frank Harris
North Carolina Troops

Pvt. Harris was wounded in the shoulder at the Battle of The Wilderness. He returned to duty and was active until the end of the war.

Miss Betty's Chicken Stew

Really sticks to your ribs!

1 large fryer, cut up
2 teaspoons salt
4 pounds potatoes, chopped
2 large onions, chopped
2 quarts canned tomatoes
2 (16-ounce) cans shoe peg
   corn

2 (16-ounce) cans green lima
   beans
1 teaspoon sugar
1 teaspoon black pepper
1 stick margarine
1 can evaporated milk

*B*oil chicken with salt until meat falls off the bone. Debone and set aside. Reserve all broth. Bring broth to a boil. Add potatoes and onions and cook until soft. Reduce heat and add tomatoes, chicken, corn, and beans. Add sugar and pepper. Simmer for 45 minutes. Add margarine and milk. Continue to simmer for 10 minutes. May be thickened with flour, if needed. Serve with corn bread. Freezes well.

★
**T. Leland Summers
Witherspoon-Barnes
Camp #1445
Lancaster, South Carolina**
★
**Great-great-grandson
4th Sgt. James Henry Therrell
Co. H, 1st South Carolina
Regulars**

James Henry Therrell grew up in Chesterfield County, South Carolina. He was sent to join the army on November 10, 1860. He served bravely until the end of the war. He returned to farming in Kershaw County, South Carolina, and died in 1912.

THE CONFEDERATE COOKBOOK

Jeff Davis Spaghetti

Fast, simple, and full of flavor

1 pound lean ground beef
1 medium onion, diced
2 garlic cloves, finely minced
3 tablespoons canola or olive
  oil
Garlic salt to taste
Salt and pepper to taste

Dried parsley
2 large cans tomato sauce
1 can tomato soup
1 can Italian stewed tomatoes
1 package Lawrey's dry
  spaghetti mix with
  mushrooms

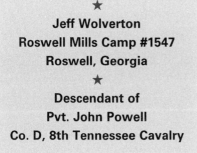

★
Jeff Wolverton
Roswell Mills Camp #1547
Roswell, Georgia
★
Descendant of
Pvt. John Powell
Co. D, 8th Tennessee Cavalry

Cook meat, garlic, and onion in canola or olive oil. When cooking meat, season with garlic salt, salt, pepper, and parsley to taste. Drain. In large cooking pot, put tomato sauce, tomato soup, and stewed tomatoes. Add dry spaghetti mix with mushrooms. Cook spaghetti, drain, and add sauce mixture. Makes 6-8 servings.

Hearty Crock Pot Clam Chowder

Turns out perfectly every time

3 cans Campbell's New
   England Clam Chowder
   soup
3 cans Campbell's Cream of
   Potato soup

1 can Campbell's Cream of
   Celery soup
3 half pints of whipping cream
2 cans minced clams, drained
Fresh ground pepper to taste

*S*tir all ingredients together in a crock pot and heat on low temperature for 4 hours or so. Serves 8-10.

I think this is the greatest clam chowder recipe ever invented. It's very easy, and ideal for a Sunday afternoon football get-together. Serve it with assorted crackers, cheeses, raw vegetables, and dip.

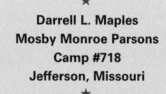

★
Darrell L. Maples
Mosby Monroe Parsons
Camp #718
Jefferson, Missouri
★
Great-great-grandson
Pvt. Bentley Barton
3rd Missouri Cavalry Battalion

Bentley Barton "crossed the river" with Gen. Sterling Price, seeing action in such places as Corinth and Iuka, Mississippi. He survived the war and returned to his home in Missouri.

Ham Pie Casserole

An old-time Southern favorite

1 cup butter or margarine
¾ cup onion, chopped
½ cup celery, chopped
½ cup bell pepper, chopped
1 tablespoon flour
2½ cups milk

1 can Cream of Chicken soup
2½ cups cooked ham, chopped
Salt and pepper to taste
Enough baking powder biscuits to cover

Sauté onion, bell pepper, and celery in butter. Add flour and stir until dissolved. Add milk and bring to a boil. Add cream soup and ham. Place in a casserole dish or pan. Place biscuits on top of casserole and bake in oven at 425 degrees until biscuits are brown. Serves 4.

This is a recipe my Mama used and has been modified through the years to adapt to the convenience of the supermarket. Leftover chicken or turkey could be used in place of ham.

★
Edwin L. Deason
Capt. Clem Vann Rogers
Camp #481
Oklahoma City, Oklahoma
★
Great-great-grandson
Pvt. John. J. Deason
Co. B, 33rd Arkansas Infantry

Crawfish Jambalaya

A meal in itself

2 tablespoons butter
2 medium onions, diced
1 tablespoon flour
2 cups water
1 (1-pound) can tomatoes, diced
Dash of garlic powder
1 tablespoon parsley, chopped

Salt and pepper
1 cup uncooked rice
¼ teaspoon thyme
1 bay leaf
1 green pepper, chopped
1 pound cooked, shelled, and de-veined crawfish tails (can substitute shrimp)

*M*elt butter in heavy skillet or kettle; add onions and sauté until browned. Add flour slowly and stir until browned. Add water, stirring constantly until a smooth paste is formed. Add all other ingredients (except crawfish). Cover kettle and cook over low heat for 15-20 minutes or until rice is tender. Add crawfish. Cover and heat thoroughly.

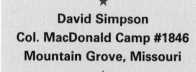

★
**David Simpson
Col. MacDonald Camp #1846
Mountain Grove, Missouri**
★
**Great-great-grandson
Pvt. Charles King Shannon
Co. B, 3rd Regiment, Missouri
Volunteer Infantry**

King Shannon served honorably in the Confederate forces. He was present at the Battle of Wilson's Creek, Lone Jack, Pea Ridge, and many other smaller engagements.

Fried Chicken and Gravy

A Sunday dinner tradition

1 chicken
1 cup flour
¹/₂ teaspoon salt

¹/₄ teaspoon pepper
Lard for frying

Wayne Simpson
Col. MacDonald Camp #1846
Mountain Grove, Missouri
★
Descendant of
Pvt. Charles King Shannon
Co. B, 3rd Regiment, Missouri
Volunteer Infantry

D ress chicken. Chill in icebox overnight, if possible. Sift flour and mix with salt and pepper. Put flour mixture in paper bag and add several pieces of chicken at a time to coat. Have about 2 inches of grease ready in large hot Dutch oven. Add the chicken. When all the chicken is in, cover for 5-7 minutes. Uncover and turn chicken when underside is golden brown. Cover again for 5-7 minutes, then remove top and cook until bottom side is brown. Reduce heat and cook 20 minutes longer. For best results, turn chicken only once.

Chicken Gravy

P our off most of the fat, leaving the brown crumbs. Add a little flour and brown. Add milk and stir until smooth and thickened. Season with salt and pepper.

This was a favorite of my mother some 60-70 years ago.
Since we were unable to have ice for the icebox at all times,
we would sometimes have to chill the chicken a short time
in the spring on our property before cooking.

Jesse's Black Bean Soup

Makes enough soup for six hungry people

1 pound black beans, soaked
  overnight in water
3 quarts water
1 pound lean veal
1 veal knucklebone with meat
4 cloves stuck in lemon pieces
1 tablespoon salt (to taste)
¼ teaspoon black pepper
2 tablespoons Worcestershire
  sauce

¼ teaspoon allspice
¼ teaspoon nutmeg
3 onions, chopped
2 tablespoons butter
1 cup sherry
1 lemon, cut in eighths
Hard-boiled eggs for garnish

★
Jesse R. Estes
Gen. Lewis A. Armistead
Camp #1847
Fort Riley, Kansas
★
Descendant of
Pvt. Joseph P. Estes
Missouri Partisan Rangers

---

*S*oak beans overnight; drain. To 3 quarts of water, add meat, knucklebone, lemon with cloves, beans, salt, pepper, Worcestershire sauce, and spices. Boil slowly until beans are mushy (3-4 hours). Remove meat and set aside. Remove lemon and cloves and discard. Press beans through a strainer or food mill. You may need to add more water to dissolve pulp or to thin soup. Shred meat and add. Fry onions in butter until brown and add to soup. Add sherry and salt and pepper to taste. Heat to boiling point. Serve 1 lemon slice and 1 slice of hard-boiled egg with each plate of soup.

Venison Steak Parmesan

Adapted from a Texas Hill Country recipe

2-pound venison round steak
(a more tender cut, such as
tenderloin, may be used)
1 cup Parmesan cheese,
grated
½ cup vegetable oil
1 medium clove of garlic,
crushed

1½ cups beef bouillon
½ cup Burgundy wine
12 small onions
1 (4-ounce) can mushrooms,
drained

Sprinkle steak with cheese. Pound with mallet. Turn steak and repeat. Continue until all cheese is used. Cut steak into serving-size pieces. Heat oil in skillet and add garlic. Sauté steaks on both sides and place in casserole. Drain oil from skillet and add bouillon to residue. Bring to a boil. Remove from heat and add wine. Pour sauce over steaks. Add onions and mushrooms; cover. Bake tender cuts of steak at 300 degrees for 1 hour. Round steaks should be cooked 1½-2 hours. Serves 4.

★

**Col. Donald G. Linton
James M. Keller Camp #648
Hot Springs, Arkansas**

★

**Second cousin
Lt. Col. Eustace Surget
7th Louisiana Infantry**

Col. Surget was adjutant to Lt. Gen. Richard Taylor. He was captured at Vicksburg and imprisoned. After the war, he went back to plantation life. He died in France.

Br'er Rabbit Stew

Makes one crock pot full

2 baking potatoes, boiled,
    peeled, and chopped
2 tablespoons butter
3 tablespoons flour
6 cups water
6 beef bouillon cubes
5 carrots, sliced

1 medium yellow onion,
    chopped
¾- to 1-pound rabbit, chopped
2 teaspoons thyme
1 (14½-ounce) can tomato
    wedges, or whole tomatoes
Salt and pepper to taste

---

*B*oil potatoes until cooked (about 30 minutes). In a large pot, melt butter on low heat. Add flour 1 tablespoon at a time and stir with melted butter to make a paste. Add 1 cup water and stir. Add 5 more cups water, turn heat on high, and add all bouillon cubes. Peel and slice carrots. Peel and chop onion. Reduce heat of large pot to medium. Trim rabbit and chop up. Heat a skillet to high and spray with cooking spray. Add rabbit pieces to skillet and cook until brown (about 2-3 minutes). Add rabbit pieces to a large pot with broth. Pour onions/carrots into skillet and stir about 6 minutes until carrots are tender and onions turn clear. Add carrots, onions, and 2 teaspoons thyme to pot. Peel and chop potatoes. Drain corn and other optional vegetables (if used) and add to pot. Add tomatoes and potatoes. Stir, bring to a boil, and reduce heat to low. Salt and pepper to taste.

Optional Ingredients
1 can lima beans or
    butterpeas

1 can whole kernel corn
1 can mixed vegetables
1 bag okra

★

Ted Brooke
Col. Hiram Parks Bell
Camp #1642
Cumming, Georgia

★

Great-great-grandson
Lt. James Brook
Co. C, 34th Georgia Infantry

Lt. Brook was killed in action at the Battle of West Harpeth River, near Franklin, Tennessee, on December 17, 1864. He was one of eight brothers who served the Confederacy.

Hot Dog Spaghetti Casserole

A one-dish meal that kids love

6 slices bacon
1 cup onion, chopped
1 (12-ounce) can whole kernel
   corn, drained
2 (10-ounce) cans condensed
   tomato soup
½ cup chili sauce

½ teaspoon oregano
¼ teaspoon basil
1 (8-ounce) package spaghetti,
   cooked
1 (16-ounce) package all-beef
   hot dogs
¾ cup sharp cheddar cheese

★

Billy K. Buck
Urquhart-Gillette Camp #1471
Newport News, Virginia

*C*ook bacon crisp, then drain and crumble. Sauté onion in drippings. Stir in corn, soup, chili sauce, oregano, and basil. Add spaghetti. Mix thoroughly. Alternate layers in ½-quart dish of hot dogs, bacon, and cheese. Pour first mixture on top. Bake in preheated oven 25 minutes at 350 degrees. Serves 6.

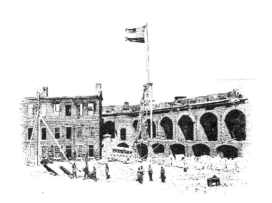

157

Southern Ham and Bean Soup

A culinary mainstay of the 5th Alabama Infantry Regiment band

1 teaspoon vegetable oil
1 large onion, diced
2 garlic cloves, diced
1 small bell pepper, diced
1 pound lean chunk ham, diced
1 teaspoon black pepper
1 can chicken stock
4 (16-ounce) cans Bush's Navy Beans

1 (8-ounce) can tomato sauce
2 medium potatoes, diced and parboiled
1 teaspoon Worcestershire sauce
1 can Ro-Tel Tomato and Green Chili, diced
Salt to taste
Tabasco to taste

Don McDaniel
Gen. Robert E. Rodes
Camp #262
Tuscaloosa, Alabama
★
Descendant of
Pvt. Charles P. Crume
Co. B, 36th Mississippi
Volunteers

*P*lace oil in a preheated, large, heavy-duty, cast-iron pot and sauté (in this order) onion, bell pepper, garlic, and ham until vegetables are tender and ham is just lightly browned. Place remaining ingredients into the pot with enough chicken stock to thin slightly, and cook on top of stove on low heat for about 1 hour. Best served with hot corn bread. It's even better the next day! Serves 4 hungry re-enactors or 5-6 civilians.

The original recipe for this soup dates back to about 1830 and comes from the Pope family plantation of Crystal Springs, Mississippi. This family gave seven sons who fought for the Confederacy. The vintage recipe called for two pounds of white beans to be soaked overnight, "covered to keep the critters out," and slow cooked about two hours. The vegetables were cooked in lard and the recipe stated that the ham should come from a "gud fat hawg." Obviously, the current recipe has been altered to meet modern day tastes and standards.

Cranberry Meatballs

Meatballs with a holiday twist

2 pounds lean ground beef
2 eggs
1/2 teaspoon pepper
1 cup corn flake crumbs
1/4 cup parsley, diced

2 tablespoons soy sauce
1/2 teaspoon garlic powder
1 (4-ounce) can diced
  mushrooms

★

Billy K. Buck
Urquhart-Gillette Camp #1471
Newport News, Virginia

*M*ix all ingredients together and form into small balls. Place on cookie sheet and brown in oven at 350 degrees for 20 minutes.

Sauce
1/3 cup catsup
1 (1-pound) can cranberry
  sauce

1 teaspoon onion, minced
2 tablespoons brown sugar
1 tablespoon lemon juice
1 (12-ounce) bottle chili sauce

*C*ombine sauce ingredients. Put meatballs in crock pot and pour sauce over them. Cook on low for 4 hours. Serve over white rice. Serves 6.

Tennessee Red Beans and Rice

Can feed a large number cheaply

2 (12-ounce) cans of red beans
(any red bean will do)
1 (12-ounce) stewed sliced or
whole tomatoes, as
preferred
1-2 green or red bell peppers
1 pound sausage (any type)
1 pound pepperoni (optional,
serves as substitute for
spicy Louisiana sausage)
½-1 pound any other meat
(round steak cut in 1-inch
chunks is fine)
Soup bone—former meat
unimportant

3 strips bacon
3 large onions (red, white, or
yellow)
2-3 shallots
1 garlic flower (use at least 4
cloves)
1 teaspoon black pepper
½ teaspoon red pepper
1-2 teaspoons oregano
Cut green beans (any amount)
Okra, cut or whole (any
amount)

★
Alton B. Lanier
Gen. N. B. Forrest Camp #215
Memphis, Tennessee
★

Great-great-grandson
Pvt. William Donaldson
Co. E (Young's Brigade), 7th
Georgia Cavalry

William was captured at
Louisa Courthouse, Virginia,
in 1864 and sent to Point
Lookout, Maryland. He was
later transferred to the prison
at Elmira, New York, where
he contracted smallpox and
lost the sight in his right eye.
He was released in July 1865.
He returned home to Bulloch
County, Virginia, and died on
December 7, 1895.

*G*et a big pot (at least a 4-quart kettle). You'll need it.
Pour in cans of red beans and cans of tomatoes,
juices and all. If you use real tomatoes, add some V-8 or
tomato juice for the proper blending of flavors. Start heating until mixture is boiling but not so hot that it is smoking. If you have leftover bones from roast, chicken, or
turkey, place them in the pot and boil for awhile (3-5 minutes). Meat should easily come off the bone. Add cut
sausage (1-inch chunks) and other meat. Remove bones
after taking off meat. Add the bacon strips—no need to cut
them up. Wash and unseed bell peppers. Cut into strips,
then 1-inch squares, and add to pot.

Peel and cut up onions. They can be left in rings—it is
not necessary to mince—and add to pot. Peel and cut up

continued on next page

shallots and add to mixture. Separate garlic cloves, peel, and cut into very thin slices, dropping them directly into kettle. Garlic will mellow while cooking. Add black and red pepper and mix well. Shake or pour in the oregano (too much is better than too little). Add your green beans or okra. Let cook or simmer on low 30 minutes.

This recipe is an "up country" meal with ingredients that can be found in any grocery store. It has more ingredients than the traditional red beans and rice served in Louisiana. We have liberally modified it, choosing not to try to duplicate Louisiana cooking. I have used it for SCV meetings, company potlucks, and as a family favorite at home. Enjoy!

Lauren Haley's Fine Fettuccine

Rich and creamy

1 package fettuccine noodles (cooked according to package directions)
¾ stick butter
1½ tablespoons flour
1 pint Half and Half

1 (8-ounce) package Velveeta
1 tablespoon sherry
1 can crab meat
1 (16-ounce) carton sour cream

Jim Evetts Haley
Dunn-Holt-Midkiff Camp #1441
Midland, Texas
★
Great-great-grandson
Pvt. William C. Evetts
Co. F, 6th Texas Infantry

*I*n a saucepan, melt butter and add flour. Add Half and Half. When thickened, add Velveeta, sherry, crab meat, and finally the sour cream. Pour the sauce over cooked pasta.

Confederate Clam Chowder

The catch of the day will be the hit of the evening!

1 dozen Little Nicks clams or
    medium-size clams
½ cup carrots, diced
½ cup celery, diced
2½ cups potatoes, diced
3 tablespoons butter
4 tablespoons onions,
    chopped

2 tablespoons flour
3 cups chicken broth
1 cup clam juice (reserved)
¾ cup cream
½ teaspoon ground pepper

★

Partick J. Griffin III
Col. William Norris
Camp #1398
Darnestown, Maryland

★

Great-great-grandson
Pvt. James Andrew
Jackson Coker
Co. H, 39th Georgia Infantry

Steam clams, pry open, and pick over. Reserve 1 cup clam juice. Place carrots, celery, and potatoes in chicken broth. Cover and boil gently until tender. Finely chop clams and sauté in butter with onions for approximately 4 minutes. Blend flour into mixture and stir into chicken broth and vegetables. Add clam juice, cream, and pepper. Reheat to boiling. Serve immediately. Yields 8 cups.

Four generations of the Griffin family have enjoyed vacationing along the Atlantic Coast in Sussex County, Delaware—a county that sent many sons to serve the Confederate cause. Over the course of thirty years, family members have set out with clam rakes and "gone clammin'" at Savage's Ditch in Rehoboth Bay. Our chowder recipe has been "tweaked" over time to the point where the children now ask, "Daddy, when are you going to make that Confederate Clam Chowder?" I think we have it right!

Granny Coleman's Brunswick Stew

Freezes well

3-4 medium white potatoes
1 pound lean ground beef or
    lean ground pork
1 tablespoon canola or olive oil
1 medium onion, chopped
1 large (14-ounce) can
    tomatoes, diced

1 (14-ounce) can creamed
    corn
1 (8-ounce) can tomato sauce
$1/2$ cup catsup
2 tablespoons cider vinegar

Cube the potatoes and cook until tender. Drain water (important) and set aside for adding later. Cook the beef or pork in a tablespoon of canola or olive oil until it starts to brown or all the red is gone. Drain off any fat. Add the onion and cook until it starts getting soft. Add tomatoes, creamed corn, tomato sauce, catsup, and vinegar. Add salt and pepper to taste and cook all for about 25-30 minutes over medium heat on the stove top. Add the cubed potatoes to the meat mixture. Do not cook any further, but keep mixture warm. Serves 4.

This recipe comes from my grandmother, Irene Scarboro Coleman, of Emanuel County, Georgia. It differs in taste from the usual Brunswick stews of Georgia and Virginia. My mother still makes this stew on a regular basis.

★

Gerald L. Engle
1st Lt. Daniel Sloan
Camp #1709
Geneva, Florida

★

Great-grandson
Pvt. Charles Matthew Coleman
Co. H, 48th Georgia Infantry

Charles Coleman was born in 1842. He saw action during the siege of Atlanta, and surrendered at Greensboro, North Carolina. After the war, he became a Methodist minister. He fathered a large family before he died in 1916.

My Guy's Smothered Venison
Deer hunter's delight

1 cup flour
Spices (your favorites)
1 pound cubed venison
$1/4$ cup Italian dressing
3 tablespoons Worcestershire
    sauce

$1/2$ cup sour cream
$1/2$ cup water or milk
Onion slices (optional)
2 cups cooked parboiled rice
    (do not substitute anything
    else)

*S*eason flour with your favorite spices. Coat venison with seasoned flour. Brown meat in skillet with *only* Italian dressing. Remove meat and add $1/4$ cup of remaining flour to skillet. Stir in Worcestershire sauce, sour cream, and water (or milk). Return meat to skillet and cover. Reduce heat and simmer for 10 minutes. For variety, add very thin onion slices before simmering. Serve on bed of rice. Serves 3-4.

★
Mason Sickel
Col. Robert G. Shaver
Camp #1655
Jonesboro, Arkansas
★
Great-great-grandson
Pvt. Daniel E. (J. D.) Ellis
Co. K, Freeman's
Missouri Cavalry

River Road Brisket of Beef

Melts in your mouth

5-6 pound boneless beef
  brisket
2 tablespoons garlic salt
2 tablespoons paprika

1 tablespoon cracked black
  pepper
1 teaspoon meat tenderizer

---

*P*reheat oven to 200 degrees. Wipe meat with a clean dish towel and dust generously with garlic salt, paprika, pepper, and meat tenderizer. Wrap securely in 2 layers of heavy aluminum foil, tucking ends tightly. Cook for 10 hours in pan in 200-degree oven. Drain juices when cool and slice.

★
**Bradford L. Alexander
Gen. Lloyd Tilghman
Camp #1495
Paducah, Kentucky**
★
**Great-great-grandson
Pvt. Elijah Moses Sayers
Co. A, 1st Alabama Cavalry**

A granddaughter described Elijah Sayers as a short, plump man whose face bore a strong resemblance to Robert E. Lee's. He was said to be always cheerful, jolly, and optimistic. He died in 1935 at the age of 87. His obituary stated that "Uncle Mose" was one of Elmore County's (Alabama) oldest and best-known citizens.

Meat Loaf à la Haley

The sauce makes the difference

1 pound ground beef (preferably chuck)
½ pound pork sausage
1 egg, beaten
1 cup corn bread crumbs

1 onion, finely chopped
1½ teaspoons salt
¼ teaspoon black pepper
½ can tomato sauce

Sauce
½ can tomato sauce
2 tablespoons prepared
  mustard

2 tablespoons brown sugar
2 tablespoons vinegar
1 cup water

Mix all meat loaf ingredients together, shape into a loaf, and place in a shallow pan. Bake at 350 degrees for 1 hour. Blend all sauce ingredients together and pour some over the meat loaf while cooking. Baste at 15-minute intervals.

★
J. Evetts Haley, Jr.
Dunn-Holt-Midkiff Camp #1441
Orlando, Florida
★
Great nephew
Pvt. John W. Haley
21st Mississippi Infantry

Pvt. Haley was mortally wounded at Cedar Creek, Virginia, in April 1864.

Opposite—John W. Haley
Private, 21st Mississippi Infantry

Prize-Winning Stuffed Cornish Hens

A festive and elegant entrée

2⅓ cups water
1 (6-ounce) package long
   grain and wild rice mix
½ cup celery, chopped
1 (5-ounce) can water chestnuts, sliced

1 (3-ounce) can chopped
   mushrooms, drained
1 tablespoon soy sauce
Salt
4 Cornish game hens
¼ cup butter, melted

★
Lee F. Smith
Pinckney D. Bowles
Camp #1840
Evergreen, Alabama
★
Descendant of
Pvt. Andrew J. York
Co. G, 11th Georgia Infantry

*M*easure the water in a 2-quart saucepan. Stir in rice and contents of seasoning packet. Bring to a boil. Cover tightly, reduce heat to low or medium-low, and simmer until all water is absorbed (about 25 minutes), then cool. Add remaining ingredients except Cornish hens. Toss lightly to mix. Salt inside of birds and stuff with rice mixture. Tie legs together. Roast, loosely covered, for 30 minutes. Cook another 60 minutes uncovered (or until done) in a 375-degree oven. If desired, baste occasionally with melted butter. Serves 4.

Missouri Cabbage Soup

Better the second day, if there is any left

½ pound lean lean beef,
  chuck or round
4 (14½-ounce) cans beef broth
1 cup green pepper, chopped
1 cup sweet onion, chopped
1 cup celery, chopped
1 ripe tomato, peeled, seeded,
  and chopped

6 cups green cabbage, coarsely
  shredded
1 (15-ounce) can kidney
  beans, drained and rinsed
Salt, pepper, hot pepper sauce
  (latter is optional)

---

*I*n a heavy pan, brown beef, stirring frequently to prevent lumps. Drain off fat. Add all the beef broth and bring to a low boil. Add pepper, onion, and celery, bring to a low boil, and cook 10 minutes. Add tomato and cabbage, bring to a low boil, and cook 20 minutes. Drain and rinse kidney beans, add to soup, and simmer about 20 minutes. Add salt and pepper to taste and a few drops of hot pepper sauce if desired. If soup is too thick for your liking, add another can of beef broth. Serves 12.

It was April in Missouri, but bone chilling with mixed rain, snow, and sleet. At lunch time I wanted a bowl of hot soup to ward off the cold. I went to a restaurant that featured a soup and salad bar. I found the soup to be very much to my liking—so much so that I ate three servings. As I ate the last bowl I used my paper napkin to make a list of the ingredients. After several attempts at home, I arrived at this recipe. We make it frequently, especially in the fall and early winter when our delicious Blue Ridge Mountain cabbage is being harvested.

★

Curtis A. Clay
Jubal Early Camp #1691
Hillsville, Virginia

★

Great-great-grandnephew
Brig. Gen. William Terry
Co. C, 4th Virginia Cavalry

William Terry, the last brigadier general of the Stonewall Brigade, was a lawyer, educator, and newspaper publisher. He graduated from the University of Virginia in 1848. After he heard about the surrender, he tried to ride up to North Carolina to join the troops that were still fighting. He was elected to the Forty-second Congress in 1877, and was a delegate to the Democratic National Convention in 1880. He drowned trying to ford Reed Creek while coming home from court in Wytheville, Virginia, in 1888.

Duck Camp Red Beans and Rice

Feeds six—unless one is my son!

1 pound dried red beans
1 tablespoon olive oil
1 large onion, minced
1 large green pepper, minced
1 large celery stalk, minced
2 cloves garlic, minced
4 cups chicken stock or white
    wine
$\frac{1}{2}$ teaspoon sage
2 large bay leaves
1 tablespoon Worcestershire
    sauce
1 tablespoon Pickapeppa
    sauce

1 pound canned tomatoes
2 smoked ham hocks
$\frac{1}{4}$ teaspoon red pepper
3 dashes Tabasco
1 teaspoon paprika
1 teaspoon thyme
$\frac{1}{2}$ teaspoon oregano
1 pound smoked sausage
1 pound Polish sausage
2 teaspoons salt
$\frac{1}{2}$ cup fresh parsley, chopped

★

**A. C. Magruder, Sr.
R. E. Lee Camp #726
Alexandria, Virginia**

★

**Descendant of
Capt. Henry A. Bowling
Adjutant (Chamblis Brigade),
4th Virginia Cavalry**

Sort and wash beans. Soak overnight in water to cover. Drain and rinse. Heal oil in 4-quart pot and sauté next 4 ingredients until soft. Add 4 cups liquid and next 13 ingredients. Stir in soaked beans and mix well. Cover pot, bring to boil, and then simmer for 2½-3 hours or until beans are tender. Stir occasionally and add additional liquid as needed.

When beans are tender, remove 1 cup of beans plus enough liquid to puree in food processor. Return pureed beans to pot. With fork, prick sausage all over and brown under broiler. Roll browned sausage in paper towels to remove as much grease as possible and slice on diagonal into bite-sized pieces. Add browned, sliced sausage to pot and remove and discard ham hocks and bay leaves. Add

continued on next page

salt and simmer until thickened. Sprinkle with parsley and serve over hot white rice.

The very best red beans and rice I ever enjoyed, bar none, was thirty years ago in a now-defunct duck camp in South Louisiana. This recipe, which combines several versions of this classic dish, is as close as possible to the real thing.

Sherried Beef
Easy and delicious

3 pounds stew beef
³/₄ cup sherry
¹/₂ package dry onion
   soup mix
¹/₂ soup can water

¹/₂-1 pound fresh mushrooms,
   sliced
Egg noodles
2 cans Campbell's Golden
   Mushroom soup

*P*ut all ingredients in a covered casserole and bake at 350 degrees for 3 hours, stirring occasionally. Serve with hot cooked noodles.

★
Bradford L. Alexander
Gen. Lloyd Tilghman
Camp #1495
Paducah, Kentucky
★
Great-great-grandson
Pvt. Elijah Moses Sayers
Co. A, 1st Alabama Cavalry

Chicken, Broccoli, and Peaches

An unusual combination that tastes great!

4-6 boneless, skinless chicken breasts
Salt and pepper
¼ cup butter
¼ cup shallots or green onions, minced
1 clove garlic, minced

1 generous teaspoon paprika
1 bunch fresh broccoli, cooked
4-6 canned cling peach halves
1 cup sour cream
¼ cup mayonnaise
¼ cup Parmesan cheese

Bradford L. Alexander
Gen. Lloyd Tilghman
Camp #1495
Paducah, Kentucky
★
Great-great-grandson
Pvt. Elijah Moses Sayers
Co. A, 1st Alabama Cavalry

*S*eason chicken with salt and pepper. Melt butter in skillet, add shallots and garlic, and sauté a few minutes. Stir in paprika and turn chicken in mixture until well coated. Put in shallow baking dish, cover loosely with foil, and bake in a preheated 375-degree oven for about 20 minutes. Arrange well-drained broccoli and peach halves along with chicken in pan. Spoon over sour cream/mayonnaise mixture. Sprinkle with cheese. Put broiler on low setting. Broil 6-8 minutes until richly flecked with golden brown.

Southern Lemon Chicken

An easy, convenient, and healthful recipe

1 roasting chicken
1 orange
1 lemon
1 lime

1 envelope dry onion soup mix
½ cup almonds, slivered
1 heaping tablespoon orange
   marmalade

Preheat oven to 350 degrees. Using either a whole chicken or parts, skin the chicken and remove as much fat as possible. Place chicken in a plastic oven browning bag. Wash and quarter orange, lemon, and lime and place into bag. Add envelope of dry onion soup mix, almonds, and orange marmalade. Seal the bag and punch a hole in it to allow pressure to escape. Place in a pan and cook for 1½-2 hours.

★
H. P. Porter
Gen. Horace Randal
Camp #1533
Carthage, Texas
★
Great-great-grandson
Pvt. Lorenzo Dow Porter
Co. D, 11th Texas Infantry

Lorenzo and his 15-year-old son were conscripted into Confederate service. The first time the conscription troops visited their farm, they came for Lorenzo. The son talked them into taking him instead so his father could remain behind to work the farm and provide for the family. They agreed. The next year, they returned for Lorenzo. Happily, both father and son survived the war.

Fried Rabbit with Mushroom Sauce

Sure to please even the most inhospitable Yankee guest

4 eggs, beaten
½ cup milk
1 fresh skinned rabbit, cut up
    (may be purchased from a
    store if you are not near a
    breeder)
4 cups flour
1 teaspoon salt or to taste
1 tablespoon black pepper

1 teaspoon fine white pepper
    (red pepper may be used
    for hotter flavor)
Vegetable oil
8 fresh mushrooms, sliced
1 can condensed mushroom
    soup
2 cups water
1 tablespoon real butter

James M. Mills
The Thomasville Rifles
Camp #172
Thomasville, North Carolina

Third cousin
Capt. Winfield Scott Lineberry
Co. M, 70th North Carolina
Troops

*M*ix eggs with milk to make egg wash. Mix dry ingredients and put into a paper bag. Run the cut up rabbit through the egg wash and then place each piece into the bag with the dry ingredients, closing the bag and shaking to coat the rabbit.

Using a skillet, fry the rabbit in vegetable oil (as you would chicken) until done and golden brown. Remove and place rabbit on a plate with paper towels to let any grease drain away. Clean and wash the frying pan and then place the rabbit back into it. Add the sliced mushrooms. Mix mushroom soup and water in a bowl and pour over rabbit and mushrooms. Add butter to the center of the rabbit dish, cover with lid, and cook in an oven at 350 degrees until the meat comes off the bones (about 45 minutes to 1 hour). Serves 3-4.

My wife prefers to use a cast-iron skillet, well seasoned over the years to prevent sticking. She also uses a glass lid in order to see the cooking process. This recipe came down through her family, some of whom rode with Gen. Nathan Bedford Forrest.

Grilled Peppered Beef

A savory main course

3 pounds eye of round roast
½ cup soy sauce
3 tablespoons lemon juice
3 tablespoons barbecue sauce

1 clove garlic, minced
2 tablespoons coarse ground
   black pepper, divided

★

Patrick J. Hardy, M.D.
Sterling Price Camp #145
Chesterfield, Missouri

★

Great-grandson
Capt. John McKim Hardy
Co. A, Col. Kenton Harper's
Regiment, Virginia

*B*utterfly roast to within ½ inch of other side. In Ziploc bag, combine soy sauce, lemon juice, barbecue sauce, and garlic. Add roast and coat. Marinate 6 hours or overnight. Remove roast; save marinade. Put on grill (I prefer charcoal to gas). Sprinkle ½ of pepper on meat (it may need more to get a good heavy coating). Cover and grill 10 minutes. Turn meat, brush with saved marinade, and sprinkle with rest of the pepper. Grill covered for 30-40 minutes. Meat temperature should read 150 degrees if you like your meat medium-well. Turn and baste occasionally. Let stand 5 minutes. Slice very thinly.

I really enjoy preparing this because it gives me a chance to show off with my grill. Also, I get to enjoy an adult beverage of my choice while grilling!

Chicken and Sausage Gumbo

A Louisiana specialty

5 cups cold water
4 (10¾-ounce) cans of chicken
   stock
½ cup cooking oil
½ cup all-purpose flour
1 cup onion, chopped
1 cup green bell pepper,
   chopped
1 cup celery, chopped
4 cloves garlic, chopped
2 tablespoons parsley,
   chopped

3 bay leaves
1½ teaspoons Tabasco
¼ teaspoon salt
⅛ teaspoon black pepper
1 teaspoon dried thyme
1 chicken, cut into pieces
1 pound hot smoked sausage,
   sliced into ½-inch rounds
½ cup green onions,
   chopped
3 cups cooked rice

★

Karlos J. Knott
Gen. Franklin Gardner
Camp #1421
Lafayette, Louisiana

★

Great-great-grandson
Pvt. Alexandre Babineaux
Co. A, 26th Louisiana Infantry

Alexandre Babineaux enlisted at the age of 17 in the 26th Louisiana, a French-speaking unit, in Lafayette, Louisiana. He was captured at Vicksburg and later paroled. He is buried at Arnaudville, Louisiana.

*I*n a large (at least 6-quart) stock pot, heat the water and chicken stock. While that is warming, heat the cooking oil in a large skillet on medium heat. Add the flour to the hot oil and cook, stirring constantly, until roux turns dark brown (about 20 minutes). Lower the heat and add the onion, green pepper, celery, garlic, and parsley to the roux and cook until vegetables are tender (about 10 minutes). Add the roux and the vegetables from the skillet, along with the bay leaves, Tabasco, salt, pepper, and thyme to the water and chicken stock in the stock pot.

Stir constantly over medium-high heat until the stock thickens (about 10 minutes). Add the chicken, sausage, and green onions and simmer uncovered, stirring occasionally for 1½ hours. For more formal occasions, you can use boneless chicken in the gumbo. Skim off any oil floating on top,

continued on next page

and correct the seasonings. Serve in individual bowls over a scoop of cooked rice.

There is a saying in Louisiana that if it flies, swims, or crawls, you can make a gumbo out of it. However, the rumor that the Audubon Zoo in New Orleans has a gumbo recipe for every one of its animals is just not true.

Crowd Chicken Casserole

Not only is it delicious, but it is ideal for a large group of people

10 cups cooked chicken, diced
2 bunches of green onions
   with tops, sliced
2 (4-ounce) cans green chilies,
   chopped
1 (5¾-ounce) can pitted ripe
   olives, drained and sliced

10 cups celery, chopped
2 cups almonds, slivered
5 cups cheddar cheese, shredded and divided
2 cups mayonnaise
2 (16-ounce) cups sour cream
5 cups potato chips, crushed

Combine the first 6 ingredients. Add 2 cups of cheese. Mix mayonnaise and sour cream; add to chicken mixture and toss. Spoon into two greased 13-inch by 9-inch baking dishes. Sprinkle with potato chips. Top with remaining cheese. Bake, uncovered, at 350 degrees for 20-25 minutes or until hot. Serves 24.

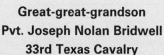

James N. Vogler, Jr.
Albert Sidney Johnston
Camp #67
Houston, Texas
★
Great-great-grandson
Pvt. Joseph Nolan Bridwell
33rd Texas Cavalry

Pvt. Birdwell's unit fought mainly along the Rio Grande border where they had not only Yankees but Mexican bandits and Indians to contend with. After the war, Joseph returned to farming.

California Style Pork Barbecue

Get ready for the best barbecue sandwich you've ever had

½ cup regular mustard
¼ cup Dijon-honey mustard
¾ cup Red Wine vinegar
1 teaspoon Worcestershire
  sauce
½ teaspoon salt
½ teaspoon pepper
¼ cup sugar

½ cup butter
½ teaspoon garlic powder
2 tablespoons chili garlic
  sauce (usually found in
  Asian/Oriental aisle of
  supermarket)
3½ pounds pork shoulder butt

★

Kent Manthorne
Father Abram J. Ryan
Camp #302
San Diego, California

★

Great-grandson
Pvt. William Anthony King
Co. C (Olmstead's),
1st Georgia Infantry

*A*dd all ingredients except pork shoulder together in small sauce pan and bring to a boil. Cover and bake pork shoulder roast at 350 degrees for 2 hours. Remove lid and bake 1 hour longer. When done, remove from oven and shred pork, using a fork. Add sauce and mix together. Tastes great served on Kaiser or onion rolls.

This recipe was a joint submission. The other contributor was John Kindred of Father Abram J. Ryan Camp #302. He is descended from Pvt. Ewel Crabtree, Co. B, 5th Tennessee Cavalry.

Opposite—William Anthony King
Private, Co. C, 1st Georgia Infantry (Olmstead's)

Southern Pasta

Chicken pasta with a hint of garlic

1 pound pasta, cooked
Olive oil
4 (6- to 8-ounce) boneless and
    skinless chicken breasts,
    cut into strips
$\frac{1}{4}$ ounce garlic, finely chopped
$\frac{1}{2}$ cup mushrooms, washed
    and sliced
2 fresh jalapeño peppers,
    sliced

1 ounce pesto basil (from
    store or homemade)
6 ounces fresh spinach,
    cleaned and chopped
$\frac{1}{2}$ cup chicken stock, canned
    or homemade
Salt and pepper to taste
Romano cheese, grated (for
    topping)
Parsley, chopped (for garnish)

While cooking pasta according to package directions, heat a skillet with olive oil and sauté the chicken breast strips until golden brown on both sides. Add the garlic, jalapeño peppers, mushrooms, pesto, spinach, and chicken stock. Simmer until half the stock is reduced. Add the cooked pasta and mix all together. Add salt and pepper if needed. Divide and place on 4 plates and top with grated cheese and parsley. Serves 4.

★
Norman J. White
19th Virginia Infantry
Camp #1493
Charlottesville, Virginia
★
Great-great-grandson
Pvt. William J. Snead
Co. K, 19th Virginia Infantry

William Snead participated in Pickett's Charge at Gettysburg and was one of the few to survive. He was at Lee's surrender at Appomattox. He lived to a ripe old age and was laid to rest in 1922 in Goshen, Virginia.

Fort Concho Frijoles

Will feed a large number of people

2 pounds pinto beans, dried
½ medium onion
1-3 raw jalapeño peppers (to taste—do not slice)
1 can whole stewed tomatoes
1 small can tomato paste
3 teaspoons Liquid Smoke
6 dashes Worcestershire sauce

2-3 pods garlic, minced
1-2 ham hocks
1-2 dashes Tabasco
1-2 dashes curry
1 bay leaf
Salt and pepper to taste
½ can beer (optional)

*R*inse and soak beans overnight. Drain off water and refill to 1 inch above the surface of the beans. Add all ingredients and heat until boiling. Reduce heat to low and cook uncovered until beans are soft. You can add seasoning ingredients as you see fit—a little experimentation is good. Add water judiciously to keep beans from becoming too dry, but do not make them watery. The goal is to have soft (not mushy) beans in a thick, tomato-y soup. You may wish to remove the ham hocks, separate the ham from the fat and bone, and return ham to the pot. You may also wish to remove the jalapeños to avoid a palatal surprise, but most of the "heat" should be gone after several hours of cooking. The beans improve with a day or two of aging in the refrigerator.

★
Leland Hamner
Gen. Tom Green Camp #1613
San Angelo, Texas
★
Great-great-grandson
Lt. Henley Hamner
Co. F, 38th Alabama Infantry

Henley's unit saw action at Chickamauga, Missionary Ridge, New Hope Church, Atlanta, and Nashville. He was wounded July 20, 1864, and died the next day in Atlanta.

181

Classic Shrimp Creole

It doesn't get any better than this!

8 slices bacon
½ stick oleo
1 cup onion, chopped
1 cup bell pepper, chopped
1 cup celery, chopped
1 tablespoon garlic, minced
1 (28-ounce) can tomatoes, chopped
1 (28-ounce) can tomato sauce

3 tablespoons Worcestershire sauce
Salt and pepper to taste
½ teaspoon oregano
Tabasco sauce to taste
2 pounds shelled and deveined raw shrimp
Hot cooked rice

★
David Moncus
Brig. Gen. John C. Carter
Camp #207
Waynesboro, Georgia
★
Great-great-grandson
Pvt. Richard Warnock
Co. B, 57th Georgia Infantry

*B*rown bacon in skillet or Dutch oven. Remove bacon and set aside. Add oleo, onion, bell pepper, celery, and garlic to the bacon drippings and sauté. Add tomatoes, tomato sauce, Worcestershire sauce, salt, pepper, oregano, and Tabasco sauce. Simmer sauce for 45 minutes to 1 hour. Add shrimp and simmer 5-10 minutes or until the shrimp turn pink. Don't cook shrimp longer or they will be too tough. Serve dish over the hot rice. Serves 6-8.

THE CONFEDERATE COOKBOOK

Easy Chicken and Dumplings

Makes enough to have seconds

5-8 boneless, skinless chicken breasts
1 large onion, finely chopped
1 teaspoon garlic powder
3 tablespoons parsley
1 can of chicken broth (if needed)

5 cups Betty Crocker Biscuit Mix (do not substitute Bisquick!)
Lemon pepper
Salt and pepper to taste

★
Elijah Coleman
Chattahoochee Guards
Camp #1639
Mableton, Georgia
★
Great-grandson
Pvt. Merick Coleman
Co. D, 36th Georgia Infantry

*B*oil chicken breast in 4-5 quarts of water until cooked thoroughly. Remove from water and tear or cut into chunks. Place chicken back into water. Add onion, garlic powder, and parsley. Bring to a rolling boil and cook until onion is tender. Taste mixture and add can of chicken broth if needed for better flavor. Mix biscuit mix with enough cold water to make a sticky dough. Drop dough from a spoon into boiling chicken broth until stew pot is full. Cover and cook for about 10 more minutes to cook dough all the way through. Be careful not to let it boil over. Serve hot in bowls and sprinkle with lemon pepper. Add salt and pepper. Serves 6-8.

Meatball Stew for a Crowd

Say the blessing and "chow down"

2½ pounds ground meat
Salt and pepper
Garlic powder
1 egg, beaten
2 tablespoons onion flakes
Flour
2 teaspoons cooking oil
   (enough to cover bottom of
   cooking pot)

3 tablespoons roux (store
   bought or homemade)
2½ cups water
1 small onion, chopped
1 small bell pepper, chopped
1 rib celery, chopped
¼ cup fresh parsley, chopped
¼ cup green onion tops,
   chopped

*S*eason meat with salt, pepper, and garlic powder. Add egg and onion flakes. Shape meatballs and lightly flour. Brown meatballs in oil, pouring off oil when done. Add water. When water is boiling, add roux and stir around to make sure all roux melts and you have a nice brown gravy consistency. Lower burner to medium and add onion, bell pepper, celery, green onion tops, and parsley. Cover and cook for 1 hour on medium heat. You can add more seasoning to suit your taste. Serve over cooked rice. Serves 8.

★
Tommy Morris, Jr.
Gen. Franklin Gardner
Camp #1421
Lafayette, Louisiana
★
Great-great-grandnephew
Henry Young, Jr.
Co. A, 4th Texas Cavalry

Henry Young was the oldest citizen of Eunice, Louisiana, when he passed away in 1927. He married four times (surviving three wives), producing 11 children. At the time of his death, he had 118 grandchildren and great-grandchildren. He remained youthful in appearance and activity until the end of his long life.

Sweet and Sour Chicken

This recipe can be used for game birds as well

2-3 whole chickens, disjointed
    and cut into sections
Soy sauce
Water
$\frac{1}{2}$-$\frac{3}{4}$ onion
10 mushrooms, sliced
1 (16-ounce) can sliced or
    diced pineapple, drained
    and juice reserved

1 bell pepper, sliced or diced
2 (12-ounce) jars sweet and
    sour sauce
Rice, cooked and served hot

---

*P*lace the chicken in baking dish(es). Sprinkle each section generously with soy sauce. Add water to baking dish to about a $\frac{1}{4}$-$\frac{1}{2}$ inch depth. In order listed, layer onion, mushrooms, pineapple, pineapple juice, bell pepper, and sweet and sour sauce on chicken, using small amounts of water to rinse sauce jars and add to dish. Bake at 400 degrees for 1 hour until done (less time usually required in gas ovens). To serve, place chicken, vegetables, and sauce on hot rice.

★
Dann Hayes
Bowen's Mounted Rifles
Camp #1759
Grinnell, Iowa
★

Great-great-grandson
Capt. Mace Andrew
Augustus Mayes
Co. C, 9th Battery, Georgia
Cavalry (Georgia State
Guards)

Capt. Mayes died in February 1906 and is buried in the family cemetery in Cobb

Catfish Stew

If you love catfish . . .

2 pounds catfish fillets	1 cup catsup
½ cup bacon, chopped	2 tablespoons Worcestershire
1 cup onion, chopped	sauce
2 (1 pound, 13 ounce) cans	2 teaspoons salt
tomatoes	1 teaspoon pepper
2 cups potatoes, diced	

*C*ut fillets into 1-inch pieces. Fry bacon until lightly browned in a large Dutch oven or kettle over low heat. Add onion and cook until tender. Add tomatoes, potatoes, catsup, and seasoning. Bring to the boiling point. Reduce heat and cook, covered, for 30 minutes, stirring occasionally. Add fish and continue cooking for 40-45 minutes or until potatoes are tender. Serves 6.

Opposite—Dickson Leland Baker
First Lieutenant, Co. B, 24th Regiment, Georgia Volunteers

"Allen, Warren & Johnny Baker were with me yesterday and took dinner with me. You cannot guess what I had for dinner. We had farce meat and corn dodger and wheat loaf, onions and coffee. Our dessert was apple dumplings and sugar. My dinner cost me, besides what I drew from government, 7 and a half dollars."

Letter from D. L. Baker to his wife, Cornelia, July 21, 1864

★
Judson Barton
Lt. Dickson L. Baker
Camp #926
Hartwell, Georgia
★

Great-great-grandson
1st Lt. Dickson Leland Baker
Co. B, 24th Georgia Infantry

Dickson Baker was a farmer in Hart County, Georgia. He and his wife, Cornelia, had five children. Dickson did not live to see the last child, born about ten days after his death. He was killed on August 16, 1864, near Front Royal, Virginia. The Bible Dickson carried in his breast pocket is still treasured today by his family. His brother-in-law, Capt. Allen S. Turner (who was in the same regiment), wrote inside: "Lieut. Dickson L. Baker, Co. B 24th Reg. Ga. Vol. was killed dead on the Field by a shot through the breast, in an engagement with the enemy at Front Royal, VA. Aug. 16, 1864. Peace to his Ashes. This book is bathed in his Blood." He is buried at Soldier's Circle, Prospect Hill Cemetery, Front Royal, Virginia.

Low Country Deviled Crab

A Charleston specialty

1 pound lump, white, or claw crab meat, cooked
2 teaspoons prepared yellow mustard
2 teaspoons horseradish
Salt
1 teaspoon pepper
½ teaspoon Texas Pete Hot Sauce
2 teaspoons Worcestershire sauce
¾ cup bread crumbs

★
**Lex Crawford
Secession Camp #4
Charleston, South Carolina**

*M*ix all ingredients in a large bowl after picking all the shell out of the crab meat. Press into individual crab shells or casserole dish. Bake at 350 degrees for 20 minutes. You can put additional bread crumbs and melted butter on top before baking.

White Sauce
3 tablespoons butter
3-4 tablespoons flour
2 cups milk

*C*ombine in heavy skillet over medium heat to make white sauce.

Southern Maryland Stuffed Ham

A closely guarded Maryland recipe

Select a cured ham weighing 10-12 pounds. A corned ham may also be used.
3 pounds kale, chopped fine (watercress may be substituted)
3 heads cabbage, chopped fine
6-8 onions, chopped fine
3 pounds mustard greens, chopped fine
6 cups celery, chopped fine
3 tablespoons salt
1 tablespoon red pepper
1 tablespoon black pepper
2 ounces celery seed
1/4 teaspoon garlic powder

*M*ix all ingredients thoroughly. With a sharp knife, cut vertically through the top of the ham and make about 6-8 pockets. Fill these pockets with the prepared ingredients. Get as much into the pockets as possible. Put the remaining stuffing on top of the ham. Place ham in a strong piece of cotton material or bag. Sew the ham in tightly to keep the stuffing in place. Boil 20 minutes per pound. Let cool and serve cold.

★

James Dunbar
Pvt. Wallace Bowling
Camp #1400
LaPlata, Maryland

★

Great-great-grandson
Sgt. Calvin Williamson
Co. D, 18th Virginia Heavy
Artillery

Despite the fact that he was a Quaker, Calvin Williamson and several of his brothers enlisted in the Confederate forces in defense of their homeland in 1862. Calvin was wounded at the Battle of Saylor's Creek two days before Appomattox and sent to Fort McHenry as a prisoner of war. After being paroled, he returned home and raised a large family.

Oyster Jambalaya

Whatever you do, don't lift the lid!

1 pound medium shrimp
$\frac{1}{2}$ teaspoon salt
3 whole breasts of chicken, boneless and skinless
$\frac{1}{2}$ pound smoked ham
24 large oysters, shucked
2 tablespoons cooking oil or lard
4 tablespoons butter
1 cup onions, coarse julienne
1 cup green pepper, coarse julienne
1 teaspoon garlic, minced
1 fresh bay leaf, minced very fine
$\frac{1}{2}$ teaspoon thyme
$1\frac{1}{2}$ cups long grain rice
$\frac{1}{4}$ teaspoon saffron
$\frac{1}{4}$ teaspoon cloves
$\frac{1}{4}$ teaspoon ground allspice
4 large fresh tomatoes, peeled, seeded, and diced into $\frac{1}{2}$-inch cubes
1 tablespoon fresh parsley, minced
$\frac{1}{4}$-$\frac{1}{2}$ teaspoon Tabasco
2 tablespoons fresh lemon juice
Salt and pepper to taste

★
Stephen Holcomb
Capt. James Iredell Waddell
Camp #1770
Orange County, California
★
Great-great-grandson
Pvt. Richard P. Sheppard
Co. K, 15th Texas Infantry

*P*lace the shrimp in a pot with 1 quart cold water and $\frac{1}{2}$ teaspoon salt. Slowly bring to a boil. Drain shrimp and reserve the liquid. Peel and de-vein shrimp. Return the shells to the liquid and simmer for 10 minutes. Strain the liquid (there should be about $3\frac{1}{2}$ cups). Add water if necessary. Cut chicken into 1-inch pieces. Cut ham into $\frac{1}{2}$-inch pieces. Shuck fresh oysters (or drain canned oysters) and set aside.

Heat oil and 2 tablespoons of butter over very low heat in a Dutch oven or heavy stew pot. Add chicken and ham and sauté, stirring often until chicken loses raw color. Add onion, green pepper, garlic, bay leaf, and thyme, and sauté until onion is translucent and tender. Add shrimp stock,

continued on next page

190

rice, saffron, cloves, allspice, tomatoes, parsley, Tabasco, lemon juice, and 1 teaspoon of salt. Mix well and bring to a boil over a moderate heat. Reduce heat as much as possible, cover pot, and simmer 20 minutes without stirring. DO NOT LIFT THE LID!

While the rice mixture is cooking, melt the remaining 2 tablespoons of butter in a heavy frying pan and sauté oysters until the edges begin to curl. When the rice mixture is done, add the shrimp and oysters, lightly tossing the mixture to mix the shrimp and oysters. Salt and pepper to taste. Keep the jambalaya on low heat until the oysters and shrimp are heated through. If the rice seems too moist, cook uncovered for a few minutes. Makes 6 generous servings.

My grandfather taught me how to make this dish when I was 12 years old. He said it would come out right every time if you don't open the lid for 20 minutes. I have been cooking this for 40 years now, and I have never had any complaints, even from people who say they don't like oysters!

Shipwreck Casserole

A good substitute for spaghetti

1 pound ground beef
Salt and pepper
2 medium potatoes, peeled
   and thinly sliced

1 onion, peeled and thinly
   sliced
1 can kidney beans
1 can tomato sauce

*B*rown ground beef and drain well. Put cooked beef in the bottom of a 2½- to 3-quart casserole dish (spray dish with Pam cooking spray first). Add salt and pepper to taste. Layer sliced potatoes and onion over meat. Pour kidney beans (including juice) over potatoes. Mix tomato sauce with ½ can of water and pour over top. Bake covered at 400 degrees for 30 minutes. Uncover and bake at 350 degrees for about 30 minutes more until potatoes stick together.

★

**Charles R. Jones
Alexander H. Stevens
Camp #78
Americus, Georgia**

★

**Great-grandson
Pvt. Jacob Chauency
Co. A, 1st Battalion, Florida
Special Cavalry**

Pvt. Chauency died in 1893 and is buried at City Point, Florida.

South Georgia Stuffed Quail

This recipe works with any game bird

12 quail

Salt and pepper to taste

1 pound bulk venison or pork
sausage

¾ stick butter, softened

1 cup onion, chopped

1 cup green pepper, chopped

1 pound fresh mushrooms,
sliced

1 (10-ounce) jar mayhaw jelly

★

**Randy Young
W. D. Mitchell Camp #163
Thomasville, Georgia**

★

**Descendant of
Cpl. Ransom C. Wheeler
Co. I, 29th Georgia
Volunteer Infantry**

Wash and dry quail. Season with salt and pepper. Preheat oven to 425 degrees. In a large skillet, brown sausage. Drain and set aside. Sauté onion, green pepper, and mushrooms in 4 tablespoons of butter. Combine vegetables and sausage. Stuff quail with sausage mixture. Rub outside of quail with 6 tablespoons softened butter. Place in a shallow roasting pan. Roast 1 hour. Baste with remaining 4 tablespoons melted butter until well browned. Melt jelly in a small saucepan and pour over quail. Serves 6-8.

Ransom Wheeler grew up in Thomas County, Georgia. He fought bravely at Chickamauga, where he was promoted to corporal. After participating in the Chattanooga campaign, he was wounded twice and captured at the Battle of Atlanta in 1864. He was held as a prisoner of war at Camp Douglas near Chicago, but was later exchanged. Still hampered by his wounds, he rejoined his regiment in March 1865. He was again wounded, this time in the left arm.

Some years after the war, Ransom experienced a sharp pain in his upper back. A doctor was summoned. The physician took out his knife and removed an object from Corporal Wheeler's back—the bullet that had lodged in his shoulder during the war! That remarkable memento is still held and treasured by members of his family.

On January 3, 1918, Ransom Wheeler was walking through a local railroad yard, taking a shortcut to his home, when a freight engine unexpectedly rolled into him. The impact knocked the elderly Confederate down, and the engine ran over both legs. Death came soon afterward.

Mexican Chicken

Ole!

1 package chicken breasts,
    boneless
Garlic
Bay leaf
½ stick margarine
1 onion, chopped
1 stalk celery, chopped
2 cans cream of chicken soup

1 can water
3 hot peppers, chopped
1 can picante taco sauce
½ cup chicken broth
1 (8-ounce) package Doritos
    chips
Velveeta cheese

_C_over chicken in skillet with additional water, garlic, and bay leaf. Cook until done. Chop cooked chicken into bite-sized pieces. Sauté onion and celery in margarine. In a bowl, mix soup, 1 can of water, peppers, picante sauce, chicken broth, and chips. Add chicken and the sautéed vegetables. Stir and pour into baking dish. Check texture for dryness and add more broth if needed. Bake covered at 350 degrees for 30 minutes. Uncover and put cheese on top. Bake until cheese melts. Serves 6-8.

★

Dr. Cecil A Fayard, Jr.
Maj. Gen. E.C. Walthall
Camp #211
Grenada, Mississippi

★

Great-great-grandson
Pvt. Sylvester (Sylvan) Fayard
Co. E, 20th Mississippi Infantry

Sylvester Fayard was from the Biloxi, Mississippi, area. He was one of five brothers who fought for the Confederacy. Only two survived. Sylvester was captured at Fort Donelson and sent to prison at Camp Douglas. He was paroled at Vicksburg and rejoined his unit to fight at the Battle of Bentonville.

Opposite—Sylvester (Sylvan) Fayard
Private, Co. E, 20th Mississippi Infantry

Seafood Gumbo

Nothing beats this on a cold winter night!

2 medium redfish
2 quarts water
4 bay leaves
2-3 pounds shrimp (peeled)
1 stalk celery, chopped
1 bell pepper, chopped
2 onions, chopped

1 (8-ounce) can tomato sauce
½ cup olive oil
1½ cups Worcestershire sauce
2 tablespoons black pepper
2 tablespoons salt
3 pounds frozen sliced okra

*B*oil the redfish in 2 quarts of water until done. Remove the skin and flake the meat from the bones. Return the flaked redfish to the broth and add all other ingredients. Bring to a full rolling boil for about 20 minutes. Reduce heat and simmer for about 4 hours. Serve over cooked rice.

★
**Landis Patrick
Stephen R. Mallory
Camp #1315
Pensacola, Florida**
★
**Great-great-grandson
Capt. Stephen Ashley
Cawthon
Co. H, 6th Florida Infantry**

Capt. Cawthon served from 1862 until the end of the war. His unit was heavily involved in the battles at Chicka-mauga, Chattanooga, and Atlanta. In later years, he was a favorite of his grandchildren. He always carried a pocket full of "penny candy" and had a walking stick that you could peer into to see a picture of the "Battle Above the Clouds." How the children loved to look at that picture! Capt. Cawthon passed away on May 12, 1918.

THE CONFEDERATE COOKBOOK

Chicken and Rice Casserole

Add a salad and you've got a meal!

3 chicken breasts, stewed
1 can cream of chicken soup
1 can cream of celery soup
1¼ cups rice, uncooked
1¼ cups chicken broth

¼ cup milk
2 tablespoons margarine
1 teaspoon paprika
Note: Low-fat soup and milk
can be substituted.

*P*ull stewed chicken meat from the bone. Mix the chicken with all ingredients except paprika. Spray a 9-inch by 11-inch casserole dish with non-stick cooking spray. Pour ingredients into the dish and spread evenly. Cook in oven at 350 degrees for 30 minutes. Remove and stir ingredients, spreading evenly. Sprinkle the paprika evenly over the top of the mixture. Cook an additional 20-30 minutes until mixture gets thick. Serves 8.

★

Alan R. Lee
William B. Bate Camp #34
Gallatin, Tennessee

★

Great-great-grandson
Pvt. James Knox Polk Buck
Co. C, 7th Tennessee Infantry

James enlisted in Confederate service in the spring of 1861 in Gallatin, Tennessee. Two of his brothers served in the same regiment. He was wounded at the Battle of Seven Pines, but recuperated in time to rejoin his regiment at Gettysburg. After the war, he returned home and became a farmer and a blacksmith. James Buck and his wife raised seven children. They are buried in Davidson County, Tennessee.

Louisiana Red Beans and Rice

If it's Monday in south Louisiana, you're eating red beans!

1 pound dried red beans
Water
1 pound hot smoked sausage,
   sliced into ½-inch rounds
2 cups onions, chopped
3 bay leaves
1 green bell pepper, chopped
4 cloves of garlic, chopped

Black pepper to taste
¾ teaspoon salt
1½ teaspoons Tabasco
1 stick margarine
2 tablespoons parsley,
   chopped
4 cups cooked rice

★

Karlos J. Knott
Gen. Franklin Gardner
Camp #1421
Lafayette, Louisiana

★

Great-great-grandson
Alexandre Babineaux
Co. A, 26th Louisiana Infantry

*R*inse and sort through beans. Combine the dried beans and water in a large, heavy pot and soak overnight. Drain the beans. Add sausage, onions, bell pepper, bay leaves, and garlic and cover with water. Bring the mixture to a boil and then turn it down to a simmer. Stir often, and simmer uncovered for about 1½ hours. You may have to add more water. Add the black pepper, salt, Tabasco, margarine, and parsley. Remove a cup or two of the beans, mash them, and then return them to the pot. Simmer for 1½ hours more, this time with the lid on the pot. Stir occasionally, making sure the beans do not stick to the bottom of the pot. When the beans are finished, they will have soaked up most of the liquid. Correct the seasonings and serve over the hot cooked rice. Serves 8.

Hot Texas Chili

If you like it hot, you'll like this!

1 pound dried pinto beans
2 pounds ground beef
2 large onions, chopped
1-2 jalapeño peppers,
  chopped
2 cloves garlic, minced
1 teaspoon celery salt
2 teaspoons pepper
1 tablespoon ground cumin

4-5 tablespoons chili powder
  seasoning blend
4 cups cocktail vegetable juice
1 (28-ounce) can tomatoes,
  undrained and chopped
1 (4-ounce) can green chilies,
  undrained and chopped
1 (15-ounce) can tomato
  sauce

★
Rodney J. Owens, Sr.
Felix H. Robertson Camp #129
Waco, Texas
★
Descendant of
Pvt. Elisha Hunter Evans
Co. D, 13th North Carolina
Battalion

Sort and wash beans, cover with water, place in oven, and bring to a boil. Cover and cook 2 minutes. Remove from heat and let stand 1 hour. Bring to a boil, reduce heat, and simmer 1 hour or until beans are tender. Drain beans and set aside. Combine ground beef, garlic, jalapeño peppers, and onions in a large Dutch oven. Cook over medium heat, stirring to crumble meat until meat is brown and onion is tender. Drain off pan drippings. Put in beans and remaining ingredients and stir well. Put on lid and simmer for 1 hour. Serves 10-12.

Southern Fried Venison and Gravy

Tender and delicious

2 tablespoons black pepper
1½ cups flour
½ cup cooking oil
3 pounds venison, sliced 3/4-inch thick (any cut)
1 large yellow onion, sliced
1 clove garlic, crushed

4 beef bouillon cubes (may substitute 2 cans beef broth)
1 heaping tablespoon Lipton's Onion Soup Mix
2 heaping tablespoons cornstarch

*M*ix the black pepper and flour in a shaker bag and coat the venison pieces. Preheat the oil in a large, deep skillet fitted with a lid. Brown the venison pieces on both sides. Remove from pan and set aside. Pour off any excess oil. Return the venison to the pan and add the onion, garlic, and bouillon cubes or broth and enough water to cover the venison by 1 inch. Add the soup mix and stir until blended.

Cover and simmer for 1 hour, 20 minutes, or until tender, stirring occasionally and maintaining the water level. Remove the venison and set aside. Make the gravy by mixing the cornstarch with 1 cup of cold water and stirring it slowly into the boiling broth until the desired thickness is achieved. Return the venison to the gravy and cover. Remove from heat and let it stand for 5 minutes, then serve. Serves 6.

When I was a small child, my mother's fried liver appealed to me about as much as the starched collar on my Sunday shirt on a hot August day. However, her liver recipe is the basis for my Southern Fried Venison—a seasonal favorite of my family, friends, and hunting buddies. I recommend serving this with mashed potatoes, pinto beans, biscuits, and iced tea.

**Sidney D. Keith
Norfolk County Grays
Camp #1549
Chesapeake, Virginia**

★

**Great-great-grandson
Pvt. Cyrus Keith
Co. B, 30th Virginia
Sharpshooters**

Cyrus was initially rejected for service because of a leg problem, but he was conscripted later on. He was eventually captured and sent to Point Lookout, Maryland. He was later released near Richmond, and had to walk home. His children did not recognize him upon his return.

Shrimp Sauce Piquante

Serve over hot rice

4 medium onions, finely chopped
4 cloves garlic, finely chopped
2 green peppers, finely chopped
4 ribs celery, finely chopped
4 tablespoons butter
4 tablespoons oil
1 small can tomato paste
Stock or chicken broth
4 lemon slices

Salt
Black pepper
$\frac{1}{4}$ teaspoon Tabasco
$\frac{1}{2}$ teaspoon thyme
1 teaspoon basil
$\frac{1}{2}$ teaspoon chili powder
1 cup sherry
2 pounds shrimp, peeled
$\frac{1}{2}$ cup green onions, chopped
2 tablespoons parsley, minced

★
Bill Myers
Beauregard Camp #130
New Orleans, Louisiana
★
Descendant of
Pvt. Charles Finney Verlander
Co. K, Confederate Guards,
Louisiana Militia

Sauté onions, garlic, green peppers, and celery in butter and oil until very soft. Add tomato paste and cook, stirring frequently, until brown. Add enough stock or chicken broth to make a thin gravy. Add lemon slices, salt, pepper, Tabasco, thyme, basil, and chili powder, and simmer for 2 hours. Stir in sherry, and 15 minutes later add shrimp. Cook for $\frac{1}{2}$ hour, then add chopped green onion and parsley.

Poppy Seed Chicken

A hit every time!

4 large whole chicken breasts, cooked, cooled, and cut into bite-sized pieces
3 cans cream of chicken soup (can substitute cream of mushroom)

1½ cups sour cream
40 Ritz crackers, crushed
1 stick margarine, melted
2 tablespoons poppy seeds

*M*ix soup and sour cream. Crumble crackers into melted margarine. Add poppy seeds to cracker mixture. Layer chicken, soup, and crackers into a 2-quart baking dish and repeat, ending with crackers on top. Bake at 350 degrees until bubbly. May be prepared the day before, refrigerated, and baked next day. Makes 12 generous servings.

★

**Ben Hestley
St. Clair Camp #308
Ashville, Alabama**

★

**Great-great-grandson
Pvt. Sanford Vandiver
Vaughan
Co. D (Orr's Regiment), 1st
South Carolina Rifles**

Sanford enlisted in 1861 at Sandy Springs, South Carolina. He was 22 years old. He succumbed to typhoid fever near Fredericksburg, Virginia, the next year and is buried in Hollywood Cemetery. He lived to see his child one time.

Oysters Johnny Reb

A specialty of the Old Southern Tea Room in Vicksburg, Mississippi

1 quart select oysters
1 tablespoon parsley, finely minced
2 tablespoons shallots, finely chopped
1/4 teaspoon salt
Red pepper to taste
1 teaspoon lemon juice
1 1/4 cups cracker crumbs (do not use cracker meal)
3/4 quart milk
3/4 stick butter

*B*utter a shallow casserole dish. Put a layer of oysters in bottom of the dish. Sprinkle parsley, shallots, salt, pepper, and a little lemon juice. Sprinkle cracker crumbs, then another layer of oysters, parsley, shallots, and crumbs. Just before baking, pour milk over contents of casserole, letting milk mix with the oysters. Dot with thin slices of butter. Bake 1/2 hour in a slow oven. Serves 6.

Traditionally, our family prepares this dish on Confederate Memorial Day. Serve with a nice spinach salad—there is nothing better!

★

**James W. Combs II
Capt. F. M. Jackson
Camp #1778
The Dalles, Oregon**

★

**4th great-grandson
1st Sgt. Wesley Combs
Co. C, 10th Kentucky Mounted
Infantry**

Wesley enlisted in 1862 in Letcher County, Kentucky. He was captured nine months later at the Battle of Gladeville in Virginia and spent time in several prisons, including Camp Douglas and Point Lookout. After eighteen months behind prison walls, he was released and walked home to Letcher County. He lived for about a year after his incarceration and died near Emmaville, Kentucky.

Viva la Chicken Tortilla Casserole

A wonderful main dish with South of the Border flair

4 whole chicken breasts
1 dozen corn tortillas
1 can cream of chicken soup
1 can cream of mushroom
   soup
1 cup milk

1 medium onion, grated
Garlic to taste
1 can green chili salsa (Ortega
   brand only)
½ pound sharp cheddar
   cheese, grated

*B*ake chicken breasts in foil for 1 hour at 400 degrees. Bone the chicken after cooking and cut into large pieces. Cut tortillas into strips or squares. Mix soups, milk, onion, garlic, and salsa. Butter a large, shallow baking dish. Place a layer of tortillas in dish, then chicken, then soup mixture. Continue layers until all ingredients are used, ending with soup mixture. Top with cheese. Refrigerate for 24 hours. Bake at 300 degrees for 1-1½ hours. Serves 8-10.

This recipe comes from my mother-in-law, Marie Watkins Bailiff, who was from Missouri and a UDC member. We have enjoyed it for years, and it goes well with a side of sour cream and guacamole.

★

Rowland R. King, Ed.D.
Gen. John B. Hood
Camp #1208
Los Angeles County, California

★

Great-grandson
Cpl. Wheeler Rufus Watson
9th Mississippi Cavalry

Wheeler Rufus Watson enlisted in Sander's 17th Tennessee Cavalry when he was just 16 years old. This unit changed names several times throughout the war, until it was finally called the 9th Mississippi Cavalry. Wheeler was a crack shot, and could hit a cornstalk at full gallop three out of six times. After the war, he returned to Strong, Mississippi, where he became an inventor and raised prize Rhode Island Red chickens.

Opposite—Wheeler Rufus Watson Corporal, 9th Mississippi Cavalry, age about 16 years

The Judge's Tex-Mex Bean Soup

Serve with corn bread for a real treat

1 cup pinto beans (wash thoroughly)
1 cup ham, chopped off the bone (may substitute bacon or sausage)
½ cup sweet white onion, chopped
½ cup bell pepper, chopped
1 pickled jalepeño pepper, chopped

2 tablespoons pickled jalepeño pepper juice
½ cup cilantro, chopped
¼ tablespoon garlic salt
¼ tablespoon lemon pepper
¼ tablespoon ground black pepper
¼ tablespoon salt (salt substitute can be used)

*W*ash pinto beans and allow them to soak in a pan of water overnight. Soaking will dissipate some of the gas in the beans. After soaking, pour away the water. Place beans in a 1-gallon sauce pan and fill with water. Add other ingredients. Bring to a boil and allow to boil for ½ hour. Add water as necessary. Cook on low for 1 hour.

★
**Judge Edward F. Butler, Sr.
Hood's Texas Brigade
Camp #1553
San Antonio, Texas**
★
**Great-great-grandson
Pvt. Benjamin Franklin
Lovelace
Co. K, 3rd Tennessee Infantry
(Clack's Regiment)**

Benjamin Lovelace, age 16, was in Tennessee visiting relatives in 1862 when he found himself suddenly conscripted into the Confederate army. He was captured during his first battle, the Battle of Chickamauga, and sent to Camp Douglas as a prisoner of war, where he remained until the surrender. Happily for his yet unborn posterity, he survived.

King Ranch Casserole

A great chicken dish

1 large chicken, cooked and
   de-boned
1 can cream of mushroom
   soup
1 can cream of chicken soup
1 can chicken broth

1 can Ro-Tel tomatoes
1 large package Fritos Corn
   chips, crushed
1 large onion, chopped
1-2 cups cheese, grated

*B*oil chicken, then de-bone and chop into small pieces. Add soups, broth, and Ro-Tel tomatoes. Add crushed chips and onion. Mix well. Top with cheese. Bake in a casserole dish at 350 degrees until bubbly and cheese is melted. Serves 8.

★

Nathaniel L. Young, Sr.
Lt. Col. William Walker
Camp #1738
Winnfield, Louisiana

★

Great-grandson
Pvt. Austin Young
Co. D, 6th Louisiana Cavalry

Austin Young was baptized Houston Lejeune, the son of Julien Lejeune and Eliza Young. By the end of the war, he had adopted the anglicized version of his name, and the family's name has been Young ever since. When my father was a boy, he didn't think his grandfather liked him. He had caught him fighting with one of his female cousins and had strongly admonished him, stating that "a gentleman does not hit a lady."

Leftover Turkey Casserole

Try this the day after Thanksgiving!

1 (8-ounce) package seasoned
   stuffing (dry)
1 cup celery, chopped fine
1 cup fresh mushrooms, sliced
   (may use 6-ounce can)
3 cups turkey, cooked and
   diced
2 (10½-ounce) cans con-
   densed cream of chicken
   soup

1½ cups sweet milk
5 eggs
¼ cup almonds, slivered
Parmesan cheese
3 tablespoons butter or margarine

Preheat oven to 375 degrees. In a lightly greased 9-inch by 12-inch baking dish, combine stuffing, celery, and mushrooms and mix well. Spread turkey evenly on the stuffing mixture. Place soup in a medium-sized mixing bowl and stir in sweet milk. Add beaten eggs, blending well. Pour evenly over turkey. Sprinkle almonds and Parmesan over the top and dot with butter or margarine. Bake uncovered for 40-45 minutes in a 375-degree oven.

★

**Allen M. Trapp, Jr.
McDaniel-Curtis Camp #165
Carrollton, Georgia**

★

**Great-great-grandnephew
Capt. Edwin Allen
Co. C, 26th Tennessee Infantry**

Capt. Edwin Allen was a gentleman farmer who organized the first Confederate recruits in Cocke County, Tennessee, in April 1861. He was killed in action at Murfreesboro, Tennessee, on January 2, 1863.

Skillet Chicken and Gravy

Country cooking at its finest

7 pieces chicken (or enough to fill the skillet)
2 teaspoons salt
¼ cup flour
¼ teaspoon pepper
3 cups water

1 teaspoon paprika
1 tablespoon lemon juice
1 tablespoon dry mustard
1 tablespoon catsup
Vegetable oil

*B*rown chicken pieces in vegetable oil. Add remaining ingredients and simmer for 1 hour. Serve with cooked rice.

★

F. Lee Hart III
Tom Smith Camp #1702
Suffolk, Virginia

★

Great-great-grandnephew
1st Lt. Benjamin T. Hart
Co. I, 15th North Carolina
Infantry

Benjamin enlisted at the age of 27 with his two brothers, Spencer Lee and Almond. He was captured in 1862 and confined at Fort Delaware until he was exchanged. He returned to duty and was wounded at Fredericksburg, and again at The Wilderness. He was paroled in 1865, and records show he never took the oath of allegiance.

Grandma Curcio's Chicken Cacciatore

Add pasta or rice for a great meal

2-3 pounds of chicken (can be a fryer cut up, or simply thighs and legs)
1 cup flour
1 cup Italian bread crumbs
1 tablespoon granulated garlic
1 tablespoon granulated onion
¼ cup plus 1 tablespoon Parmesan cheese
2-3 tablespoons Italian spice mix
1 teaspoon black pepper
1 teaspoon hot red pepper flakes (optional)

3-5 tablespoons olive oil
2-3 garlic cloves, minced
1 medium Walla Walla sweet onion
⅔ cup sliced mushrooms (fresh or canned)
Bell peppers (red or green)
3-4 sprigs parsley, chopped fine
2 cups tomato sauce
1 cup of your favorite dry wine (red or white)
2 bay leaves

**John Griffin
J. K. McNeill Camp #674
Moultrie, Georgia**

**Descendant of
Pvt. John Jackson Griffin
Co. I, 50th Georgia Infantry**

Wash and gently dry (not completely, though) the chicken. Mix flour, bread crumbs, granulated garlic, granulated onion, 1 tablespoon Parmesan cheese, 1 tablespoon Italian spice mix, black pepper, and red pepper flakes in a plastic bag, drop the chicken pieces in, and shake around to coat the chicken with the mix.

In an electric skillet, heat 3-4 tablespoons olive oil at about 325 degrees, along with 1-2 minced garlic cloves (to taste). Add the coated chicken. Cook the chicken until golden brown on all sides. When chicken is cooked, remove from pan and drain on a paper towel.

In the skillet, add 1 minced garlic clove, sweet onion, bell pepper, and mushrooms to leftover oil and chicken

continued on next page

drippings. When this mixture is slightly browned, add parsley, tomato sauce, $1/4$ cup Parmesan cheese, and wine. Stir briskly and scrape all "flavorings" you can from the pan. Add the chicken, bay leaves, and remaining Italian spices to pan. Allow the mixture to cook down into a more thickened sauce, turning the chicken so that it does not burn.

When the sauce is thickened to desired consistency, remove from heat and remove the bay leaves. Transfer all the contents of the skillet into a baking dish. Cover with aluminum foil and bake in an oven for 30-45 minutes until chicken is so tender it flakes away from the bone by touch.

Chicken Crunch Casserole

A good addition to a Sunday brunch

3 cups cooked chicken, diced
2 hard-boiled eggs, chopped
1 small can sliced mushrooms
$3/4$ cup celery, diced
$1/2$ cup almonds, slivered
1 tablespoon onion, chopped
1 can cream of chicken soup
$3/4$ cup mayonnaise
1 cup chow mein noodles

Mix first 6 ingredients. Combine soup and mayonnaise and toss with chicken mixture. Turn into an 8-inch by 8-inch by 2-inch casserole. Top with noodles. Bake 30 minutes at 350 degrees.

★
Roger W. Ridings
Hood's Texas Brigade
Camp #153
San Antonio, Texas
★
Great-grandson
Pvt. Pleasant Henry Ridings
3rd Mississippi Infantry

Pleasant Ridings survived the war and died on August 30, 1881. He is buried in Liberty Cemetery in Monroe County, Mississippi.

Old Virginia Brunswick Stew

Small game may be substituted for chicken

2 tablespoons bacon grease
2 onions
1 frying chicken (2-2½
   pounds), cut into pieces
   and seasoned
3 cups water
½ cup sherry

1 large can crushed tomatoes
2 teaspoons Worcestershire
   sauce
1 pound fresh lima beans
1 can okra
1 large can whole kernel corn
Salt and pepper to taste

*B*rown the onions in the bacon grease, then add the chicken. When the chicken is done, pour off the grease and put chicken and onions into Dutch oven. Add the water, tomatoes, sherry, and Worcestershire sauce. Cook slowly over low flame for 1 hour, then add the lima beans, corn, and okra. Let simmer for 2 hours. Salt and pepper to taste.

★
**Edward J. Bennett
Fincastle Rifles Camp #1326
Roanoke, Virginia**
★
**Great-great-grandson
Pvt. Franklin Bennett
Co. G. 57th Virginia Infantry**

Franklin Bennett served in numerous campaigns leading up to Pickett's famous charge at Gettysburg. The 57th was one of the few units to break the Federal lines, and Franklin was shot in the leg just before going over the wall defended by Federal troops. His leg was amputated by a Yankee surgeon on the field following the Confederate retreat. He was taken prisoner and later exchanged. Upon returning to the family farm, he married and had two children before dying in 1870 of complications from his war wounds. He is buried in the family cemetery in Franklin County, Virginia.

Hungry Soldier Bean Soup

An easy, delicious soup from the authors of The South Was Right !

2 cans Campbell's Bean with
  Bacon soup
2 cans Great Northern Beans
1 large onion, chopped

2 cans Pinto beans with
  jalapeño
1 bell pepper, chopped
Smoked link sausage, sliced

*M*ix all ingredients (except sausage) in a large pot and stir well. Add smoked link sausage to taste (we use a lot!) and cook 15 to 30 minutes.
  Note: Cook this soup over an open fire for the best flavor.

General Lee once alluded to the fact that the only dependable friend of his hungry soldiers was the common field peas of the South. Both during and after the War, peas and beans have been nutritious staples for hungry Southerners. This recipe has been used often by the Kennedy brothers to feed a hungry army of Southern "War Between the States" reenactors.

★
**James Ronald Kennedy
Beauregard Camp #130
New Orleans, Louisiana**
★
**Walter Donald Kennedy
Sgt. James W. Nicholson
Camp #1478
Ruston, Louisiana**
★
**Great-grandsons
Pvt. John Wesley Kennedy
Co. F, 38th Mississippi
Volunteer Infantry**

John Wesley Kennedy always stated that he and "the boys" blew up a Yankee gunboat in the Yazoo River during the War. The Federal gunboat *Cairo* was raised from the depths of the Yazoo in the late 1950s. The Federal government had always maintained that an accidental boiler explosion was the cause of the sinking of the *Cairo*. However, modern day inspection of the wreck proved that the boat was indeed sunk by a Confederate mine or torpedo.

Vegetables
and
Side Dishes

Grits with an Attitude
Best Broccoli Casserole
Rebel Yell Southern Sweet Potatoes
Sweet and Sour Green Beans
Spicy Eggplant Casserole
Squash Fritters
Tasty Texas Hash
Southern Firehouse Beans
Vidalia Onion Casserole
Okra Casserole
Stuffed Zucchini
Aunt Jinki's Sweet Potato Casserole
Carol's Cheese Grits Casserole
Mashed Potato Casserole
Sweet Potato Soufflé
Mrs. Toney's Molasses Baked Beans
Grandmother's Cheese Grits
Black-Eyed Peas
Crock Pot Macaroni and Cheese
Sharon's Sweet Onion Casserole
Grillades and Grits
Heidi's Famous Fresh Tomato Pie
Butter Bean Casserole
Sausage and Rice Casserole
Janie's Tasty Sweet Potatoes
Microwave Stuffed Onions
Great Granny's Confederate Sweet Potato
    Soufflé
Black Beans Cuban Style (Frijoles Negros)
Squash Casserole
Southern-Style Corn Casserole
Confederate Collard Greens
Main Course Macaroni and Cheese
Sweet Potato Crunch
Easy Squash Casserole
Independence Day Baked Beans

Barton Family Tomato Dressing
Rebel Rice
Confederate Cranberry Delight
Hoppin' John
Fried Green Tomatoes
Corn Pudding
So Easy Squash Casserole
Sweet Potato Surprise
Margie's Ultra-Super Veg-All Casserole
Squash Puppies
Scalloped Corn
Celery Casserole
Carrots Maretto
Soufflé of Spinach
Libby's Spicy Fried Squash
Hot and Spicy Tofu Stir Fry
Green Bean Casserole
Wreck on the Mountain
Corn Pudding
All Day Beans
Eggplant Creole
Three-Layer Cabbage Casserole
Rhonda's Favorite Rebel Eye Gravy
Copper Carrot Pennies
Stuffed Yellow Squash
Cheese Grits Casserole
Charleston Red Rice
Eggplant Casserole
Robert E. Lee Natural Bridge Sweet Tater
    Pone
Calcasieu Tigers Eggplant Parmesan
Cheese Onion Pie
Confederate Squash
Mama's Sweet Potato Soufflé
Marinated Carrots
Stuffed Pumpkin

Grits with an Attitude

Even those who don't care for grits will like this!

4 cups water
1 garlic clove, crushed
Fresh ground pepper to taste
1 cup quick cooking grits
2 tablespoons butter

1¼ cups cheddar cheese,
   shredded
2 eggs, beaten
½ cup milk

★
D. Keith Baker
Robert E. Lee Camp #726
Alexandria, Virginia
★
Great-grandson
2nd Sgt. Calvin Luther Peek
Co. I, 61st Virginia Infantry

*B*ring the water to a boil in a large saucepan. Add the garlic and pepper. Gradually stir in the grits. Lower the heat and simmer for about 5 minutes. Stir a couple of times. Remove the pan from the heat. Mix in 1 cup of cheddar cheese and the butter. Mix the eggs with the milk and combine with the grits. Pour the mixture into a greased 2-quart casserole. Sprinkle the remaining ¼ cup of cheddar cheese on top. Bake in a 350-degree oven for an hour (or until set and browned on top). Serves 4.

Best Broccoli Casserole

A traditional Southern favorite that goes with anything

2 boxes frozen broccoli florets
(can use 3-4 cups fresh
broccoli)
1 egg, beaten
1 cup mayonnaise
1 can cream of mushroom
soup

2 tablespoons finely chopped
onion
1 cup grated cheddar cheese
½ stick butter or margarine
20 Ritz crackers

C ook broccoli according to package directions. If fresh broccoli is used, cook until very tender. Drain well. Mix egg, mayonnaise, soup, onion, and cheese together. Stir in broccoli. Put in 2-quart casserole. Bake at 350 degrees for 30-40 minutes. During last 15-20 minutes of baking, melt ½ stick of butter and add 20 crumbled Ritz crackers. Toss together and then spread on top of casserole and continue baking. Serves 6.

★
Phillip B. Issacs
Col. Samuel H. Walkup
Camp #1375
Monroe, North Carolina
★
Great-great-grandson
Pvt. Godfrey Isaacs
Co. A, 28th Regiment, North Carolina Troops

Rebel Yell Southern Sweet Potatoes

Yams with a little something extra

3 pounds sweet potatoes
4 ounces margarine or butter
¾ teaspoon of ground cinnamon
½ teaspoon of ground nutmeg
1 teaspoon salt
½ cup milk

1½ ounces of Rebel Yell bourbon whiskey
4 additional tablespoons of margarine
¼ cup light brown sugar, packed

James L. Speicher
B. G. William Steele
Camp #1857
Leavenworth, Kansas

Descendant of
Quartermaster
Sgt. Nathan R. Ensign
11th Battery,
Georgia Light Artillery

Preheat oven to 350 degrees. Peel the potatoes and boil for approximately 20 minutes until very tender, or bake for 1 hour at 350 degrees. While the potatoes are still warm, mash them with a mixer, adding the margarine, cinnamon, nutmeg, and salt. Beat until smooth. Add milk and Rebel Yell and mix well. Place potato mixture in a greased casserole dish. Scatter 4 one-tablespoon dollops of margarine on top. Sprinkle the entire top with the brown sugar. Place in preheated oven and bake for 45 minutes or until heated through.

Note: Additional ingredients such as raisins, pecans, or chopped pineapple may be added to suit your taste. Miniature marshmallows may also be used as a topping to be added at the end of baking so that they melt and turn light brown on top.

Sweet and Sour Green Beans

Has a tasty, tangy flavor

1½ cups fresh green beans or 4 cans

4 slices bacon

2 medium onions, sliced thin

1 tablespoon dry mustard

1 teaspoon salt

2 tablespoons brown sugar

2 tablespoons sugar

¼ cup vinegar

Cook fresh beans until crisp. Drain and reserve 1 cup liquid. Cook bacon and reserve drippings in skillet. Crumble bacon and set aside. Sauté onions in drippings until tender, gradually stirring in mustard. Combine salt, both types of sugar, reserved bean liquid, and vinegar and pour over onion. Bring to a boil and stir to blend well. Add beans and bacon. Cover and simmer 15 minutes. Serves 6.

★

Samuel Terrell ("Terry") Rowell
Jasper County Grays
Camp #1349
Heidelberg, Mississippi

★

Great-great-grandnephew
Lt. Col. James Stephens Terral
7th Mississippi Battalion

Spicy Eggplant Casserole

Eggplant that doesn't taste like eggplant

1 large eggplant, diced
1 teaspoon salt
½ teaspoon pepper
2 tablespoons green pepper, chopped
1 medium onion, chopped
¾ cup bread crumbs

1 egg, beaten
1 cup creamed corn
Dash of garlic powder (optional)
½ cup jalapeño cheese, shredded

Peel and cook eggplant until tender. Drain and mash slightly. Combine with all other ingredients except cheese. Mix well. Sprinkle cheese on top. Bake at 350 degrees for 30 minutes or until golden brown. Serves 4.

★
Eric Hague
Madison Starke Perry
Camp #1424
Lake Geneva, Florida
★
Descendant of
Archibald Hague
Co. C, 7th Florida Infantry

Squash Fritters

A different way to cook squash

2 medium-sized yellow squash, grated
¼ cup onion, diced
2 tablespoons green bell pepper, diced
1 teaspoon brown sugar

1 teaspoon salt
1 tablespoon all-purpose flour
1 large egg, lightly beaten
2 teaspoons butter, melted
½ cup olive oil

Stir together first 8 ingredients. Heat olive oil in a large, heavy skillet. Drop by tablespoons into hot oil. Fry until golden brown. Drain on paper towel and serve hot.

★
Donald W. Brickey
Gen. William B. Bate Camp
#34
Gallatin, Tennessee
★
1st cousin,
three times removed
Gen. Robert E. Lee
Commander in Chief of the
Confederate Forces

Tasty Texas Hash

Good alternative to dirty rice

1 pound hamburger meat
2 onions, diced
2 green bell peppers
1 hot pepper
3 tablespoons shortening
1 cup cooked brown rice
1 cup uncooked white rice

2 cups cooked tomatoes
1 teaspoon salt
1 tablespoon Worcestershire
   sauce
$\frac{1}{4}$ teaspoon pepper
1 teaspoon chili powder

Brown hamburger meat. Drain. Sauté onions, bell peppers, and hot pepper slowly in shortening until onions are yellow. Add meat and cook until blended. Add cooked brown rice, uncooked white rice, tomatoes, and seasonings in casserole dish with above mixture. Bake in moderately hot oven (375 degrees) for 45 minutes to 1 hour. Serves 8.

★
Leonard Q. Varner
Lt. T. D. Falls Camp #1768
Fallston, North Carolina
★
3rd great-grandson
Pvt. Harmon Thomas Eugene
Lovelace
Co. D, 55th Regiment, North
Carolina Infantry

Harmon Lovelace enlisted with the "Cleveland Farmers" in May 1862, and saw action at Chancellorsville, Petersburg, The Wilderness, and Gettysburg, where he was wounded. After the war, in 1884, he and his oldest son, Drury, purchased land in Kings Mountain, North Carolina, where he lived until his death on April 8, 1913. He and his wife, Ann Hamrick Lovelace, had nine children.

THE CONFEDERATE COOKBOOK

Southern Firehouse Beans

A tasty recipe from a retired firefighter

1 pound ground beef
2 #10 cans pork and beans
1 #10 can red kidney beans

1 cup brown sugar
1 small bottle catsup
1 package dry onion soup mix

Brown and drain ground beef. Combine all ingredients in a large baking dish or roaster. Stir well. Bake at 350 degrees for 1 hour. Serve hot. Serves 4-6.

★
James K. Phillabaum
Maj. Gen. William D. McCain
HQ Camp #584
Columbia, Tennessee
★
Great-great-grandnephew
Pvt. Nimrod Anderson Wills
"Orphan's Brigade," Kentucky

After the war, Nimrod was active in local politics and continued the operation of an inn (established by his father and located in Menifee County, Kentucky) called Traveler's Rest. He is buried in the family cemetery near the old inn.

Vidalia Onion Casserole

Has a mild, sweet flavor

2 pounds thinly sliced Vidalia
    or sweet onions (approxi-
    mately 6)
4 tablespoons butter or oleo
3 eggs, beaten

1 cup sour cream
¼ cup Parmesan cheese
½ cup cheddar cheese, grated
Salt and pepper to taste

★
John F. Ewell
John S. Mosby Camp #1237
Front Royal, Virginia
★
**1st cousin, four times
removed
Lt. Gen. Richard S. Ewell**

Preheat oven to 350 degrees. Grease a large casserole dish and set aside. In a large saucepan, sauté onions in butter over medium heat until they turn pale and are tender. In a medium bowl, beat eggs. Add sour cream and Parmesan cheese. Mix well. Place onions in prepared casserole dish. Pour egg mixture over onions. Sprinkle top with grated cheddar cheese. Bake uncovered for 45 minutes in preheated oven. Serves 8.

Okra Casserole

A simple casserole that serves a crowd

1 pound fresh okra, sliced
1 large onion, sliced
2 medium tomatoes, sliced
1 cup cheddar cheese,
  shredded

1 cup cracker crumbs or bread
  crumbs
Salt and pepper to taste
1/4 stick oleo or butter, melted

---

*L*ayer onion, okra, tomatoes, cheese, and crumbs (in that order) in a casserole dish. Sprinkle a pinch of salt and pepper on each layer. Pour melted butter over top of crumbs and bake at 350 degrees for 45 minutes. Makes 8-12 servings.

This recipe was created in the 1930s by my maternal grandmother, Jewell Givens Kelley, and has been a family favorite ever since.

★

Richard B. Davis
Gen. Lloyd Tilghman
Camp #1492
Paducah, Kentucky

★

Great-great-grandson
Pvt. Benjamin Dekalb Kelley
Co. K, 4th Alabama Cavalry
(Roddey's Regiment)

Pvt. Kelley entered the service with four of his brothers in 1861 and served until the end of the war. He participated in several major battles, including Shiloh and Chickamauga. He was captured near the Black Warrior River in northern Alabama at the close of the war, but was released after the Federal soldiers could not tell if he was a soldier or a beggar because of the worn condition of his uniform. He returned home to Walker County, Alabama, and reared a large family. Some of his descendants live there to this day.

Stuffed Zucchini

Can also be served as a main dish

1 large zucchini (at least 12 inches in length)
2 ounces (¼ cup) bulk pork sausage
1 tablespoon chopped celery
1 tablespoon chopped onion

½ cup Ritz cracker crumbs (can substitute garlic croutons)
½ cup grated cheese (cheddar, mozzarella, or Monterey Jack)

Trim ends of zucchini and boil in salted water until crisp-tender (8-10 minutes). Drain. Cut zucchini lengthwise and carefully scoop out center, saving the skin whole. Chop or blend center of zucchini. Fry sausage; add celery and onion and cook until they are sautéed; drain. Mix the fried items into the zucchini mixture and add cracker crumbs and ¼ cup of cheese. Divide mixture and shape each half into empty zucchini skins. Bake uncovered at 350 degrees for 20 minutes. Cover each with the rest of the cheese. Bake 5 minutes more. Serve hot. Each zucchini serves 2 people, so simply double recipe as needed to serve the required number of guests.

★

**Brett Bradshaw
Capt. John M. Kinard
Camp #35
Little Mountain, Georgia**

★

**Great-grandson
3rd Lt. John Wesley Dotson
12th Tennessee Cavalry
Battalion**

Lt. Dotson survived the war, and died in 1899.

Aunt Jinki's Sweet Potato Casserole

It's Goooooooood!

3 cups cooked sweet potatoes, mashed

$\frac{1}{2}$ stick butter or margarine, melted

$\frac{1}{2}$ cup brown sugar

$\frac{1}{2}$ cup white sugar

2 eggs, beaten

$\frac{1}{2}$ teaspoon salt

$\frac{1}{2}$ cup milk

$\frac{1}{2}$ teaspoon vanilla

Combine all ingredients and pour into baking dish. Top with the following:

$\frac{1}{2}$ cup flour

1 cup brown sugar

1 cup nuts

$\frac{1}{2}$ stick butter or margarine, melted

Combine all ingredients and spread topping over sweet potato mix. Bake 35 minutes at 350 degrees. Serves 8-12. May be prepared in advance and frozen. Simply defrost and bake as directed.

Every holiday it is a requirement that we all fill up with Aunt Jinki's Sweet Potato Casserole. It's a traditional Southern recipe—easy to make with no regard for calories!

★

**R. Scott Prochaska
Gen. Jo Shelby Camp #1414
Harrison, Arkansas**

★

**3rd great-grandson
Pvt. Robert Israel Mathews
Co. D, 49th Virginia Infantry
(Extra Billy Smith's Boys)**

Carol's Cheese Grits Casserole

Good at breakfast or anytime

1 cup quick grits
½ teaspoon salt
4 cups boiling water
¼ pound butter or margarine

½ pound grated cheese
2 eggs, well beaten
¼ cup milk

★
Joseph R. Ferguson, Jr.
Urquhart-Gillette Camp #1471
Franklin, Virginia

*S*lowly stir grits and salt into 4 cups of briskly boiling water. Reduce heat to medium-low; cover. Cook 5-7 minutes or until thickened, stirring occasionally. Remove from heat. Add butter and cheese and mix well. Add eggs and milk. Mix and pour into greased casserole. Bake 45 minutes in 425-degree oven. Serves 8.

Mashed Potato Casserole

A meal in itself!

3 large potatoes
⅓ cup sour cream or yogurt
1 teaspoon salt
Dash of black pepper
½ teaspoon sugar
¼ cup margarine

Milk
⅛ teaspoon dill seed
2 teaspoons chives, chopped
1 cup cooked spinach, well
    drained and chopped
½ cup grated cheese

★
Steven W. McFarlane
Matthew Fontaine Maury
Camp #1722
Fredericksburg, Virginia
★

Great-great-grandson
Pvt. Augustus McFarlane
Co. I, 34th Battalion,
Virginia Cavalry

Cook and mash potatoes. Add next 5 ingredients and mix well, then add just enough milk to reach desired consistency. Whip. Stir in dill seed, chives, and spinach. Pour into greased casserole dish. Top with cheddar cheese. Bake at 400 degrees for 20 minutes. This dish freezes well and can be made 1-2 days ahead. Serves 6-8.

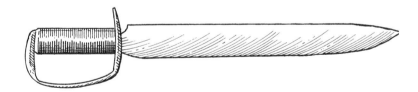

Sweet Potato Soufflé

Can be used as a vegetable or a dessert

3 cups mashed sweet potatoes
2 eggs
1 teaspoon vanilla
1 cup sugar
½ cup sweet milk
½ stick butter
1 cup coconut

Topping
1 cup brown sugar
½ stick butter
½ cup self-rising flour
1 cup pecans

*M*ix first 7 ingredients. Add topping. Bake at 350 degrees for 45 minutes or until brown. Serves 15.

★
James D. Ramey
Maj. Wm. E. Simmons
Camp #96
Lawrenceville, Georgia
★

Great-great-grandson
Pvt. Jack Asa Whidby
Co. F, 24th Georgia Infantry

Pvt. Whidby was captured at Gettysburg, paroled, and then recaptured at Cold Harbor, Virginia, in 1864. He was sent to prison at Point Lookout, Maryland, and later transferred to Elmira Prison. He was finally released in June 1865. Jack returned home to rear a family of five children. He died in 1883.

THE CONFEDERATE COOKBOOK

Mrs. Toney's Molasses Baked Beans

The finest tasting beans in the South

½ pound ground beef
2 (16-ounce) cans pork and
    beans
1 (16-ounce) can barbecued
    beans
1 medium onion, chopped
½ cup green pepper, chopped
½ cup brown sugar, firmly
    packed
¼ cup molasses

¼ cup catsup
2 tablespoons prepared mus-
    tard
1 tablespoon Worcestershire
    sauce
1 clove garlic, crushed
1 teaspoon seasoned salt
½ teaspoon lemon pepper sea-
    soning
4-5 slices bacon

Cook ground beef until browned; drain well. Combine all ingredients except bacon and mix well. Pour into a 13-inch by 9-inch baking dish and top with bacon. Bake at 350 degrees for 2 hours. Serves 8.

★

Jim Steeley
Clement A. Evans Camp #64
Waycross, Georgia
★

Great-great-grandson
Pvt. Green Berry Franklin
Co. F, 10th Alabama Infantry

Pvt. Franklin was a native of Jefferson County, Alabama. He was captured at Gettysburg. After his release, he returned home to rear a family. He died in 1881.

Grandmother's Cheese Grits

A versatile dish that can be used for breakfast, lunch, or dinner

2 cups grits
1½ quarts water
Cheddar cheese (12-ounce
    block), cut into cubes
½ cup milk
4 eggs, beaten

½ cup margarine
1 cup sour cream
Paprika
Salt and pepper to taste
Parmesan cheese, grated

Preheat oven to 300 degrees. Cook grits in water. Add cheese, milk, eggs, margarine, sour cream, salt, and pepper. Pour into a buttered 4-quart casserole. Sprinkle with Parmesan cheese and paprika. Bake for 30-45 minutes. Serves 10.

This recipe has been a favorite of our family for generations. It may be easily halved or doubled and freezes beautifully. Whenever there is a covered dish gathering, the family knows my wife will bring her famous cheese grits!

★
Richard E. Hager
Kirby-Smith Camp #1209
Jacksonville, Florida
★
Grandson
Pvt. Burwell S. Hager
Co. D, 36th Virginia Infantry

Burwell Hager was born in 1843. He was captured at Newhope and imprisoned at Camp Morton. After he was paroled, he made his way back to Logan County, West Virginia, where he married and had six children. He is buried in the family cemetery on his homeplace in Big Creek, West Virginia.

THE CONFEDERATE COOKBOOK

Black-Eyed Peas

Put the pot on early and it will be ready by noon

8 ounces dried black-eyed peas
1 slice bacon
1 (14½-ounce) can whole
tomatoes
¼-½ fresh, hot green pepper
pod

Salt and pepper to taste
½ pound scrambled, browned
hamburger meat
½ small to medium onion,
chopped

★

Keith Thomason
Chief Clinton Camp #366
Abilene, Texas

★

Great-grandson
Pvt. Jessie James Cotter
3rd Battery, Maryland Artillery

Wash dried black-eyed peas well. Drain. Place peas, bacon, tomatoes, green pepper pod (to taste), and salt and pepper into a large pan. Bring to a boil and lower heat to medium. Cook about 2 hours or until peas soften. Add cooked hamburger meat and chopped onion. Cook about 10 more minutes. Serve with corn bread. Serves 6-8.

Tastes great with a side dish of sliced onion, fresh tomatoes, radishes, and cucumbers, or whatever fresh vegetable is in season.

233

Crock Pot Macaroni and Cheese

Rich and creamy

1 (8-ounce) package elbow
  macaroni (cooked and
  drained)
1 (12-ounce) can evaporated
  milk
1½ cups milk
1 teaspoon salt
Black pepper to taste

1 cup medium cheddar
  cheese, grated
2 cups sharp cheddar cheese,
  grated
½ cup melted butter or oleo
2 eggs, beaten
Additional grated cheese for
  topping (optional)

*C*oat crock pot with non-stick cooking spray. Combine all ingredients and pour into pot. Cook for 3½ hours on low. Don't stir. Serves 6-8.

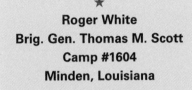

★
Roger White
Brig. Gen. Thomas M. Scott
Camp #1604
Minden, Louisiana
★
Descendant of
Edward Eugene Pratt
Co. G, 8th Louisiana Infantry

Edward succumbed to wounds received at Manassas, Virginia, in 1861. His brother Clarence survived the fighting only to be killed in a duel in New Orleans shortly after the end of the war.

Sharon's Sweet Onion Casserole

This is wonderful!

½ cup unsalted butter, room
   temperature, divided
4 large Vidalia onions or sweet
   onions, sliced into rings
1½ packages butter-flavored
   crackers (50-60 crackers),
   crushed

8 ounces sharp cheddar
   cheese, shredded
Salt and pepper to taste
3 large eggs, beaten
1 cup milk
Paprika to taste

---

*P*reheat oven to 350 degrees. Sauté onion rings in ¼
cup butter. Combine remaining butter with cracker
crumbs. Reserve ¼ cup crumb mixture for topping and
layer remaining crumbs into bottom of creased 9-inch by
13-inch casserole. Spread sautéed onion rings over crumb
layer and sprinkle with cheese. Salt and pepper to taste.
Combine eggs and milk and pour over layers. Top with
reserved crumbs and paprika and bake 35-40 minutes.
Serves 8-10.

*This dish can be prepared in advance and refrigerated
until ready to pop in the oven.*

★

**Joseph W. Halsey
Col. Harry W. Gilmore
Camp #1388
Baltimore, Maryland**

★

**Great-grandson
Cpl. William Halsey
Co. I, 51st Virginia Infantry**

William Halsey was known as
"Sheep Bill" because he
raised sheep for a living. He
was captured at the Battle of
Waynesboro and sent to
prison at Fort Delaware. He
refused to sign the Oath of
Allegiance, and was imprisoned until June 1865. He
died in 1901 and has many
descendants.

Grillades and Grits

An old New Orleans specialty

2 pounds veal or beef round,
 ³/₄-inch thick
5 tablespoons shortening
1¼ cups celery, chopped
½ cup green or white onions,
 chopped
1 toe garlic, chopped
5 tablespoons flour
3 cups water
1 teaspoon salt

¼ teaspoon black pepper
1 teaspoon thyme
½ teaspoon Tabasco
1 bay leaf
3 tablespoons parsley,
 chopped
3 tablespoons tomato sauce
Grits, cooked according to
 package directions

*P*ound meat on both sides to ½-inch thickness, then sauté in shortening until brown. Remove and lightly season. Sauté celery, onions, and garlic for 6-8 minutes, then remove. Add shortening if necessary to make a total of 5 tablespoons, then add flour and brown. Add water and blend. Return meat and vegetables to skillet. Add salt, pepper, thyme, Tabasco, and bay leaf and simmer for 30 minutes, adding 1 cup of water if necessary. Add parsley and tomato sauce and simmer for 4 minutes more. Serve over hot cooked grits.

★
**Bill Myers
Beauregard Camp #130
New Orleans, Louisiana**
★
**Great-great-grandson
Pvt. Charles Finney
Vanderlander
Co. K, Confederate Guards,
Louisiana Militia**

Charles Vanderlander was born in New York in 1833. He married in 1858 in New Orleans, where he earned his living as a riverboat pilot. Just before the fall of New Orleans to Federal troops in 1862, he was sent with his ship to Vicksburg, where he ferried troops and supplies back and forth across the river. He died in New Orleans in 1891.

Heidi's Famous Fresh Tomato Pie

Worth the wait for the first fresh tomatoes to come off the vine

1 deep-dish pie shell, cooked per package instructions
3 large tomatoes, peeled, sliced, and drained*
2-3 green onions, chopped
1 tablespoon fresh basil, chopped
1 tablespoon fresh chives, chopped
1 cup mayonnaise (salad dressing may be used)
1 cup sharp cheddar cheese, grated
Salt and pepper to taste

*M*ake layers in pie shell beginning with tomato, top with half the green onions, half the basil, and chives. Repeat, then top with remaining tomato slices. Mix mayonnaise and cheese. Spread on top. Bake for 30 minutes at 350 degrees. Makes 6-8 servings.

To drain tomatoes, peel, slice, and lay out slices on paper towels; sprinkle with salt and let drain for 15-20 minutes.

The first three vine-ripened tomatoes that come out of my garden go into this recipe. My wife makes at least one of these pies a week throughout the summer.

★
Steven Mills
Franklin Rifles Camp #310
Louisburg, North Carolina
★

3rd great-grandson
Pvt. John Addison Mills
51st North Carolina Home Guard

John Mills was captured during the Federal pursuit of Jefferson Davis. He was paroled at Salisbury, North Carolina.

Butter Bean Casserole

Serve with salad and a roast

2 tablespoons onions,
    chopped
2 tablespoons green pepper,
    chopped
1 tablespoon butter or
    margarine

1 can tomato soup
1 tablespoon brown sugar
1 tablespoon vinegar
2 packages frozen butter
    beans

*P*reheat oven to 350 degrees. Sauté onions and green pepper in butter or margarine. Add all ingredients as listed. Place in casserole dish and bake for approximately 1 hour.

★

Allen M. Trapp, Jr.
McDaniel-Curtis Camp #165
Carrollton, Georgia

★

Great-great-grandnephew
Capt. Edwin Allen
Co. C, 26th Tennessee Infantry

Sausage and Rice Casserole

These ingredients compliment each other beautifully to make a delicious casserole

1 pound ground sausage,
    cooked and drained (mild
    or spicy, to your taste
1 medium bell pepper,
    chopped
1 medium onion, chopped

½ cup celery, chopped
½ cup regular white rice,
    uncooked
2 packages Lipton's Chicken
    Noodle Soup mix (dry)

*B*rown and drain ground sausage and set aside. Cook bell pepper, onion, celery, soup mix, and rice in 4 cups of boiling water for about 7 minutes (will be soupy). Add the cooked sausage and bake at 350 degrees in a buttered 9-inch by 13-inch covered casserole dish for about 35 minutes. Serves 6.

★

Maitland O. Westbrook III
Gen. William McCain
Headquarters Camp #584
Columbia, Tennessee

★

Great-grandnephew
Pvt. John W. P. Westbrook
Co. E, 16 th Virginia Infantry

Pvt. Westbrook was killed at the Battle of the Crater on July 30, 1864. He was buried in a mass grave on the field of battle near Petersburg, Virginia.

238

Janie's Tasty Sweet Potatoes

Even picky kids like this!

3 cups sweet potatoes
½ cup sugar
½ cup butter
2 eggs
1 teaspoon vanilla
⅓ cup milk (may use a little less)

Topping
⅓ cup melted butter
1 cup brown sugar
½ cup flour
1 cup pecans

★

**Jarrell D. Clark
Gen. Franklin Gardner
Camp #1421
Lafayette, Louisiana**

★

**Descendant of
Pvt. William Elisha Upshaw
Blake's Scouts, Georgia**

*B*oil and mash sweet potatoes. If using canned, heat in syrup, then pour off syrup and mash. Add rest of ingredients, but use just enough milk to make sweet potatoes soft (not runny). Pour into deep casserole (5 quart). Spread topping over all. Bake 25 minutes at 350 degrees.

Microwave Stuffed Onions

Try this for something really different

4 small onions (preferably
   Vidalia)
1 tablespoon butter
$\frac{1}{4}$ teaspoon salt

$\frac{1}{8}$ teaspoon pepper
1 cup herb-seasoned stuffing
   mix
$\frac{1}{4}$ cup beef broth

---

*P*lace a piece of plastic wrap large enough to cover onions in a 1$\frac{1}{2}$-quart casserole. Slice onions crosswise into 3 layers. Place bottom of each onion on plastic wrap in casserole. Place butter in a 4-cup microwaveable measure. Microwave on *high* 20 seconds to melt. Stir in salt, pepper, stuffing mix, and beef broth. Place a little of the stuffing mixture on onion slice. Place center onion slice on top of stuffing, place a little more stuffing on this slice, and top with the remaining onion slice. Cover with plastic wrap and microwave on *high* for 6-7 minutes.

★

Allen M. Trapp, Jr.
McDaniel-Curtis Camp #165
Carrollton, Georgia

★

Great-great-grandnephew
Capt. Edwin Allen
Co. C, 26th Tennessee Infantry

Great Granny's Confederate Sweet Potato Soufflé

An old-fashioned Southern favorite

4-5 large sweet potatoes
2 eggs, beaten
1-1¼ cups sugar
½ stick butter
1 teaspoon nutmeg

1 teaspoon vanilla flavoring
¼-½ teaspoon salt
Milk
Marshmallows

---

*B*oil sweet potatoes. Peel while still hot and whip in a mixing bowl. Add remaining ingredients except milk and marshmallows to the whipped potatoes. Add just enough milk to make a soft consistency. For variety, you can also add pecans, coconut, raisins, or drained pineapple chunks. Stir well. Bake at 350 degrees for 30-35 minutes. Top with marshmallows and heat for another couple of minutes. Serves 6-8.

I first had this wonderful dish when I was a small child. I loved it the first time I had it, and to this day I would rather eat this preparation than anything else I have ever tasted.

★
Robert Parker Hurst
David Lang Camp #1314
Tallahassee, Florida
★
Great-great-grandson
Capt. John Henry Hurst
Co. L, McCain's Alabama
Guard

For reasons unknown, John Henry Hurst hanged himself in 1867. He left a wife and four children. He lies buried in the Old Concord Cemetery in Clay County, Alabama.

Black Beans Cuban Style (Frijoles Negros)

Easy to make in the crock pot

1 pound black beans
2 tablespoons olive oil
1 whole ripe tomato
1 whole onion
1 whole green pepper
1 garlic clove, unpeeled and crushed
1 bay leaf
½ cup plus 2 tablespoons olive oil

1 garlic clove, minced
1 medium onion, chopped
½ green pepper, chopped
1 teaspoon oregano, crushed
¼ teaspoon cumin
2 tablespoons wine vinegar (or red wine, if you prefer)
1 teaspoon salt
½ teaspoon hot pepper sauce

Wash beans and discard imperfect ones. Place in a deep bowl and cover with water 2 inches above beans. Soak overnight. The next day, pour beans and water they soaked in into a crock pot (a 3-4 quart kettle can be substituted). If necessary, add more water so beans will be covered by 1 inch of water. Add 2 tablespoons of olive oil, whole tomato, whole onion, whole green pepper, crushed garlic clove, and bay leaf. In a crock pot, cook for about 2 hours on high, then about 6 more hours on low until done.

In a skillet, heat ½ cup olive oil and sauté the chopped onion and green pepper until onion is transparent. Add the minced garlic, crushed oregano, cumin, wine or wine vinegar, and salt. Use wooden spoon to stir well and cook 2 minutes longer. Add to beans. Stir in hot pepper sauce and correct seasoning to taste, if necessary. Before serving,

continued on next page

★
Scott L. Peeler, Jr.
John T. Lesley Camp #1282
Tampa, Florida
★
Great-great-grandson
Pvt. John Moore
Capt. Andrew J. Williams' Co.
(Ogeechee Rifles), Georgia
Troops

John Moore enlisted in Savannah, Georgia, and spent part of his service in the shipyard as a carpenter working on a floating battery. He died in Screven County, Georgia, on June 12, 1888.

remove bay leaf and what is left of the whole tomato, onion, pepper, and garlic. Serve hot over cooked long grain white rice with raw chopped onions on top. Put a mixture of olive oil and vinegar on top also.

Many Cubans, Spaniards, and Sicilians emigrated to Tampa, Florida, to work in the cigar industry. With them came the delicious foods that are extremely popular among the residents of this area today. This dish is traditionally served with roast pork, yucca, plantains, and a tossed salad.

Squash Casserole
Just a good old Southern thing!

1 pan crumbled Mexican corn bread (prepare according to package directions)
1 cup onions, chopped
½ cup bell pepper, chopped

2 cups boiled squash
2 eggs
1 stick of butter or margarine
Salt and pepper to taste

Combine all ingredients and bake in a buttered casserole at 350 degrees for 40-45 minutes.

★
Roger White
Brig. Gen. Thomas M. Scott
Camp #1604
Minden, Louisiana
★
Descendant of
Pvt. Edward Eugene Pratt
Co. G, 8th Louisiana Infantry

Southern-Style Corn Casserole

Has a pudding-like texture

1 can whole kernel corn,
   drained
1 can cream-style corn
2 eggs, slightly beaten
³/₄ teaspoon salt
¹/₈ teaspoon pepper

³/₄ tablespoon sugar
1¹/₂ tablespoons butter or margarine, melted
³/₄ cup scalded milk
1 tablespoon flour

*M*ix ingredients and pour into a buttered baking dish. Bake at 335 degrees until firm (about 50 minutes).

★
**Scott L. Peeler, Jr.
John T. Lesley Camp #1282
Tampa, Florida**
★
**Descendant of
Pvt. Leander J. Garren
Co. G, 59th Tennessee
Mounted Infantry (Cooke's
Regiment)**

Leander Garren was born in Monroe County, Tennessee, on May 8, 1818, the son of Adam Garren (a veteran of the War of 1812) and his first wife, a Cherokee Indian whose name is unknown. Leander was shot and killed on the Old Federal Road in Monroe County on January 17, 1865, at the age of 46. He is buried at Notchey Creek Baptist Church Cemetery, southeast of Madisonville, Tennessee.

Confederate Collard Greens

So good they'll make you sit up and whistle Dixie!

1 large bunch of collard greens (exposed to frost best) or 3-4 pounds fresh mixed greens (turnip and mustard)

1 meaty ham hock
1-2 cups water
2 tablespoons Br'er Rabbit molasses

★
Miles Jackson
Confederate Memorial
Camp #1432
Stone Mountain, Georgia
★
Great-grandson
Allen Stephens Alford
Co. B, Blount's Battalion,
Georgia Militia

*P*ut ham hock in large pot with water and bring to boil while preparing greens. Wash and pick over greens, removing large stems. If cooking collards, cut large leaves across leaf with kitchen shears to about 1-inch in width. Add greens to pot as they are washed, cover with tight-fitting lid, and allow to steam down to make room for more greens. Continue until all greens have been added to pot. Reduce heat and simmer for about 45 minutes to 1 hour or until greens are tender. Watch water so that pot does not dry and greens stick.

When greens are nearly done, add molasses for a wonderful flavor. Lift greens onto a shallow serving dish, draining as much liquid as possible (collards should be cooked until most liquid is gone). Cut greens in crisscross pattern so that no large leaves are intact. Remove skin and bone from ham hock, and lay lean ham on side of bowl to serve. Serve 6-8.

Tastes great with a bottle of hot pepper sauce and a big plate of corn bread!

Main Course Macaroni and Cheese

Makes a great main course—just add Caesar salad

1 (7-ounce) package or 2 cups
  uncooked elbow macaroni
2 cups mild cheddar cheese,
  shredded and divided

1¾ cups whole milk
3 large eggs
½ teaspoon salt
½ stick butter or margarine

★

Tad D. Shelfer
John B. Hood Camp #50
Houston, Texas

★

3rd great-grandson
Pvt. Levi Shelfer
Co. G, 2nd Florida Cavalry

Preheat oven to 350 degrees. Cook macaroni as package directs just until tender. Drain water from pot. Add remaining ingredients to cooked macaroni except for ½ cup cheese. Mix well. Cook and stir over medium heat until the cheese melts (about 5 minutes). Turn into a greased 1½-quart baking dish. Top with remaining cheese. Bake 25-30 minutes or until bubbly. Serves 8 as a side dish.

Sweet Potato Crunch

A holiday favorite that really puts the pounds on!

3 cups sweet potatoes, mashed
1 cup sugar
1 teaspoon vanilla
¼ stick butter, melted

¼ teaspoon cinnamon
⅓ cup milk
½ teaspoon salt
2 eggs, beaten

*M*ix ingredients and pour in baking dish.

Topping
1 cup brown sugar
1 cup pecans, chopped

⅓ stick butter, melted
⅓ cup plain flour

*M*ix topping ingredients and place on top of sweet potato mixture. Bake at 350 degrees for 30-35 minutes. Serves 6-8.

★

**Jerry P. Adams
Gen. States Rights Gist
Camp #1451
Bogansville, South Carolina**

★

**Great-grandson
Pvt. Jasper Newton Adams
Co. C, 2nd South Carolina
Rifles**

Jasper Adams was born in 1831 in the Pickens District of South Carolina. He served the Confederacy from 1862 to 1865, and was wounded at the Battle of Chickahominy River. Jasper returned home to farm and rear a family of ten children. He died in 1908 and is buried in the Adams Family Cemetery in Westminster, South Carolina.

Easy Squash Casserole
Great cheesy flavor

6-8 squash, sliced
2 onions, chopped
1 teaspoon salt
½ teaspoon lemon pepper
½ stick margarine
½ cup cheddar cheese,
  grated and divided

½ cup Ritz crackers, crushed
  and divided
1 egg, beaten
½ cup milk
Salt and pepper to taste

---

*B*oil squash and onions until tender. Drain. Add 1 teaspoon salt, lemon pepper, margarine, ¼ cup of the cheddar cheese, ¼ cup of the crushed crackers, and more salt and pepper to taste. Mix the egg with the milk and add to the squash mixture. Mix and pour into a casserole dish and top with the remainder of the cheese and crushed crackers (don't use too many crackers). Bake at 350 degrees for about 30 minutes. Serves 8.

★
**William B. Bennett
A. P. Hill Camp #167
Chester, Virginia**
★
**Great-grandson
Pvt. John Albert Bennett
Co. C, 9th Virginia Infantry**

Pvt. Bennett was wounded at the Battle of Chester Station. He was later captured at Five Forks, Virginia, and sent to Point Lookout, Maryland, as a prisoner of war. He died in 1918 at the age of 77.

THE CONFEDERATE COOKBOOK

Independence Day Baked Beans

When plain canned just won't do

1 large can baked beans (Van Camp's is best)
1 teaspoon hearty brown mustard
4 tablespoons honey
⅓ cup onion, finely chopped

1 tablespoon dried bell pepper flakes
1 tablespoon ketchup
1 tablespoon bacon grease or margarine
Bacon bits to taste

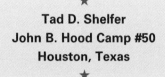

★
Tad D. Shelfer
John B. Hood Camp #50
Houston, Texas
★
3rd great-grandson
Pvt. Levi Shelfer
Co. G, 2nd Florida Cavalry

*P*reheat oven to 350 degrees. Combine all ingredients (reserve bacon bits) in a 1½-quart casserole dish. Bake uncovered for 1 hour. Sprinkle bacon bits on top for the last 10 minutes. Serves 6.

I first ate these beans several years ago at my in-laws' house on the Fourth of July. It was served along with pork barbecued sandwiches, coleslaw, potato salad, Golden Flake potato chips, dill pickles, and watermelon. What a Southern feast! Even now our Independence Day celebration is not complete without this dish.

Barton Family Tomato Dressing

Passed down in the Barton family for over 100 years

Make one large pone of black-skillet corn bread first.

Corn bread Recipe

1½ cups stone-ground corn meal

1 cup all-purpose flour

1½ teaspoons baking powder

¼ teaspoon baking soda

½ teaspoon salt

1 cup buttermilk

1 egg

¼ cup vegetable oil

---

*P*reheat oven to 400 degrees. Grease skillet well. Mix liquid ingredients separately from dry ingredients. Then mix them together and pour in skillet. Bake at 375-400 degrees until lightly browned on top.

Dressing

1 pone corn bread (see above)

1 can cream of celery soup

1 can tomatoes, diced with the juice

½ onion, chopped

6 green onions (use all)

½ bell pepper, chopped

⅓ can chicken broth

1-2 slices white bread, broken into pieces

4 pieces raw bacon

---

*C*rumble corn bread into a bowl. Add all other ingredients except bacon. Mix well with potato masher and pour into a slightly greased baking pan. Salt and pepper to taste. Place strips of bacon on top. Bake at 350-375 degrees, stirring slightly every 5-7 minutes so that bacon drippings are well mixed into the dressing for seasoning. When bacon is brown (after 25-30 minutes), the dressing is done.

★

Aubrey Hayden
Lt. Col. William Walker
Camp #1738
Winnfield, Louisiana

★

Great-great-grandson
Sgt. James Madison Rogers
Co. H, 15th Mississippi
Infantry

Sgt. James Madison Rogers was present at Appomattox Courthouse when Gen. Robert E. Lee surrendered his army to Grant. He put a piece of the apple tree under which Lee first met with Grant into his pocket and walked home to Mississippi. When he arrived home, he packed up the few belongings he had left and moved with his wife to Winn Parish, Louisiana, where he scratched out a living at farming until his early death in 1885. His wife kept the piece of the apple tree, showing it to children, grandchildren, and great-grandchildren until it literally turned to dust.

Rebel Rice

So yummy you'll get Rebel yells from your guests

1 cup white rice
1 stick real butter
1 whole onion, chopped
1 cup fresh mushrooms,
   chopped

1 can Campbell's Beef
   Consommé
1 cup tap water

Brown ½ stick butter and 1 cup rice in skillet on top of stove (not more than 5 minutes over medium heat). Pour into a bowl; set aside. Take other ½ stick of butter in same skillet and sauté onion (same cooking time). Add browned rice and all remaining ingredients to sautéed onions. Place uncovered skillet immediately into a preheated oven (350 degrees) for 45 minutes. Remove from oven and fluff with fork. Serves 8.

★

Ken and Vic Stanton
Admiral Semmes Camp #11
Mobile, Alabama

★

Grandnephews
1st Lt. Benjamin Charles
Foster, Jr.
Co. E, 11th Alabama Infantry
(Grove Hill Guard)

Benjamin Foster came from a military family. His father was a colonel in the War of 1812. Benjamin was reported killed in action. He disappeared from the muster rolls after Shiloh, and it is believed that it was there that he met his death.

Confederate Cranberry Delight

Wonderful with turkey dinner

1 large package of cherry
   Jell-O
1 cup walnuts, finely diced

1 cup celery, finely cut
1 can of whole or jelly cranberry sauce

---

*F*ollow directions on Jell-O, reducing hot water to 1½ cups and cold water to 2 cups. Dissolve Jell-O in hot water, cool, and refrigerate when Jell-O starts to set (shakes like jelly). Add all above ingredients and put in large Jell-O mold. Put in refrigerator and let set. Serves 15.

This recipe has been in our family for many years, has a wonderful flavor, and has always been a hit at holiday time.

★
**Jeff Wolverton
Roswell Mills Camp #1547
Roswell, Georgia**
★
**Great-grandnephew
Pvt. John Powell
Co. D, 8th (Smith's)
Tennessee Cavalry**

John Powell was from Woodbury, Tennessee. Little is known of his service record, but apparently he was left behind at some point by retreating troops, as he was "sick and unable to be removed." He survived the war.

Hoppin' John

A simple side dish that goes with anything

½ pound bacon or salt pork
1 cup black-eyed peas (if using
   dried peas, soak overnight)
1 quart water

Hot peppers (if desired)
Salt to taste
1 cup uncooked rice

★
Boris Bulatkin
Gen. Albert Pike
Camp #1439
Wichita, Kansas
★
Descendant of
James Grandville Morrow
Co. E, 4th Missouri Infantry

Put everything but the rice in a covered pot. Bring to a boil and then simmer until peas are tender—about 1½ hours. Add salt, but check broth first—bacon or salt pork can be mighty salty by itself. Add the rice and simmer until it's tender, about another ½ hour. You might have to add more water as it simmers, especially if you haven't covered the pot. Serves 6.

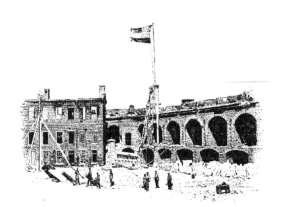

Fried Green Tomatoes

Delicious with fried chicken, sausage, or what have you

Several large, green (throughout), firm tomatoes
Salt and pepper to taste

Sugar to taste
Corn meal
Bacon grease

*S*lice tomatoes ¼-inch thick. Discard end and stem slices. Sprinkle with salt, pepper, and sugar. Dip in corn meal and fry in enough bacon grease to cover. Have the fat hot when tomatoes are added, then reduce flame and brown on one side. Turn and brown other side.

★
Paul L. Harrison
Colonels Lewis & Harrison
Camp #1854
Lawrence, Kansas
★
Descendant of
Galliten Mosby
Civilian prisoner

Corn Pudding

Kids really like this one

3 eggs
2 cups milk
½ cup evaporated milk
1 tablespoon sugar
1 teaspoon salt

2 cups fresh corn, cut from
cob
½ cup bread crumbs
2 tablespoons butter, melted

*G*rease a 1½-quart casserole dish. Beat eggs until light and fluffy. Add milk, evaporated milk, sugar, and salt, mixing well. Stir in corn, crumbs, and butter. Pour into dish and place in a pan of boiling water. Put all in oven and bake at 350 degrees for 50-60 minutes or until custard is set.

★
Larry E. Beeson
Stokes County Troops
Camp #1540
King, North Carolina
★
Great-great-grandson
Cpl. John Frazier
Co. D, 57th Regiment, North
Carolina Troops

254

So Easy Squash Casserole

Rich and delicious

1 quart of squash, cut up	1¼ cups cheddar cheese, grated
1 can cream of mushroom soup, undiluted	¾ cup buttered bread crumbs

*C*ook squash until tender in a small amount of salted water; drain thoroughly. Fold in soup and 1 cup of cheese and mix lightly. Place in buttered casserole dish. Top with buttered bread crumbs and remaining cheese. Bake at 350 degrees for 30 minutes.

★

**Eric E. Martin
J. M. ("Matt") Barton
Camp #441
Sulphur Springs, Texas**

★

**3rd great-grandson
Pvt. Charles H. Martin
Co. C, 4th Mississippi Cavalry**

The 4th Mississippi Cavalry fought in many skirmishes and campaigns under the command of Gen. Nathan Bedford Forrest. Charles Martin survived the war and was discharged near Grenada, Mississippi, after the surrender.

Sweet Potato Surprise

The coconut is the secret!

2 cups sweet potatoes, mashed
1 cup sugar
¼ cup milk
1 cup coconut

2 eggs
1 teaspoon vanilla
¼ stick margarine

Melt margarine and mix all ingredients together. Place in glass baking dish.

Topping
1 cup pecans
1 stick melted margarine

½ cup flour
1 cup brown sugar

Mix together and spread over first mixture. Bake at 350 degrees for 20 minutes.

★
Larry Smith
M. M. Parson's Camp #718
Eugene, Missouri
★
3rd great-grandson
Pvt. Silas Stewart
54th Virginia Infantry
(Marshall's Brigade)

Margie's Ultra-Super Veg-All Casserole

Simple to make, store, and reheat

1 (15-ounce) can Veg-All
   Mixed Vegetables, drained
1 (15-ounce) can whole kernel
   corn, drained
1 (8-ounce) carton sour cream
½ cup premium mayonnaise

½ onion, chopped
8 ounces mild cheddar cheese,
   grated
2 tubes Ritz crackers, crushed
1 stick soft or melted butter

*M*ix all ingredients together and put in 9-inch by 13-inch casserole dish. Mix together Ritz crackers and butter and spread over mixture. Cook at 350 degrees for about 25 minutes.

My wife makes this casserole whenever we go to a covered dish supper. Every time she makes it she is asked for the recipe.

★

Clyde D. Wright
James P. Douglas Camp #124
Tyler, Texas

★

Great-grandnephew
Pvt. George S. Alder
1st Regiment,
Arkansas Infantry

On May 20, 1862, George Alder enlisted in the Confederate army in Sulphur Springs, Arkansas, at the age of 19. Not long after his enlistment, he was seriously wounded, and died in Little Rock at St. John's Hospital in July 1862.

Squash Puppies

A good alternative to hush puppies

1 cup cooked squash, drained
    and mashed fine
½ cup corn meal
½ cup self-rising flour

½ teaspoon salt
1 medium onion
1 egg

---

*C*ombine all ingredients. Add water (drained from squash, if needed) for consistency. Drop with a tablespoon in deep fat to form balls about the size of hush puppies. Makes about 12-14 puppies.

★

**Charles Stoudemire, Jr.
15th Regiment South Carolina
Volunteers Camp #51
Lexington County, South
Carolina**

★

**Great-great-grandson
Pvt. Elias Stoudemire
6th South Carolina State
Troops**

Elias Stoudemire was a farmer who served in the South Carolina Home Guard because of his age when the fighting broke out. He was captured by Sherman's troops as they burnt their way through South Carolina and spent the remainder of the war in Point Lookout Prison. He was 54 years of age. His stepson also served the Confederacy and was killed at Gettysburg.

Scalloped Corn

Hearty and delicious

1 tube of Ritz crackers,
   crumbled
2 eggs
³/₄ cup milk (skim or whole)

2 cans cream-style corn
4 pats of butter or margarine
Dash of pepper

★

Shannon R. Walgamotte
Beauregard Camp #130
New Orleans, Louisiana

★

4th great-grandson
Pvt. Thomas L. Walgamotte
Co. C, 5th Louisiana Infantry
(Bienville Guards)

*M*ix crumbled crackers, eggs, and milk. Mixture should have a thick, creamy consistency. Add cream-style corn, butter, and a dash of pepper. Bake at 375 degrees for about 45 minutes or until firm and brown on top. Serves 8.

This recipe came from my friend Marilyn Clark Gilhuly at the Georgia Civil War Commission. It was passed down from her great-grandmother, who was married to a surgeon assigned to the Army of Tennessee.

Thomas Walgamotte was a New Orleans policeman who volunteered to serve the Confederate cause in 1861. He was detailed for a time at Chimborazo Hospital but joined the march to Gettysburg, where he was captured on July 3, 1863, and sent to Fort Delaware as a prisoner of war. In 1865, he made his way back to New Orleans and rejoined the police force. He was on duty when the Mechanic's Institute Riot of 1866 broke out.

It was a fight that signaled the beginning of harsh Reconstruction rule in New Orleans. Ironically, Thomas survived four years of deprivation, war, and prison only to become the one policeman in the riot to die in the line of duty. It was a scorching July day, and in the midst of the fray he dropped dead of exhaustion and sunstroke—a victim of his depleted physical condition and his hot wool uniform. He was 40 years old and left a widow and three small sons.

Celery Casserole

A family favorite at Christmas for many years

4 cups celery, chopped into 1-
    inch pieces
Water
1 (10¾-ounce) can cream of
    chicken soup

¼ cup pimientos, diced
    (optional)
½ cup fresh bread crumbs
¼ cup almonds, slivered
2 tablespoons butter, melted

---

*B*oil celery in water about 8 minutes; drain. Add soup and pimientos. Pour mixture into a greased 1-quart casserole dish. Top with bread crumbs and almonds. Pour melted butter on top of casserole. Bake in a 350-degree oven for 35 minutes. Serves 4-6.

Note: Do not double recipe. Make 2 separate casseroles.

★
**Patrick J. Hardy, M.D.
Sterling Price Camp #145
Chesterfield, Missouri**
★
**Great-grandson
Capt. John McKim Hardy
Co. A, Col. Kenton Harper's
Regiment, Virginia**

Capt. John Hardy was born in 1831 in Winchester, Virginia. As a young man, he moved to Staunton, where he established J.M. Hardy and Sons Wagon Works, a major wagon factory doing business in all 33 states. During the war, the Federals attempted to burn the brick factory on several occasions. Capt. Hardy participated in many battles throughout Virginia with his unit while keeping the factory busy producing wagons for the Confederate army. After the war, he rebuilt his factory without ever signing the Oath.

Soufflé of Spinach

Will change any youthful protest about spinach into cries of "More!"

2 eggs, separated
1 teaspoon salt
20 ounces frozen chopped
    spinach, cooked, drained,
    and cooled

3 tablespoons Parmesan
    cheese, grated
1 cup heavy cream

★

Ralph Green
Gen. W. L. Cabell Camp #1313
Dallas, Texas

*P*reheat oven to 325 degrees. Butter 7-inch soufflé dish. In small mixing bowl, beat egg whites until soft peaks form. Set aside. In blender, puree spinach, egg yolks, cheese, and salt. Slowly add cream until blended. Pour into medium bowl and fold in egg whites. Place mixture in prepared dish. Bake 40 minutes or until knife inserted into center comes out clean. Serve immediately. Serves 6.

Carrots Maretto

Has a great almond flavor

1 pound carrots, sliced ⅛ inch
    thick
2 ounces butter (¼ stick)

2 ounces almonds, sliced
¼ cup Amaretto liqueur
Salt and pepper to taste

★

Patrick J. Hardy, M.D.
Sterling Price Camp #145
Chesterfield, Missouri
★

Great-grandson
Capt. John McKim Hardy
Co. A, Col. Kenton Harper's
Regiment, Virginia

*S*auté carrots in butter in a large skillet until lightly cooked. Add almonds. When carrots are *al dente*, add Amaretto and heat through. Salt and pepper to taste. Serves 6-8.

Libby's Spicy Fried Squash

An interesting substitute for fried okra

1 egg
3 medium-sized yellow squash
1½ cups flour
Salt to taste
1 teaspoon black pepper

Red pepper to taste
Canola oil (may use peanut oil)
Texas Pete to taste (may substitute Tabasco)

*B*eat egg in bowl and set aside. Wash and then cut squash lengthwise in thin strips about 2 inches long. Mix flour, salt, and pepper. Dip squash strips in egg, then coat with flour. Fry in frying pan over medium heat in enough canola or peanut oil to cover until squash is brown on both sides. Remove from frying pan and sprinkle lightly with Texas Pete. Serves 3-4.

★
Timothy T. Casstevens
Yadkin Gray Eagles
Camp #1765
Yadkinville, North Carolina
★
Great-grandnephew
Sgt. Samuel Speer Harding
Co. I, 28th North Carolina
Regiment

Sgt. Harding was killed at Reams Station, Virginia, on August 25, 1864.

Hot and Spicy Tofu Stir Fry

Healthful and delicious

4 (2-inch) cubes of tofu
6 ounces ground meat (pork, beef, or turkey)
3 tablespoons cooking oil
1 teaspoon chopped garlic
1 tablespoon hot red chili paste

2 tablespoons soy sauce
1 teaspoon salt
1 tablespoon green onion, chopped
2 tablespoons cornstarch
1 tablespoon black pepper

Drain tofu and cut into ½-inch cubes. Stir fry ground meat in oil. Add garlic, hot chili paste, soy sauce, and salt, stirring constantly. Add chopped tofu, then stir and cook for 3-4 minutes. Add green onion, then thicken with cornstarch and remove to platter. Sprinkle black pepper over tofu and serve hot. Serves 4.

★
Peter Griffin
Col. William Norris
Camp #1398
Gaithersburg, Maryland
★
Great-great-grandson
Pvt. James Andrew
Jackson Coker
Co. H, 39th Georgia Infantry

On April 16, 1863, Pvt. Coker was wounded and taken prisoner at the Battle of Baker's Creek, Mississippi. After he was paroled, he was captured a second time at Lookout Mountain, Georgia, and sent to Camp Morton, Indiana. After the war, he returned to life as a farmer. He died in 1874.

Green Bean Casserole

No holiday is complete without this

2 (10-ounce) packages of
   frozen, french-style green
   beans
2 tablespoons flour
2 tablespoons butter, melted
2 teaspoons sugar
1 teaspoon salt

3-4 teaspoons onion, finely
   grated
1 pint sour cream
1 (8-ounce) package Swiss
   cheese, shredded
Crushed corn flakes

---

*C*ook beans according to package directions, drain, and reserve. Make a paste of flour and butter. When smooth, add sugar, salt, and onion. Beat in sour cream and Swiss cheese. Gently fold in beans. Sprinkle with crushed flakes to cover. Bake in a preheated 350-degree oven until hot throughout (about 25 minutes). Serves 8.

**Conwill Randolph Casey
Old Free State Camp #1746
Victoria, Virginia**

**Great-grandson
Pvt. Barzilla Harris Mixson
Co. H, 53rd Alabama Mounted
Infantry**

Barzilla Mixson fought with Forrest's troopers in the Tennessee Valley and in the Atlanta Campaign. He followed Sherman to the sea and fought at Camden. He died in January 1914 near Elba, Alabama.

Wreck on the Mountain

We're not sure how it got its name, but it sure is good!

2 tablespoons of cooking oil or
   lard
½ head of red cabbage
4 medium to large potatoes,
   peeled

1 large onion
Salt and pepper to taste

Put oil or lard in a large skillet. Finely chop up all the ingredients. Fry until done (make sure potatoes are done). Serve with any meat or by itself, with ketchup, or pinto beans, and corn bread. Salt and pepper to taste. Serves 4-6.

★

Tim Casstevens
Yadkin Gray Eagles
Camp #1765
Yadkinville, North Carolina

★

Great-grandnephew
Sgt. Samuel Speer Harding
Co. I, 28th North Carolina
Infantry

Corn Pudding

Easy to prepare in the microwave

1 can cream-style corn
2 tablespoons sugar
2 tablespoons butter, melted
1 small can pimientos

2 tablespoons flour
1 teaspoon salt
2 eggs
½ pound cheese, grated

Mix all ingredients (except cheese) together. Put half the mixture in a baking dish. Then sprinkle cheese over the mixture, add the remaining mixture, and top with cheese. Bake at 350 degrees for 1 hour or bake in a microwave for 12-14 minutes.

★

Richard D. Lockhart
Flat Top Copperheads
Camp #1694
Princeton, West Virginia

★

Descendant of
Pvt. Benjamin H. Lockhart
16th Regiment,
Virginia Cavalry

All Day Beans

Don't let the long cooking time deter you—this dish is well worth the effort!

72 ounces pork and beans
6 slices bacon, chopped
1½ large green peppers, chopped
2 large onions, chopped
4 cloves garlic, minced
3 tablespoons brown sugar, packed

1 tablespoon New Mexico ground chilies (not chili powder)
1½ cups catsup
1½ cups water
1 tablespoon Dijon mustard
2 cans green chilies, chopped

★
**William Nelms
Hood's Texas Brigade
Camp #153
San Antonio, Texas**
★
**Descendant of
Pvt. Martin Ransom Gwyn
Co. D, 16th Tennessee Infantry**

*M*ix all ingredients well in large pan, well-greased. My wife uses her old enameled turkey roaster. Bake, covered, at 325 degrees for 3 hours, stirring from time to time. Lower heat to 225 degrees. Uncover and bake an additional 2 hours until very thick, stirring more frequently to keep from burning. The long, slow process allows the ingredients to caramelize somewhat, giving an extra flavor boost. Serves 14 easily.

Eggplant Creole
Eggplant prepared Louisiana style

3 strips bacon
1 cup onion, diced
1 cup green pepper,
   diced
1 (15-ounce) can tomatoes,
   diced

1 medium eggplant, peeled
   and diced into 1/4-inch
   cubes
1 tablespoon brown sugar
1 cup water
Salt and pepper to taste

★
F. Lawrence McFall, Jr.
Cabell-Graves Camp #1402
Danville, Virginia
★
Great-great-grandson
Pvt. Lewis Nostrandt
Co. H, 14th Louisiana Infantry

Cook bacon in a 10-inch skillet until crisp. Remove from pan and set aside on a paper towel to drain. Do not drain skillet. Sauté onion and peppers in the same skillet until translucent. Add diced tomatoes, water, eggplant, and brown sugar. Cover and simmer on low heat until eggplant turns dark in color (about 20 minutes). Salt and pepper to taste. Before serving, garnish with the 3 strips of crushed bacon. Serves 4.

Lewis Nostrandt was born in Schoharie County, New York. He moved to New Orleans prior to 1860. He volunteered to serve the Confederate cause in 1861 and suffered a severe stomach wound at the Battle of Gaines Mill. While he recuperated in the CSA General Hospital in Danville, Virginia, he was cared for by a nurse, Martha Mann Royster, whose husband was also in the Confederate army. Lewis returned to his regiment in 1863. He had to have his left hand amputated because of a gunshot wound in the wrist during the Battle of Cedar Creek. He received a certificate of disability and returned to Danville, where he found his former nurse a widow after her husband's death at the Battle of Bristoe Station. They were married seven days later. Many of their descendants still live in Danville, Virginia. Lewis had two brothers who remained in New York and joined the Union army. One of them died in Andersonville Prison.

Three-Layer Cabbage Casserole

Cheap, filling comfort food

Cooked cabbage, seasoned to taste

Bread crumbs (best if from leftover biscuits)

Pork gravy

---

*I*n the bottom of a deep casserole dish, put a layer of cooked cabbage. The second layer should be bread crumbs. Pour the prepared gravy on top. Top with more bread crumbs and brown in a hot oven.

Gravy Recipe
Pork drippings

Flour
Milk

---

*S*tir pork dripping and flour together over a low flame until it makes a paste, then add milk to correct consistency and stir.

In the early 1920s, my grandmother made this dish for my mother and her siblings after many a hard day's work in the fields.

★

**Elijah S. Coleman
Chattahoochee Guards
Camp #1639
Mableton, Georgia**

★

**Great-great-grandson
Pvt. Merick Coleman
Co. D, 36th Georgia Infantry**

Rhonda's Favorite Rebel Eye Gravy

A mouth-watering gravy with a tomato base

1 pound/roll hot sausage
  (Tennessee Pride preferred)
3 tablespoons flour
1 (6-ounce) can Pet
  Evaporated Milk
2-4 ounces water

3 medium vine-ripe tomatoes,
  peeled and pureed
Pinch of sugar (to reduce
  acidity of tomatoes)
Salt, black pepper, and
  cayenne to taste

*B*rown and crumble sausage in large cast-iron skillet over medium heat; drain on paper towels. Leave 3 tablespoons of drippings in skillet. Add flour, stirring constantly to make a medium roux. Turn heat to medium low; add water, evaporated milk, and tomatoes, stirring until desired consistency. Add sausage and season to taste with sugar, salt, and pepper. Cook on low heat for 2-3 minutes, adding more water if mixture thickens too quickly. Ladle over your favorite biscuits or grits. Serves 8-10.

My wife has served this gravy over her homemade biscuits and grits for years. We had requested sausage gravy for breakfast one morning when she discovered she was out of milk. She saw three vine-ripe tomatoes on the kitchen counter and the rest is history. The gravy was such a hit that she modified the next batch and added a little evaporated milk to make it creamier. In order to differentiate between which sausage gravy we wanted, she suggested that we call it "Rebel Eye Gravy." It has become my daughter Rhonda's favorite. Thank God for Southern mothers!

★

Ronald H. Miller
John B. Gordon Camp #46
Atlanta, Georgia

★

Great-grandnephew
Pvt. John W. Rudolph
Co. B, 3rd Kentucky Mounted
Infantry (Forest Cavalry
Troops)

John Rudolph, aged 21, enlisted on April 4, 1864, in Ballard County, Kentucky, and met history and General Forrest the next day in Tennessee. Rudolph fought in every major battle remaining for Forrest, including Forrest's stunning victory at Brice's Cross Roads. Rudolph was paroled in May 1865 at Columbus, Mississippi. In our family history book, he mentions only the Confederate victories he participated in, and none of the defeats.

Copper Carrot Pennies

A tangy, tasteful Southern dish

2 pounds carrots
1 green pepper,
    sliced in rings

1 Vidalia onion,
    sliced in rings

Scrape, slice, and boil carrots in salt water until tender (about 10 minutes). Drain and cool. In bowl, alternate layers of carrots, green pepper, and onion rings. Combine marinade ingredients and pour over vegetables. Cover and refrigerate. Serve cold. Flavor is even better if made a day or so ahead. Serves 10-12.

Marinade
1 can tomato soup
½ cup salad oil
¾ cup vinegar
1 cup sugar

1 teaspoon regular mustard
1 teaspoon Worcestershire
    sauce
Salt and pepper to taste

★
Robert L. Seay
Fincastle Rifles Camp #1326
Roanoke, Virginia
★
Great-great-grandson
Pvt. James Lewis Seay
Co. D, 13th Virginia Infantry

James Seay was wounded in August 1862 at Cedar Mountain, but recovered to rejoin his regiment after Gettysburg. In 1912, he was living in the Old Soldier's Home in Richmond, Virginia. His grave site is currently unknown.

Stuffed Yellow Squash

Even folks who don't like squash will like this!

6 yellow squash
6 slices of bacon, crisply
  cooked
½ cup green onions

1 cup cheese, shredded
Salt, pepper, and butter to
  taste

Cook squash whole in boiling water until pierceable with a fork (not mushy). Cut off stems and chop them into cubes. Slice remaining squash sections lengthwise. Gently scoop out insides, leaving little boats intact. Combine chopped stems and scooped out insides with bacon, green onions, cheese, butter, salt, and pepper. Place in boats. Bake until bubbly, approximately 10-15 minutes at 350 degrees.

★
The Reverend M. Don Majors
James P. Douglas Camp #124
Tyler, Texas
★
Great-great-grandson
Pvt. Ephraim Majors
Co. B, 19th Texas Cavalry

Ephraim Majors was one of five brothers who fought for the Confederacy. He died at Mount Vernon, Texas, in 1908.

Cheese Grits Casserole

The secret is in the garlic

1 cup grits
1 teaspoon salt
4 cups water
½ cup margarine
1 (6-ounce) roll garlic cheese

2 eggs
Milk
1 cup cheddar cheese, grated
Cornflake crumbs

Cook grits and salt in water. Melt margarine and garlic cheese and add to grits. Beat eggs, put in a 1-cup measuring cup, and fill to top with milk. Add to grits and pour into greased 2-quart casserole. Top with cheddar cheese and cover with enough cornflake crumbs to make a good topping. Bake at 350 degrees for approximately 25 minutes.

★

David R. Hereford
Col. Andrew Jackson May
Camp #1897
Prestonsburg, Kentucky

★

Great-great-grandnephew
Col. Andrew Jackson May
10th Kentucky Infantry

Andrew Jackson May was the leading Confederate in Big Sandy Valley. He set up a recruiting station and campground at his childhood home, which was the first brick house in Prestonsburg, Kentucky. After the war, he married and settled in Tazewell, Virginia, where he became a prominent attorney. He died in 1901. Col. May's home in Prestonsburg is now a museum and is open to the public.

Charleston Red Rice

A Low Country specialty

6 strips cooked bacon, crumbled
1 onion, minced
1 tablespoon salt
2 teaspoons sugar
1 teaspoon pepper

1 (6-ounce) can tomato paste
1/2 teaspoon Texas Pete Hot Sauce
1 1/2 cups water
2 cups raw rice

*C*ook bacon and remove from pan. Pour out 1/3 of grease. Cook onion in grease until clear. Add salt, sugar, pepper, tomato paste, hot sauce, and water. Cook for 15 minutes on medium heat. Put mixture in top of rice steamer with 2 cups of rice. Cook for 45 minutes on medium-high heat. Add bacon the last 5 minutes of cooking. Stir with a fork before serving. Don't let water boil out of the bottom of rice steamer.

★

**Lex Crawford
Secession Camp #4
Charleston, South Carolina**

★

**Great-grandson
Sgt. Maj. John Marcus
Smither
5th Texas Infantry**

John enlisted at age 17 in Huntsville, Texas. He was promoted to sergeant after the Battle of Sharpsburg and fought until the surrender. After the war, he became a judge in Huntsville and lived a long and successful life.

Eggplant Casserole

An easy way to prepare eggplant

1 eggplant, peeled, cubed, cooked, and drained

1 cup milk

2 eggs, beaten

1 cup sharp cheddar cheese, grated

1 cup bread crumbs (crouton sized)

1 tablespoon margarine or butter

½ teaspoon salt

Pepper to taste

Combine all ingredients well, pour into a greased casserole, and bake 40 minutes at 350 degrees. Serves 4.

★
Will Mason
Gen. Richard Taylor
Camp #1308
Shreveport, Louisiana
★
Grandson
Pvt. Andrew Dorrie Mason
Co. D, 19th Louisiana Infantry

Andrew Mason had to have a letter of permission from his mother when he enlisted at the age of 17. His brother was killed at Fredericksburg. After he was paroled at Meridian, Mississippi, he had to walk down the Natchez Trace to Natchez to ford the Mississippi, and then continue on north to his home in Minden, Louisiana. He died in 1928.

Robert E. Lee Natural Bridge Sweet Tater Pone

The name is a mystery, but it sure is tasty!

3 cups raw sweet potatoes,
   grated
1 teaspoon nutmeg
1 cup sugar

³⁄₄ cup pecans
1 cup milk
1 egg, beaten
3 tablespoons butter

Grease a 1¹⁄₂-quart baking dish. In a mixing bowl, combine the sweet potatoes, nutmeg, sugar, and ¹⁄₂ cup pecans. Add the milk and egg. Pour into the prepared baking dish and sprinkle with remaining pecans. Dot with butter. Bake in a 350-degree oven for 45-60 minutes. Serves 4-6.

★
Mark Craig
Fincastle Rifles Camp #1326
Roanoke, Virginia
★
Great-grandson
Pvt. William Giles Mitchell
Co. D, 28th Virginia Infantry

Pvt. Mitchell was taken prisoner at Newport News, Virginia, and released in June 1865. He is buried in Bedford County, Virginia.

Calcasieu Tigers Eggplant Parmesan

Take this to your next potluck supper

1 eggplant
2 eggs
½ cup milk
2 cups bread crumbs

1 (32-ounce) jar pasta sauce
1 large package mozzarella
    cheese

---

*P*eel and slice the eggplant into thin slices. Mix eggs and milk. Dip slices into egg mixture, then cover with bread crumbs. Fry until browned. Get a medium-size casserole dish and place alternating layers of pasta sauce, eggplant, and mozzarella. Bake at 350 degrees for 15 minutes.

★

**Michael Jones
Capt. James W. Bryan
Camp #1390
Iowa, Louisiana**

★

**Great-grandson
Pvt. William C. Annis
Co. B, 9th Battalion,
Louisiana Infantry**

William Annis was born in Bayou Sara, Louisiana, in 1840. He fought in the Battle of Baton Rouge, at Port Hudson, and in a number of small skirmishes late in the war. He was the publisher of the *Baton Rouge Advocate* from 1872 to 1881 and was city editor at the time of his death in 1903. He was elected to the Baton Rouge city council and the Democratic central committee. He was a member of the United Confederate Veterans, a volunteer firefighter, and a Mason.

Cheese Onion Pie

Similar to quiche, but not as heavy

1 stick butter
1¼ cups cracker crumbs, crushed
2½ cups onions, thinly sliced
3 eggs, beaten

2 cups sharp cheddar cheese, grated
1¼ cups milk
1 teaspoon salt
¼ teaspoon pepper

*M*elt butter in skillet and pour all but about 2 tablespoons into a bowl with cracker crumbs. Mix well and pat into a large-sized pie pan, covering the bottom and sides of the pan. Slice the onions thinly into a skillet with the rest of the butter. Cook gently until transparent. Place onions evenly in pie plate atop the cracker crumbs. Preheat oven to 350 degrees. Combine eggs, cheese, milk, salt, and pepper in a bowl and pour the mixture over the onions and crumbs in plate. Bake for about 45 minutes or until knife in center comes out clean. Serves 6.

My wife serves this dish every Christmas Eve. It is a great substitute for potatoes and is delicious served with roast beef or steak.

★

Donald Beck
Col. William Norris
Camp #1398
Gaithersburg, Maryland

★

Great-grandson
Pvt. Thomas David Beck
Co. B, Cobb's Legion, Georgia Troops

Mr. Beck was the last surviving Confederate soldier from Carroll County, Georgia. He suffered a leg wound at Chancellorsville, and had the end of his chin shot off at the Battle of South Mountain in Maryland (he later covered this with a beard). On his pension application, he stressed that he had never been captured. He died in 1941.

Confederate Squash

Causes a delightful, ecstatic secretion of the salivary glands

5 medium white onions
  (Vidalia preferred)
½ stick butter
4 tablespoons extra virgin
  olive oil
1 large green pepper, diced

1 large red pepper, diced
1 hot red, green, or jalapeño
  pepper (optional)
Whole pepper corns, ground
12 summer baby squash (no
  longer than 6 inches)

Slice onions ¼-inch thick and then cut in quarters. Place in frying pan with ¼ stick of butter and enough olive oil to coat the bottom of the pan. Heat on low, stirring often. Dice peppers and place in pan. Grind pepper corns to cover the ingredients. Cover and cook on medium heat until heated through, then reduce heat to simmer. While simmering, slice squash ¼-inch thick. Place in pan with remaining 1/4-inch stick of butter and grind more pepper to cover ingredients. While stirring frequently, continue to heat on low until heated through (approximately 45 minutes). Serves 4-6.

★
David A. Denisch
Gen. Isaac Ridgeway Trimble
Camp #1836
Ellicott City, Maryland
★
Great-grandnephew
Pvt. James Luther Castle
Co. C, 2nd Maryland Infantry

A native of Frederick, Maryland, Luther was 19 years old when he slipped through the Federal lines to enlist in the Confederate forces after the Battle of Sharpsburg. He was wounded and captured at Gettysburg. After his parole from prison, he reenlisted and was wounded again at Petersburg. When the war was over, Luther had served time in a total of five different Federal prisons. He died in 1907 in the Old Soldier's Home in Baltimore, Maryland.

Mama's Sweet Potato Soufflé

Unusual corn flake topping

2 cups mashed sweet potatoes
  (can substitute pumpkin)
1¼ cups sugar
¼ stick butter

½ teaspoon nutmeg
2 eggs
1 cup canned milk
½ teaspoon cinnamon

*M*ix all ingredients and pour into a buttered baking dish. Bake at 400 degrees for about 20 minutes or until firm on top. Remove from oven.

Topping
⅔ cup pecans
¼ cup butter, softened
½ cup brown sugar

¾ cup corn flakes (Frosted Flakes for a sweeter topping), crumbled

*M*ix all topping ingredients and pour on top of baked soufflé. Do not mix baked soufflé and topping together. Return to the oven and bake until topping is brown. Serves 4-6.

★

**Chris S. Knapp
Albert Sidney Johnston
Camp #67
Houston, Texas**

★

**Great-great-grandson
Pvt. William Mosby Eastland
Co. B, 17th Texas Infantry
(Allen's Regiment)**

William Eastland was born in the Republic of Texas in 1843. He was in a group of Texans on their way to Vicksburg when it surrendered. He became ill and was furloughed to go home and recover. When he got home (he had walked all the way), his own father didn't recognize him. When he returned to the army, he was transferred to the cavalry. Mr. Eastland died in 1933 at the age of 90 and is buried in the family cemetery in Bastrop.

Marinated Carrots

Easy to fix the day before

2 bunches of carrots, cut in ½-inch slices
1 bell pepper, chopped
1 onion, chopped
1 can tomato soup
¾ cup sugar
½ cup Wesson Oil
2 teaspoons Worcestershire sauce
½ cup vinegar
1 teaspoon salt

---

*C*ook carrots in salted water until tender. Drain and place in dish or jar. Add peppers and onions on top, but do not stir. Heat soup, sugar, oil, Worcestershire sauce, vinegar, and salt. Pour this mixture over carrots, peppers, and onions. Refrigerate overnight. Serve cold.

Note: Leftover juice makes a good salad dressing after carrots have been served.

★
**Jeffrey K. Wright
Camp McDonald #1552
Kennesaw, Georgia**
★

**3rd great-grandson
2nd Lt. William Stafford
Co. E, 65th Georgia Infantry**

William Stafford was from Fannin County, Georgia. Due to chronic health problems, he was eventually forced to resign his commission. He was a blacksmith by trade.

Stuffed Pumpkin

A great Native American recipe

4-5 pound sugar pumpkin
2 teaspoons salt
$\frac{1}{2}$ teaspoon dry mustard
1-2 tablespoons vegetable oil
    or rendered fat
1 pound ground venison
1 pound ground pork sausage

1 medium onion, chopped
2 bunches green onions,
    chopped
1 cup wild rice, cooked
3 eggs, beaten
1 teaspoon crushed dried sage
$\frac{1}{4}$ teaspoon pepper

Preheat oven to 350 degrees. Cut the top from the pumpkin and remove seeds and strings. Prick cavity with a fork and rub with 1 teaspoon of salt and the mustard. Heat oil in a large skillet. Add meat and onions and sauté over medium-high heat until browned. Remove from heat, stir in wild rice, eggs, remaining salt, sage, and pepper. Stuff pumpkin with this mixture. Place $\frac{1}{2}$-inch water in the bottom of a shallow baking pan. Put pumpkin in the pan and bake for $1\frac{1}{2}$ hours or until tender. Add more water to the pan as necessary to avoid sticking. Cut pumpkin into wedges, including both pumpkin and stuffing in each. Serves 6-8.

★

G. Scott Thorn
Capt. J.W. Bryan Camp #1390
Lake Charles, Louisiana

★

Great-great-grandson
Pvt. Edmund William Hodges
Webb's Company, Louisiana
Cavalry

Edmund Hodges, the son of a cotton planter, enlisted in 1863 at the age of 18. He served under Nathan Bedford Forrest and was present at the battle of Brice's Cross Roads. After the war, he took over the operation of the family plantation and also entered the mercantile business. He reared a family of eight children, and died in 1920.

Sweets

Pinckney Welsh Pie
Edna's Almond Pound Cake
General de Polignac's Gingersnap Pudding
Best Apple Sauce Cake
The Ultimate Chocolate Chip Cookies
Blue Ribbon Cheesecake
Mississippi Mud
Aunt Dorothy's Coconut Custard Pie
Mamie's Orange Cookies
Never Fail Chocolate Pie
Monster Cookies
Bread Pudding with Lemon Sauce
Blockade Runner's Pie
Date Nut Candy
Lila's Simple Fruit Cake
Carrot Cake
Polly's Old-Fashioned Pound Cake
Grandma's Fruit Cocktail Cake
Opal Varner's Peanut Butter Cookies
Mama Hewitt's Chocolate Cake
Grandma Curcio's King-Size Applesauce
    Cake
Charlotte Russe
Ann's Famous Carrot Cake
Molasses Stack Cake
Virginia Applesauce Cake
Ann's Fresh Pumpkin Pie
Poor Man's Cake
Date Pecan Pie
Chocolate Chess Pie
Orange Date Cake
Vanilla Fudge Squares
Mama Ruth's Blackberry Jam Cake
Buttermilk Chocolate Cake
Cream Cheese Cookie Delights
Chocolate Cake Pudding
Old Fashioned Dark Chocolate Cake
One Step Pound Cake
General Washington's Virginia Cherry Pie
Honey Mammy's Jerusalem Cookies
Original Banana Cookie Pudding
Ice Box Cookies
General Lee's Eggnog

Miss Nancy's Famous Coconut Cake
Easy Lemon Pie
Raw Apple Cake
Persimmon Pudding
Old-Fashioned Peppermint Ice Cream
Peach Fried Pies
Cold Oven Pound Cake
Southern Power Cookies
Tipsy Custard
Mama's Old-Fashioned Tea Cakes
Bonton's Bread Pudding
Gingerbread Boys
Matt's Easy SCV Dessert
Chocolate Gravy
Beverly's Strawberry Jell-O Pie
Yankee Cannon Balls
So Good Peach Cobbler
Chocolate Oatmeal Cookies
Apple-Lokshen Kugel
Butter Roll Pie
Tomato Soup Cake
The Easiest Cheesecake
Lynda's Cookie Puddin'
Sister's Scrumptious Southern
    Pecan Pie
Fried Apple Pies
Lemonade Pie
Gingersnaps
Fruit Cocktail Cake
Aunt Faye's Chocolate Pie
Microwave Pralines
Old-Fashioned Coconut Cake
Zucchini Pineapple Cake
Blueberry Cream Pie
Seven-Up Pound Cake
Crème Brulee
Missouri Confederate Cake
Sweet Potato Loaf Cake
Persimmon Cookies
No Bake Peanut Butter Pie
Tea Cakes
No Crust Coconut Pie

Pinckney Welch Pie

A tasty pie full of fall flavor

½ cup butter
2 cups light brown sugar
4 egg yolks
2 tablespoons flour
1 teaspoon cinnamon
½ teaspoon allspice
1 teaspoon nutmeg, freshly
   grated

1 cup heavy cream
½ cup dates, chopped
½ cup raisins
½ cup pecans, broken
1 baked pie shell (store bought
   or homemade)
Meringue or whipped cream
   for topping

Preheat oven to 325 degrees. Mix butter and brown sugar. Beat in egg yolks and mix well. Add flour, cinnamon, allspice, and nutmeg. Stir in cream, dates, raisins, and pecans. Fill the shell with the mixture and bake until set (about 30 minutes). When cool, top with either meringue or fresh whipped cream. Makes one 9-inch pie.

**Hon. Richard B. Abell
Robert E. Lee Camp #726
Alexandria, Virginia**

**Great-great-grandson
Pvt. Richard Pinckney Welch
Co. E, 31st Alabama Volunteer
Infantry**

Pinckney Welch enlisted in 1862 and served until the end of the war. He was one of only 15 men (out of 1100) remaining in his regiment at the surrender. He returned to farming in Clay County, Alabama, and had a family of nine children. He died in 1914.

Edna's Almond Pound Cake

This pound cake has a wonderful almond flavor

1 cup butter
½ cup butter-flavored Crisco
    stick
3 cups sugar
5 eggs
½ teaspoon baking powder

3 cups sifted all-purpose flour
1 cup milk
1 teaspoon vanilla extract
1 teaspoon lemon extract
1 teaspoon almond flavoring

Lewis Cowder Lawrence
Robert E. Lee Camp #803
Sanford, North Carolina

Great-grandson
Robert Boyd Thornton
68th North Carolina Troops

---

*C*ream together butter and Crisco. Gradually add sugar; beat until light and fluffy. Add eggs, one at a time, beating well. Stir in the dry ingredients, milk, and flavorings, ⅓ at a time. Beat one minute only—do not over-beat. Pour into a greased, non-stick tube pan. Start in cold oven. Bake at 325 degrees for 1 hour and 20-30 minutes or until cake tester comes out clean. Wait about 30 minutes or until only warm before turning out on rack to cool.

THE CONFEDERATE COOKBOOK

General de Polignac's Gingersnap Pudding

A mouth-watering treat from the dining room of the Federal Reserve Bank in Dallas, Texas

½ pound gingersnaps, crushed into crumbs
2½ cups powdered sugar
1 stick softened butter
3 fresh eggs
3 or 4 small bananas

1 (20-ounce) can crushed pineapple, well-drained
1 cup chopped pecans
1 cup whipped cream (or whipped topping)

Roll gingersnaps into crumbs. Place in heavily buttered, 10-inch by 13-inch Pyrex dish. Chill. Cream powdered sugar and butter. Add whole eggs 1 at a time, creaming after each. Continue beating until fluffy. Spread over chilled crumbs and replace in refrigerator. Dice bananas; mix with pineapple and pecans. Fold mixture into whipped cream. Spread over other layers and sprinkle with a few gingersnap crumbs. Chill at least 2 hours before serving.

It is our family's tradition that anyone honored with a birthday, anniversary, or other special occasion may select the meal and dessert to be served. This is one of the most requested desserts, year after year!

★

**Phil E. Johnson
General de Polignac
Camp #1648
Arlington, Texas**

★

**Great-great-grandson
Pvt. William Thomas Dunn
Co. B, 19th Texas Cavalry**

Pvt. Dunn survived the war and died in February 1908.

287

Best Applesauce Cake

A holiday favorite

4 eggs
2 cups applesauce
2 cups sugar
2 sticks margarine (melted)
4 cups flour
2 teaspoons cinnamon
$\frac{1}{2}$ teaspoon nutmeg

$\frac{1}{4}$ teaspoon salt
1 pound shelled walnuts
1 (16-ounce) box raisins
   (lightly floured so they will
   not clump)
2 teaspoons baking soda

★
Robert C. Nail
Turner Ashby Camp #1567
Winchester, Virginia
★
Great-great-grandson
Pvt. Branson McInturff
Co. D, 18th Virginia Cavalry

*B*eat eggs in a large mixing bowl. Add applesauce, sugar, and margarine. Stir. Add all remaining ingredients except the baking soda. Dissolve baking soda in $\frac{1}{4}$ cup hot water. Pour into mixture and mix well. Bake in a well-greased and floured mold for $1\frac{1}{2}$ hours at 350 degrees. Serves 12-15.

This recipe was my mother's favorite at Christmas time.
After baking the cake, she would wrap it in a tea towel
that had been dipped in wine and store it in a
tin container. Delicious!

The Ultimate Chocolate Chip Cookies

Combine with a glass of cold milk for the perfect midnight snack

¾ cup Butter Flavor Crisco or
    regular Crisco
1¼ cups firmly packed light
    brown sugar
2 tablespoons milk
1 tablespoon vanilla

1 egg
1¾ cups all-purpose flour
1 teaspoon salt
¾ teaspoon baking soda
1 bag chocolate chips
1 cup pecans, chopped

★
Sidney J. Hullum
Johnson-Sayers-Nettles
Camp #1012
Teague, Texas
★
Descendant of
Pvt. Benjamin M. Hullum
Co. L, 13th Tennessee Infantry

*C*ombine Crisco, brown sugar, milk, and vanilla. Add egg and cream well. Add flour, salt, and baking soda. Mix into creamed mixture. Stir in chocolate chips and pecans. Drop by tablespoon onto greased cookie sheet or ungreased Teflon pan. Mash flat with a floured glass. Bake at 375 degrees for 10-13 minutes. Makes about 3 dozen cookies.

Blue Ribbon Cheesecake

This tasty cheesecake won a blue ribbon at the North Carolina State Fair

½ of 13½-ounce package
   graham cracker crumbs
4 (8-ounce) packages cream
   cheese (2 Philadelphia
   brand and 2 store brand)

2 cups sugar
8 eggs
1 (16-ounce) carton sour
   cream
2 teaspoons vanilla

*U*se a very well-greased angel food cake (tube) pan. Pour graham cracker crumbs in bottom of the pan to about ¼-inch deep. Set aside a few pinches to sprinkle on top of cake later. In a very large bowl, cream softened cream cheese and sugar together with an electric mixer. Add eggs 1 at a time, beating for 1 minute after each. Add sour cream gradually, but mix thoroughly. Add vanilla and mix well. Gently pour cream cheese mixture into tube pan on top of cracker crumbs. Sprinkle the crumbs set aside earlier on top of the mixture before putting in the oven. Bake at 350 degrees for 40 minutes, then turn oven off but do not open the door. Cake should stay in hot oven for another 1½ hours. Open the door and leave cake 30 more minutes before removing. Chill at least overnight before serving. Makes 16 servings.

★

**Steven Mills
Franklin Rifles Camp #310
Louisburg, North Carolina**

★

**3rd great-grandson
Pvt. Charles Benton Dudley
Co. E, 14th North Carolina
Infantry**

Charles Dudley survived the war, lived to be 101 years of age, and attributed his long life to drinking a quart of buttermilk every day.

Mississippi Mud

A delightful treat at holiday time

2 cups sugar	1½ cups nuts
3 tablespoons cocoa	1½ cups flour
2 sticks margarine	1 teaspoon baking powder
4 eggs	1 teaspoon vanilla
1½ cups coconut	1 pint marshmallow cream

Cream sugar, cocoa, and margarine. Add eggs, coconut, and nuts. Add flour, baking powder, and vanilla. Beat 1-2 minutes. Bake in 9-inch by 13-inch pan at 350 degrees for 30-45 minutes. While still hot, spread the marshmallow cream over the top and allow it to cool.

Frosting

1 stick margarine	½ cup Pet milk
1 box powdered sugar	1/4-½ cup cocoa (or to taste)
	1 teaspoon vanilla

Combine all ingredients, mix well, and spread.

★

R. W. P. Patterson
Gen. J. H. McBride Camp #632
Springfield, Missouri

★

Great-grandnephew
Sgt. W. W. Cupit
Co. E, 7th Mississippi Infantry

Sgt. Cupit gave his life for the Confederate cause at the Battle of Murfreesboro, Tennessee.

Aunt Dorothy's Coconut Custard Pie

An all-time favorite

1½ cups shredded, sweetened coconut, packed tight into measure
1 cup evaporated milk
2 eggs, beaten

1½ cups sugar
1 teaspoon vanilla
4 tablespoons butter, melted
1 unbaked pie shell

★
John W. Adams
CSS *Florida* Camp #102
Orlando, Florida
★
Great-great-grandson
2nd Lt. Sylvester G. Martin
Co. K, 19th Virginia Infantry

*P*reheat oven to 350 degrees. Put coconut into a bowl and pour evaporated milk over it. In another bowl, beat eggs, and add sugar, vanilla, and melted butter. Add to coconut-milk mixture and mix thoroughly. Pour into the pie shell. Bake for 30-40 minutes or until top is golden brown and filling is almost completely set. Pie will set further when cooled in a refrigerator. Best served cold. Makes one 9-inch pie.

Mamie's Orange Cookies

A must on your cookie list

½ **cup cream shortening**	¼ **teaspoon salt**
¾ **cup sugar**	½ **teaspoon baking powder**
1 **egg**	½ **teaspoon orange juice**
1¼ **cups flour**	1½ **teaspoons orange rind**

*M*ix all ingredients in a large bowl. Roll out dough and cut into cookie shapes. Bake at 350 degrees on a greased and floured cookie sheet for 8-10 minutes. Cool before icing.

Cookie Topping   **2 teaspoons orange juice**
¼ **cup sugar**

*A*dd orange juice slowly to sugar and mix well until smooth. Thinly ice cooled cookies.

Mama, Mamie Stubbs, made these cookies for the family as long as I can remember. I never figured out how all the neighborhood kids showed up just as the pans were being taken out of the oven. Mama knew what to expect, so she always made enough for all to have some.

★
Norman Stubbs
Captain J. L. Halbert
Camp #359
Corsicana, Texas
★
Descendant of
Pvt. Samuel Elkins Hand
Co. C, Texas Militia

Never Fail Chocolate Pie

The perfect addition to any special occasion

1½ cups sugar
2 tablespoons cocoa
3 tablespoons flour
Dash of salt

3 egg yolks
1½ cups milk
½ stick butter or margarine

---

*M*ix all ingredients well and cook over slow burner, stirring constantly until thick.

Topping
3 egg whites
½ teaspoon vanilla

3 teaspoons water
Chopped pecans
3 tablespoons sugar

---

*B*eat egg whites, vanilla, and water until peaks form. Gradually add 3 tablespoons of sugar. Beat until stiff. Top with chopped pecans. Bake until brown.

Monster Cookies

Makes a great Halloween treat

1 pound butter
2 pounds brown sugar
2 cups white sugar
12 eggs
1 tablespoon vanilla
6 teaspoons baking soda
3 pounds peanut butter
18 cups oats (quick-cooking
   oatmeal best)

2 large packages chocolate
   chips
1 large package M&M's (plain
   work best, but peanut okay)
1 cup of your favorite nuts
   (optional)
1 cup raisins or dates
   (optional)

★
John Griffin
J. K. McNeill Camp #674
Moultrie, Georgia
★
Descendant of
Pvt. John Jackson Griffin
Co. I, 50th Georgia Infantry

Preheat oven to 375 degrees. Mix butter, sugars, eggs, vanilla, and baking soda. Then add peanut butter. Mix well into a batter. Add the oats, then add the chocolate chips and M&M's. If you use the optional ingredients, add them now and mix well. Scoop out the dough with an ice cream scoop and place on a non-stick cookie sheet. Flatten down the balls of dough. Bake for about 12 minutes until light brown. Remove from oven and allow to cool. Makes about 3 dozen cookies.

Try 2 cookies with a slab of vanilla ice cream in between.
Delicious!

Bread Pudding with Lemon Sauce

Delicious bread pudding with an unusual twist!

Bread Pudding

4 slices bread, slightly toasted
½ cup raisins
1 cup Pet Evaporated Milk
1 cup boiling water
½ cup sugar
¼ teaspoon salt
2 eggs slightly beaten
1 teaspoon vanilla
1 teaspoon cinnamon

Cube bread and place in a 2-quart greased casserole dish. Sprinkle raisins on top. Mix together sugar, milk, salt, and water and pour over bread. Let stand for 10 minutes. In a smaller bowl, mix eggs, vanilla, and cinnamon. After the bread mixture has set for 10 minutes, add the egg mixture to it. Mix well by hand. Bake at 350 degrees for 25 or 30 minutes or until knife inserted in center comes out clean. Allow to cool approximately 30 minutes before serving, but not any longer. Serve warm. Makes about 4 servings.

Lemon Sauce

½ cup sugar
1½ tablespoons cornstarch
1 cup hot tap water
2 tablespoons butter
1 tablespoon lemon juice (real lemon juice only)
1-2 teaspoons grated lemon rind
1-2 drops yellow food coloring, if desired

In small pot stir together sugar, cornstarch, and water until smooth. Cook over medium-high heat until mixture comes to a boil and is thickened. Remove from heat. Stir in butter, lemon juice, and rind until well blended. Add

continued on next page

★

Phillip B. Isaacs
Col. Samuel H. Wolkup
Camp #1375
Monroe, North Carolina

★

Great-great-grandson
Pvt. James Snow
Co. I, 18th North Carolina
Regiment (Branch's Brigade)

Pvt. Snow participated in battles at Harper's Ferry and Sharpsburg. He died of typhoid fever at the age of 24 while serving in the Confederate army. He left behind a wife and two small children. His young widow never remarried. One of James' sons, Byrd Winfield Snow, had 26 children, so James has many descendants.

THE CONFEDERATE COOKBOOK

yellow food coloring if desired. In a small bowl put a couple of scoops of warm bread pudding and top with a spoonful or two of lemon sauce and enjoy!

This recipe was given to me by my mother-in-law, Tommie Wilmoth. While scanning an antique cookbook, she discovered the lemon sauce recipe and got the idea to combine it with her wonderful bread pudding. Delicious!

Blockade Runner's Pie

After a successful run through the Yankee blockade, you will enjoy this!

1 can sweetened condensed
   milk
$^1/_3$ cup fresh lemon juice
$^1/_3$ cup maraschino cherries
$^1/_3$ cup pecans, chopped

$^1/_3$ cup pineapple, crushed
1 prepared pie shell (graham
   cracker is good)
1 container whipped cream or
   Cool Whip

*B*lend condensed milk and lemon juice. Stir in cherries, pecans, and pineapple. Mix well and spoon into pie shell. Chill for 2 hours and spread on whipped cream or Cool Whip.

★
R. W. P. Patterson
Gen. J. H. McBride Camp #632
Springfield, Missouri
★
Great-grandnephew
Sgt. W. W. Cupit
Co. E, 7th Mississippi Infantry

Date Nut Candy

This is heavenly candy!

2 cups pecans, chopped
1 (8-ounce) package dates,
    chopped
⅓ stick butter

3 cups sugar
1 cup sweet milk
1 teaspoon vanilla

Chop pecans and put in a little bowl (you must be prepared to move quickly after mixture cooks). Empty package of dates in another bowl. Get vanilla out and ready with a mixing spoon. Get linen or terrycloth tea towel and soak with cold water, then wring out and put in refrigerator for rolling the candy in later. Butter sides of a large saucepan so sugar crystals won't stick. Put sugar, butter, and milk in saucepan and cook on high until mixture forms a soft ball (almost hard ball) when dropped in a cup of cool water. This takes about 30 minutes of cooking and stirring occasionally with a wooden spoon.

Remove from heat and add dates. Beat with spoon until dates are melted well into sugar. Add vanilla and nuts and stir well. Boil until sides of pan are lukewarm to touch (about 30 minutes), but don't let candy harden at all. Pour out in a long strip on the cold, wet cloth and gradually fold cloth over and over, shaping roll with your hands until candy is in a long loaf form. Let chill an hour until thick enough to cut into slices.

★
Peter Orlebeke
Gaston-Gregg Camp #1384
Dallas, Texas
★
Great-grandson
5th Sgt. Wilborn Curry
Co. A, 37th Arkansas Infantry

Lila's Simple Fruit Cake

A delicious fruit cake recipe that is also quite simple

2½ cups sifted self-rising
  flour
1 can Eagle Brand milk
1 (28-ounce) jar of mincemeat

Chopped candied fruit (large
  package)
2 eggs, well beaten
1 cup pecans

Combine all dry ingredients. Fold all liquid ingredients into the dry ones. Bake at 300 degrees. Cook less than 2 hours or until done.

★
Bob G. Davis
Col. George R. Reeves
Camp #349
Sherman, Texas
★
Descendant of
Pvt. Robert R. Bogle
Co. F, 7th Tennessee Infantry

Carrot Cake

A classic

Cake

1⅓ cups Wesson oil
4 eggs
3 cups raw carrots, grated
2 cups flour
2 cups sugar
1½ teaspoons baking soda
2 teaspoons cinnamon
½ teaspoon nutmeg

Sift dry ingredients. Add oil and eggs one at a time. Blend well. Add carrots and mix well. Bake at 350 degrees in two- or three-layer pans, greased and floured, until layers test done. Ice with frosting below. Serves 12.

Frosting

1 (8-ounce) package cream cheese, softened
½ cup oleo, softened
1 (16-ounce) box powdered sugar, sifted
1 cup chopped nuts
1 teaspoon vanilla

Combine all ingredients and beat until smooth. Frost cake.

★
**John Mauk Hilliard
Gen. A. Gracie Camp #985
New York, New York**
★
**3rd great-grandson
Cpl. James Lemon Miller
Co. B, 19th Texas Cavalry**

Cpl. James Miller saw heavy fighting with his regiment in Arkansas and northern Louisiana along the White and Cache Rivers. He returned to his family and resumed farming in Dallas County, Texas, after the war. He died in July 1881.

Polly's Old-Fashioned Pound Cake

A favorite in the Chastain family for over 100 years

2 cups butter, softened
2 cups sugar

10 eggs, separated
4 cups all-purpose flour

Cream butter in a large mixing bowl. Gradually add sugar, beating until light and fluffy and sugar is dissolved. Add egg yolks, 1 at a time, beating well after each addition. Add flour, beating only until blended. Beat egg whites (at room temperature) until soft peaks form and fold into batter. Spoon batter into a greased and floured 10-inch tube pan. Place in a cold oven and bake at 350 degrees for 1 hour and 15 minutes or until cake tests done. Cool 10 minutes and remove from pan. Combine all glaze ingredients and mix well. Spoon glaze over cake.

Glaze
1½ cups powdered sugar

2 tablespoons water
½ teaspoon vanilla extract

★

**David Chastain
McDonald Camp #1552
Kennesaw, Georgia**

★

**Great-great-grandson
1st Lt. Jason Coward
25th Georgia Infantry**

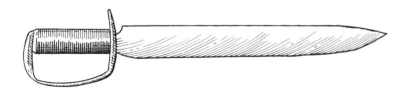

Grandma's Fruit Cocktail Cake

A recipe that is truly a family heirloom

2 eggs
1 (15-ounce) can fruit cocktail
1 teaspoon vanilla
1½ cups sugar
2 cups flour

½ teaspoon salt
2 teaspoons baking soda
½ cup brown sugar
½ cup coconut

★
Ben Head
Lt. Gen. Richard Taylor
Camp #1308
Shreveport, Louisiana

*B*eat the eggs first until thick and lemon colored, then add fruit cocktail and vanilla. Gradually add sifted together dry ingredients and mix thoroughly. Pour into 13-inch by 9-inch greased and floured pan. Sprinkle the top with brown sugar and coconut. Bake at 350 degrees for 30 minutes or until firm. Serves about 10.

*This recipe was passed down from my wife's
great-grandmother Mamie Howard Young. Her
grandmother Elsie Young Wright made this for every
family reunion I can remember attending!
It has long been a Young family favorite.*

THE CONFEDERATE COOKBOOK

Opal Varner's Peanut Butter Cookies

You won't be able to keep them out of the cookie jar!

½ cup oil
½ cup peanut butter
½ cup sugar
½ cup brown sugar

1 egg
1 teaspoon vanilla
1¼ cups self-rising flour

*M*ix oil, peanut butter, and both sugars. Add egg and vanilla. Beat well. Blend in sifted flour. Mix well. Chill dough. When ready to bake, form small balls and place on lightly greased pan. Flatten with fork dipped in flour, making crisscrossed pattern. Bake at 375 degrees for 10-12 minutes. Makes 4 dozen cookies.

★
Leonard Q. Varner
Lt. T. D. Falls Camp #1768
Fallston, North Carolina
★
3rd great-grandson
Pvt. Thomas Lovelace
Co. D, 55th North Carolina
Infantry

My wife's ancestor, Pvt. George H. Wright, 12th Regiment, North Carolina Infantry, enlisted in the Cleveland Guards on April 22, 1861. He was wounded in the right leg at Chancellorsville, and later wounded again at Spotslyvania Court House and left to die. He gave his pocketwatch to someone to take back to his family, but he later reached home before the watch did!

Mama Hewitt's Chocolate Cake

Southern comfort food at its finest!

Cake
1 (16-ounce) can Hershey's
   Chocolate Syrup
1 cup all-purpose flour
1 cup sugar
1 teaspoon baking powder
4 eggs
1 stick butter, melted

Mix all ingredients together and pour into a 9-inch by 13-inch greased and floured pan. Bake at 350 degrees for 35 minutes. Serves 12.

Frosting
½ stick butter, melted
½ box powdered sugar
3 tablespoons milk
1 teaspoon vanilla

Mix ingredients together until smooth and pour over warm cake.

★
R. Scott Prochaska
Gen. Jo Shelby Camp #1414
Harrison, Arkansas
★
3rd great-grandson
Pvt. Robert Israel Mathews
Co. D, 48th Virginia Infantry
(Extra Billy Smith's Boys)

Pvt. Mathews was wounded at Fredericksburg, Virginia, in 1862, and again (this time severely) in The Wilderness Campaign. He became a prisoner of war and was paroled in 1865. He died in 1888 in Warren County, Virginia.

This recipe comes from my grandmother, known as Mama Hewitt. My brother and I spent almost every summer at her place in the small town of Newton-Conover, North Carolina. She has since passed on, but this cake rekindles fond memories of her and the wonderful times we spent together. Have big piece of this incredible chocolate cake with a cold glass of milk, and you'll start whistling "Dixie."

Grandma Curcio's King-Size Applesauce Cake

Flavor improves with age

1 cup shortening
2 cups sugar
2 teaspoons baking soda
1 teaspoon cinnamon
1 teaspoon allspice
1 teaspoon salt
1 tablespoon ground
  chocolate
1/3 cup brandy

2 cups unsweetened apple-
  sauce
1 cup raisins (can use 2/3 cup
  currents if preferred)
2½ cups flour
1 cup walnuts, chopped
Apple juice
1 cup candied fruit mix
  (optional)

★
John Griffin
J. K. McNeill Camp #674
Moultrie, Georgia
★
Descendant of
Pvt. John Jackson Griffin
Co. I, 50th Georgia Infantry

*M*ix shortening, sugar, soda, spices, brandy, and warm apple sauce, then add raisins and walnuts. Finally, add flour to make a good batter. You may put in a little apple juice if the mix is dry. Batter should be thick but well mixed. This is the time to put in the candied fruit, if you decide to use it.

Bake in greased pan at 350-375 degrees for 1 hour. Cake may be served plain or with a frosting, or you can dust with powdered sugar. Store in a tight container in a cool, dry place.

Charlotte Russe

An Old South dessert you'll be proud to serve

1 pint whipping cream	¼ cup cold milk
½ cup sugar	¼ cup warm milk
1 teaspoon vanilla	5 egg whites
Sherry	Lady Fingers, split
½ tablespoon gelatin	

Whip the cream until stiff, then add sugar and vanilla. Add sherry to personal taste. Soften gelatin in cold milk and then dissolve in warm milk. When cool, add to the above mixture, beating the cream all the while. Add beaten egg whites and pour entire contents into bowl or dessert glasses lined with Lady Fingers. Serves 6-8.

★
Mark Choate
Sam Davis Camp #1293
Dickson, Tennessee
★
Great-grandson
Pvt. James Marion Choate
Co. A, L. S. Ross'
Calvary Brigade

After the war, James Choate returned to farming in Charlotte, Tennessee. He reared a family of nine children and died in 1910 at the age of 68.

Opposite—James Marion Choate
Private, Co. A, L. S. Ross' Cavalry Brigade

Ann's Famous Carrot Cake

Ann says this cake is still going "hot" after three generations

2 cups all-purpose flour, sifted
2 teaspoons baking soda
$\frac{1}{2}$ teaspoon salt
2 cups sugar

1 teaspoon ground cinnamon
$1\frac{1}{2}$ cups vegetable oil
4 eggs, well beaten
3 cups carrots, grated

---

*S*tir together flour, soda, salt, sugar, and cinnamon. Add oil, eggs, and carrots. Beat well. Pour batter into 3 greased and floured 8-inch pans. Bake at 350 degrees for 30 minutes or until a wooden pick inserted in center comes out clean. Cool on cake racks until completely cool.

Cream Cheese Icing

1 (8-ounce) package cream
  cheese
$\frac{1}{2}$ cup butter

2 teaspoons vanilla
$3\frac{1}{2}$ cups confectioner's sugar,
  sifted

---

*S*often cheese. Blend in remaining ingredients until smooth. Spread on top of cake and between layers.

★
**Giles J. Duplechin
Beauregard Camp #130
New Orleans, Louisiana**
★
**Great-grandson
Pvt. Giles A. Glasscock
Co. G, 1st Louisiana Cavalry**

Giles Glasscock saw action at Shiloh, the Battle of Nashville, and many other places in Kentucky and Tennessee. He was captured at Irvine, Kentucky, in 1863, and spent the remainder of the war at Camp Chase prison, where he declined an offer to "galvanize" and join the Indian fighters in the West. After the war, he became a riverboat pilot. He died in 1904 and is buried in Marksville, Louisiana.

Molasses Stack Cake

An old-time Southern favorite

1 cup Crisco shortening (may use butter instead)
1 cup sugar
1 cup molasses
2 eggs
6 cups sifted all-purpose flour
1 teaspoon nutmeg

1 teaspoon baking soda
2 teaspoons baking powder
2 teaspoons ginger
2 teaspoons cloves
3 teaspoons cinnamon
1 jar apple butter (add extra spices and sugar to taste)

Cream shortening and sugar, add molasses, and beat well. Add eggs and beat. Sift all other ingredients together and add to first mixture. Chill for 1½ hours. Roll dough into thin (the thinner the better), round, cake-size "pancakes" and bake at 350 degrees on a cookie sheet (about 3 minutes each). Assemble 20 or more layers, alternating each with a thick layer of apple butter. The final layer, or "topper," should be the thickest "pancake" and should not be topped with apple butter. Age for at least a day before serving.

This recipe was handed down through our family by a Real Daughter, Nannie Belle Gothard.

★
Brett Bradshaw
Capt. John M. Kinard
Camp #35
Newberry, South Carolina
★
Great-grandson
Pvt. Augustus Henry Gothard
Co. C, 16th Tennessee
Cavalry Battalion

Henry Gothard ran away from home at age 17 to enlist in the Confederate army. After fighting in the Battle of Perryville, he was sent home for being underage. He soon joined his 55-year-old father, Larkin Gothard, in Co. C of the 16th Tennessee Cavalry Battalion. They fought from Chickamauga, Georgia, to York, Pennsylvania, with Early's Raiders. Henry was eventually severely wounded by shrapnel, and went through the rest of his life with a silver plate where he lost a piece of his skull, behind his right ear. Henry led the parade, carrying the flag at the grand opening of the Chickamauga National Battlefield Park. He lived until 1932, and was the long-time gatekeeper at Chattanooga's cemetery.

Virginia Applesauce Cake

A moist, flavorful treat—perfect for a fall Sunday dinner

5 cups flour
3 tablespoons cocoa
4 teaspoons baking soda
½ teaspoon salt
2 teaspoons ground cloves
2 teaspoons cinnamon
1 teaspoon nutmeg

1 cup butter
2 cups sugar
3 cups Virginia applesauce
2 tablespoons distilled white
  vinegar
2 cups raisins
2 cups chopped walnuts

★

Joseph R. Ferguson, Jr.
Urquhart-Gillette Camp #1471
Franklin, Virginia

★

Descendant of
John Charles Smith
Co. E, 41st Virginia Infantry

Preheat oven to 350 degrees. Mix first seven ingredients together in a medium bowl. In a large bowl, cream butter. Add sugar, applesauce, and vinegar. Mix in the dry ingredients until thoroughly moistened. Add raisins and walnuts. Pour batter into a 10-inch by 4-inch tube pan. Do not flour pan. Cover top of pan with aluminum foil and bake for 2 hours. Sprinkle cooled cake with powdered sugar if desired.

Ann's Fresh Pumpkin Pie

For those who prefer a more delicate taste

2 cups fresh sugar pumpkin
  puree (may substitute butternut squash)
2 large eggs, beaten
¾ cup coffee cream
⅓ cup dark maple syrup

¼ cup sugar
¾ teaspoon cinnamon
¼ teaspoon cloves
¼ teaspoon ginger
¼ teaspoon nutmeg
1 prepared graham pie crust

★

**Father Alister Anderson
Jefferson Davis Camp #305
Washington, D.C.**

★

**1st cousin,
three times removed
Capt. Aristides Doggett
Co. A, 3rd Florida Infantry**

Prepare the puree by roasting the pumpkin, in a glass dish, in the oven at 350 degrees. The pumpkin is done when either it collapses or a knife can be easily inserted. Remove the peel, and when cool, puree in a food processor. This can be frozen for a long time, several months if necessary. One sugar pumpkin is usually enough for one pie. Add the puree to eggs, then add other ingredients and mix well.

Prepare the pie crust by brushing it with beaten egg white and baking it in the oven at 350 degrees for 5 minutes. Pour the puree into the pie crust and cook at 375 degrees for 10 minutes. Turn the oven down to 350 degrees and cook for up to a further 45 minutes. Test by inserting a knife into the center. If it comes out clean, the pie is done. This is often the case in less than the allotted time. After cooling, garnish with whipped cream. Serves 8.

Poor Man's Cake

Simple but delicious

2 eggs
1 cup sugar
1 cup flour
1 teaspoon baking powder
½ teaspoon salt
1 teaspoon vanilla
½ cup milk

2 tablespoons butter
3 tablespoons butter, melted
2 tablespoons whipping cream
5 tablespoons light brown
   sugar
½ cup sweetened, shredded
   coconut

*P*reheat oven to 350 degrees. Beat eggs well in a large bowl. Add sugar, flour, baking powder, salt, and vanilla. Beat well until smooth. In a small pan over medium heat, simmer milk and butter until butter has melted. Do not boil. Stir hot milk mixture into egg mixture. Pour into an 8-inch square cake pan and bake for 30 minutes. Remove from oven, but leave cake in pan. While cake is still warm, mix together melted butter, cream, brown sugar, and coconut. Spread evenly over cake. Place cake under broiler just long enough for frosting to start to bubble and brown very slightly.

★
John Walker Adams
CSS *Florida* Camp #102
Orlando, Florida
★
Great-great-grandson
2nd Lt. Sylvester G. Martin
Co. K, 19th Virginia Infantry

Sylvester Martin was wounded and captured in Pickett's Charge at Gettysburg and imprisoned at Johnson's Island until the end of the war. His mess mates plotted and executed the daring "escape over the ice," an attempt to cross frozen Lake Erie into Canada. He was left behind, probably because of his leg wound. Most of the escapees were captured or killed. After the war, Martin returned to Virginia, where he earned a living as a farmer.

Date Pecan Pie

Can be prepared pie style or baked in a pan and cut into squares

3 egg whites
1 cup sugar
½ cup graham cracker crumbs
1 cup pecans, chopped

½ cup dates, chopped
1 teaspoon vanilla
Whipped cream for topping

---

*P*reheat oven to 350 degrees. Beat the egg whites until stiff, gradually sprinkling in the sugar while beating. Fold in the graham cracker crumbs, followed by pecans and dates. Stir in the vanilla. Spread the mixture evenly in a buttered Pyrex pan, round or square, and bake 30 minutes. Serve warm, topping each piece with whipped cream.

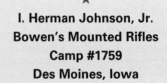

★

I. Herman Johnson, Jr.
Bowen's Mounted Rifles
Camp #1759
Des Moines, Iowa

★

Great-grandson
Pvt. Micajah Tucker
Co. A, 61st Georgia Infantry

Micajah Tucker, a planter, died in 1897 at the age of 75. He had twenty children by two wives.

Chocolate Chess Pie

Pie for chocolate lovers

1 (9-inch) pie shell, unbaked
1½ cups sugar
3 tablespoons cocoa
¼ cup margarine or butter,
  melted
2 eggs, slightly beaten

⅛ teaspoon salt
1 (5.33-ounce) can evaporated
  milk
1 teaspoon vanilla
½-¾ cup chopped pecans
  (optional)

*P*repare unbaked pie shell. Mix sugar, cocoa, and butter. Stir well. Add eggs and beat with electric mixer for 2 ½ minutes. Add salt, milk, and vanilla. Stir in pecans if desired. Pour filling into pie shell. Bake at 350 degrees for 35-45 minutes. If you underbake it slightly, it will make the pie very creamy.

★
**Steven W. McFarlane
Matthew Fontaine Maury
Camp #1722
Fredericksburg, Virginia**
★
**Great-great-grandson
Pvt. Augustus McFarlane
Co. I, 34th Battalion, Virginia
Cavalry**

Augustus McFarlane was born in 1798 and was 64 when he fought at the Battle of Gettysburg. After the war, he served as a constable and sheriff in Russell County, Virginia. He died in 1890.

Orange Date Cake

A good substitute for fruit cake

Cake
1 teaspoon baking soda
1½ cups buttermilk
1 cup shortening
2 cups sugar
4 eggs

1 package dates
1 cup pecans
2 tablespoons grated orange
   peel
4 cups flour

---

*P*reheat oven to 300 degrees. Dissolve baking soda in buttermilk. Mix well with the other ingredients and pour into a greased and floured tube pan. Bake for 1 ½ hours.

Filling
2 cups sugar
1 cup orange juice

2 heaping tablespoons grated
   orange peel

---

*M*ix ingredients. Make sure sugar is dissolved in the juice. Let stand until you remove cake from oven, then immediately punch holes in the top of the cake and pour filling over it while cake is still hot. Let cool in the pan. Cake serves 10-12.

This cake is amazing in that it transports so well. In 1954, I received this cake in Germany after it was shipped from Texas by surface means (approximately four weeks). It remained delicious and moist.

Compatriot William J. Willmann passed away on March 1, 2000.

**William J. Willmann
Major K. M. VanZandt
Camp #1351
Fort Worth, Texas**

**Descendant of
Pvt. John L. Leggett
Co. D, 8th Arkansas Infantry**

John Leggett enlisted in the Confederate forces when he was 16 years old. In 1862, he was discharged for being underage and sent home. He rejoined in 1863 and participated in the Great Missouri Raid. He also saw action at the Battle of Shiloh and the siege of Corinth, Mississippi. After the war, he became a physician and practiced in Bald Knob, Arkansas.

Vanilla Fudge Squares

Rich and creamy

2 cups sugar
1 cup evaporated milk (whole milk can be substituted)

²/₃ stick margarine or butter
2 teaspoons vanilla
1½ cups pecan halves

*A*dd sugar and milk to large cast-iron skillet. Cook over medium heat until ¼ teaspoonful of candy placed in cup of cold water will form soft ball. Remove from heat. Add butter. Place in large mixing bowl. Beat at high speed with electric mixer until candy begins to cool. Add pecans and vanilla. Grease a large platter with margarine. Pour candy onto platter. Let candy sit for several hours or overnight. Slice into squares.

This recipe came from my mother-in-law, Lois Wheeler.
She had cows on her farm, so she used whole milk
instead of evaporated milk. However,
candy is extra creamy if evaporated milk is used.

★

Keith Thomason
Chief Clinton Camp #366
Abilene, Texas

★

Great-grandson
Pvt. Jessie James Cotter
3rd Battery, Maryland Artillery

Mama Ruth's Blackberry Jam Cake

A blackberry delight

1 cup vegetable oil	1 teaspoon baking soda
1 cup buttermilk	1 teaspoon allspice
1½ cups sugar	1 teaspoon cinnamon
3 eggs	1 teaspoon nutmeg
1 teaspoon vanilla	1 cup seedless blackberry jam
2 cups flour	1 cup pecans

Cream first 5 ingredients together in a large mixing bowl. Sift next 5 ingredients together in a separate bowl. Slowly add sifted ingredients to creamed ingredients while beating. Add blackberry jam and beat together. Stir in pecans. Bake 1 hour in a greased and floured bundt pan at 350 degrees. Serves 12.

★

Raymond Driver
Col. William Norris
Camp #1398
Gaithersburg, Maryland

★

Great-grandson
Cpl. George Washington Small
Co. A, 55th Virginia Infantry

George Small enlisted in the 55th Virginia Infantry in May 1861. He was promoted to corporal after the Battle of Chancellorsville. He was taken prisoner at Cashtown, Pennsylvania (near Gettysburg). His unit was part of A.P. Hill's Third Corps, which played a big part in Pickett's Charge. After the war, George returned to Essex County, Virginia, to resume his life as a farmer. He married twice and had seven children. He died on February 22, 1925, his namesake's birthday.

Buttermilk Chocolate Cake

A chocoholic's dream

Cake
2 sticks butter
4 tablespoons cocoa
1 cup water
2 cups flour
2 cups sugar

1 teaspoon soda
$\frac{1}{2}$ teaspoon salt
$\frac{1}{2}$ cup buttermilk
1 teaspoon vanilla
2 eggs, slightly beaten

Preheat oven to 350 degrees. Combine butter, cocoa, and water in saucepan, bring to a boil, and set aside. Mix flour, sugar, soda, and salt together and add boiled mixture. Add buttermilk, vanilla, and eggs. Bake in 9-inch by 13-inch pan about 22 minutes.

Buttermilk Frosting
1 stick butter
6 tablespoons buttermilk
4 tablespoons cocoa

1 (1-pound) box powdered
   sugar
1 teaspoon vanilla
1 cup chopped nuts (optional)

Combine butter, buttermilk, and cocoa in saucepan and bring to a boil. Remove from heat and add remaining ingredients. Stir until smooth. Pour over top of cake while still warm. Cake and frosting can be hot.

I have known people to drive a long way to get a piece of this cake. Some of these same people have "borrowed" the recipe and are now claiming it as their own!

★
Jarrell D. Clark
Gen. Franklin Gardner
Camp #1421
Lafayette, Louisiana
★
Descendant of
William Elisha Upshaw
Blake's Scouts, Georgia

William Upshaw was taken prisoner at the Battle of Vicksburg.

THE CONFEDERATE COOKBOOK

Cream Cheese Cookie Delights

Easy and quick

2 sticks butter or margarine
3 (8-ounce) packages of cream
   cheese
1½ cups sugar

1 egg yolk
½ teaspoon vanilla
2½ cups sifted flour
Jelly topping as desired

*P*reheat oven to 350 degrees. Cream first 3 ingredients. Add egg yolk and vanilla. Mix in sifted flour. Lightly roll dough into balls of about 1 inch in diameter and place on cookie sheet with 2 inches of space between balls. Add a ½-teaspoon dollop of jelly topping, making indentation into dough ball with spoon if desired. Bake for 10-12 minutes. Makes about 2 dozen cookies.

This is a recipe given to me by my daughter, Carla, about 30 years ago. I don't know its origin, but it's mighty good! These taste best when they are hot right out of the oven. Later, this effect can be recreated by heating in a microwave oven for a few seconds.

★
Carl Fallen
Chief Black Dog Camp #1829
Coffeyville, Kansas
★
Descendant of
1st Lt. James S. Guinn
Co. I, 10th Regiment,
Kentucky Infantry

Chocolate Cake Pudding

Tastes like a hot fudge brownie without the ice cream

Cake
3/4 cup sugar
1 cup flour
2 tablespoons cocoa

1/2 cup milk
3 tablespoons butter, melted
1 teaspoon vanilla

*M*ix together and bake in same square baking pan.

★
**Phillip Bickerstaff
James R. Chalmers
Camp #1312
Memphis, Tennessee**
★
**Great-great-grandson
Pvt. William N. Harris
Co. A, 24th Tennessee Infantry**

Topping
1/2 cup sugar
1/2 cup brown sugar

1/4 cup cocoa
1 1/2 cups water

*M*ix dry ingredients together and sprinkle over cake. Pour water over cake in pan. Bake at 350 degrees for 45 minutes. Serve warm. Serves 6-8.

THE CONFEDERATE COOKBOOK

Old-Fashioned Dark Chocolate Cake

A rich, heavy cake that keeps well

2 cups sifted all-purpose flour
3 teaspoons baking powder
½ teaspoon salt
½ cup butter, softened
1¾ cups sugar
2 eggs

4 squares unsweetened chocolate, melted
1½ cups milk
2 teaspoons vanilla
1 cup pecans, finely chopped

Father Alister Anderson
Jefferson Davis Camp #305
Washington, D.C.

1st cousin,
three times removed
Capt. Aristides Doggett
Co. A, 3rd Florida Infantry

*S*ift flour once, measure, add baking powder and salt, then sift again. Cream butter, gradually add sugar, and cream until light and fluffy. Add eggs 1 at a time, beating thoroughly after each. Add melted chocolate and blend. Add the flour alternately with the milk, beating after each addition until smooth. Add vanilla and nuts and blend. Pour batter into a greased and floured 10-inch tube pan and bake at 350 degrees for 55-60 minutes or until a pick inserted comes out clean. Cool completely in the pan. Serves 12.

For the frosting, melt the chocolate pieces over hot water, then stir in sour cream.

Frosting
5 ounces semi-sweet chocolate pieces

Hot water
½ cup regular sour cream (do
   not use low-fat)

This cake has been a birthday favorite in our family for at least thirty years, and it is better the second day.

One Step Pound Cake

A strawberry festival prize winner

1 cup sour cream (or 8 ounces any flavor yogurt), room temperature

4 eggs, room temperature

2 sticks butter or margarine, softened

2¼ cups flour, sifted

2 cups sugar

½ teaspoon salt

½ teaspoon baking soda

1 teaspoon vanilla

---

*H*eat oven to 325 degrees. Grease and flour a tube pan or 2 loaf pans. Blend all ingredients for 1 minute, beat for 3 minutes. Pour into pan. Bake 60-70 minutes, making sure center is cooked.

This recipe (using strawberry yogurt) won first place and best of category at the strawberry festival held annually in Plant City, Florida. I love making this recipe using orange yogurt. It won a blue ribbon at the same festival.

★

Scott L. Peeler, Jr.
John T. Lesley Camp #1282
Tampa, Florida

★

Descendant of
The Reverend Joseph Peeler
Chaplain, 3rd Lillard's
Tennessee Mounted Infantry

The Reverend Joseph Peeler was born about 1808 in Elbert County, Georgia. He was a Cumberland Presbyterian minister and founded several churches. Family tradition states that Reverend Peeler took part in the Battle of Chattanooga and swam across the Tennessee River with his coat pockets full of Bibles. He died at the age of 63 in March 1871. He has hundreds of descendants today.

Opposite—The Reverend Joseph Peeler Chaplain, 3rd Lillard's Tennessee Mounted Infantry

General Washington's Virginia Cherry Pie

A savory winter treat

4 cups seeded sour cherries, well drained	1 teaspoon cinnamon
⅔ cup sugar	2 shakes nutmeg
3 tablespoons flour	Butter
	Milk

Fold cherries with sugar. Add flour, cinnamon, and nutmeg, and toss lightly. Place cherry mixture in pie crust. Dot with butter. Top with second crust. Brush crust with milk. Bake 15 minutes at 425 degrees, then turn down to 375 for 30 minutes more. Should be golden brown at finish. Serves 6-8.

Crust	
2 cups flour	1 cup Crisco
Pinch salt	1 cup cold water

Add salt to flour. Cut in shortening with pastry blender until "crumbly." Measure 1 cup cold water (use ice cubes to chill water, but remove cubes before adding to flour mixture). With fork, add enough water to flour mixture to form 2 equal balls. Use 1 ball for each crust. Flour rolling pin and clean surface. Roll out crust ⅛-inch thick. Roll crust back over pin, and then roll back into pie plate for the bottom and over cherries for top crust.

This pie is dear to me and my family. For generations, in honor of the first president's birthday on February 22, we have salivated over this pie, which we make with cherries from our own trees. Honestly, I can't think of anything I'd rather eat!

★
Gregg Clemmer
Col. William Norris
Camp #1398
Gaithersburg, Maryland
★
Great-great-grandson
1st Lt. Mathew Bolling Clay
Co. C, 9th Virginia Infantry

Lt. Clay, a second cousin once removed of Sen. Henry Clay of Kentucky, was captured in Pickett's Charge at Gettysburg on July 3, 1863. He was imprisoned at Johnson's Island, then exchanged to his regiment. He served in the Petersburg siege until captured a second time at Five Forks, Virginia, in 1865.

Opposite—Mathew Bolling Clay
1st Lieutenant, Co. C,
9th Virginia Infantry

Honey Mammy's Jerusalem Cookies

Perfect for holiday baking

1 pound butter	1 pound nuts, chopped
3 large eggs	(pecans are best)
2 quarts flour	1 pound powdered sugar
1⅓ cups sugar	½ box cinnamon
1 cup whiskey, wine, or vanilla	
(as preferred)	

Preheat oven to 350 degrees. Blend all ingredients to make cookie dough. Shape dough into crescent shapes. Bake cookies for about 15 minutes or until dough begins to brown. While still piping hot from oven, dip cookies into powdered sugar/cinnamon mixture. Dip once again after cookies have cooled.

This recipe was passed down from my great-grandmother Annie Lou "Honey Mammy" Miller Almon. While experimenting with her mother in the kitchen as a small child, Honey Mammy came up with this cookie recipe—making it a true Southern treat dating back to about 1875.

★

**Hudson Alexander
Maj. Gen. William D. McCain
Camp #584
Columbia, Tennessee**

★

**Great-great-grandson
Thomas E. Miller
Co. C, 26th Mississippi Infantry**

Thomas Miller was captured after the fall of Fort Donelson in February 1862. He was sent to prison at Camp Morton in Indianapolis. After being exchanged at Vicksburg, he reenlisted, but was captured again while fighting in the Eastern Theatre. He was paroled from Hart's Island Prison in New York in 1865. After the war, he became very involved in the United Confederate Veterans and attended many reunions. Up until his death in 1906, one of his favorite holiday treats was Honey Mammy's Jerusalem Cookies.

Original Banana Cookie Pudding

A classic childhood favorite

¾ cup granulated sugar
⅓ cup all-purpose flour
Dash of salt
4 eggs, separated (room
   temperature)
2 cups milk
½ teaspoon vanilla (can use a
   little more, if preferred)

35-50 vanilla wafer cookies
   (reserve 10 for garnish)
5 or 6 fully ripe bananas,
   sliced (reserve 1 banana for
   garnish)

★

**William Frank Lee III
Irvin Toombs Camp #511
Washington, Georgia**

★

**Great-grandson
Lt. Richard Nixon Westbrook
Co. H, 5th Georgia Infantry**

Combine ½ cup sugar, flour, and salt in top of double boiler. Stir in 4 egg yolks and milk and blend well. Cook, uncovered over boiling water, stirring constantly until thickened. Reduce heat and cook, stirring occasionally, for 5 minutes. Remove the custard from heat and add vanilla. Spread small amount of this mixture on the bottom of a 1½-quart casserole dish and cover with a layer of cookies. Top with a layer of bananas. Pour about ⅓ of custard over bananas.

Continue to layer cookies, bananas, and custard to make 3 layers of each, ending with custard. Beat egg whites until stiff, but not dry. Gradually add remaining sugar and beat until stiff peaks form. Spoon on top of pudding, spreading meringue to cover surface and extending to edges. Bake at 425 degrees for 5 minutes or until meringue is lightly browned. Cool slightly or chill before serving. Just before serving, garnish with sliced banana and cookies around the edges of the dish. Makes 16 servings.

Ice Box Cookies

A delicate, understated flavor

½ cup butter
1 cup brown sugar
1 egg
½ teaspoon vanilla flavoring

2 cups flour
½ teaspoon baking soda
½ teaspoon cream of tartar
½ cup black walnuts, chopped

*C*ream butter and sugar. Add egg and vanilla, mixing well. Combine flour, baking soda, and cream of tartar and stir into creamed mixture. Add black walnuts. Divide dough in half and roll into 2 logs about 1½ inch in diameter. Wrap in waxed paper and store in refrigerator. When thoroughly chilled, cut into ¼-inch slices and place on ungreased cookie sheet. Bake at 325 degrees until lightly browned, about 8-10 minutes.

★

Larry E. Beeson
Stokes County Troops
Camp #1540
King, North Carolina

★

Great-great-grandson
Cpl. John Frazier
Co. D, 57th
North Carolina Troops

John Frazier, a native of Stokes County, North Carolina, was captured by Federal troops twice. During an engagement near the Rappahannock River in 1863, he was captured, sent to Point Lookout Prison, and then released. He rejoined his regiment and was recaptured at the third Battle of Winchester. Again, he was sent to Point Lookout. He died there on February 2, 1865.

General Lee's Eggnog

A Southern holiday tradition

12 eggs
1 pound sugar
1 quart bourbon whiskey
½ pint Jamaican rum

½ pint brandy
1 quart whole milk
1 quart whipping cream

*S*eparate eggs and refrigerate whites. Beat egg yolks until light yellow, slowly beat in sugar, then *very* slowly add whiskey while beating constantly. Continue beating while adding rest of ingredients, except egg whites. Pour into quart jars (about 5), cover, refrigerate, and allow to mellow for 2 days. When ready to serve, pour mixture into a serving bowl. In a separate bowl, beat egg whites until they form soft peaks, then fold into rest of mixture.

★

P. James Kurapka
Gen. Isaac Ridgeway Trimble
Camp #1836
Catonsville, Maryland

★

Great-grandson
Pvt. David McConas Jayne
Co. D, 25th Virginia Cavalry

David Jayne was a stonemason, carpenter, and farmer by trade. He was the blacksmith for his unit during the war. He was very proud of his Confederate service and often spoke of his wartime experiences with family and friends. He was present at the Battle of Gettysburg and vividly described the cannonade during Pickett's Charge as an "overarching canopy of flame." He died in 1923 and is buried in Scott County, Virginia.

Miss Nancy's Famous Coconut Cake

A classic dessert

2¼ cups sifted flour
1½ teaspoons baking powder
½ teaspoon baking soda
¾ teaspoon salt
½ cup unsalted butter
1¼ cups sugar

3 eggs
½ cup angel flake coconut
1¼ cups buttermilk
1½ teaspoons vanilla
Seven-Minute Frosting
Coconut

*S*ift together the dry ingredients. Cream butter and sugar. Add the eggs one at a time to the creamed mixture. Beat well after each addition. Combine the ½ cup coconut and the buttermilk. Add alternately with flour mixture to sugar mixture (on slow speed if using mixer). Add vanilla. Pour into 2 greased and floured 9-inch cake pans. Bake at 375 degrees for 25 to 30 minutes. This can be made in 3 layers with the cooking time shortened. Serves 12 or more.

Filling
2 egg whites
½ cup non-alcoholic pina
    colada mix

1½ cups angel flake coconut
4 tablespoons confectioners'
    sugar

*B*eat egg whites until stiff. Add other ingredients to egg whites. Mix gently with spoon. Do not cook. Spread between cake layers. Ice cake with Seven-Minute Frosting. Sprinkle cake with coconut.

★
Dr. Milburn Calhoun
Beauregard Camp #130
New Orleans, Louisiana
★
Great-grandson
Pvt. Malcolm Calhoun
Co. E, 19th Louisiana Infantry

Malcolm Calhoun enlisted in the army at Monroe, Louisiana. After his company completed training at Camp Moore, they were sent by train to Shiloh, where they fought in the first great battle of the West. Malcolm survived heavy fighting at Shiloh and Chickamauga, but was killed in action at Atlanta in 1864. His gravesite remains unknown. He left a wife and several small children.

continued on next page

Seven-Minute Frosting
1½ cups sugar
¼ cup water
2 egg whites

2 tablespoons light corn syrup
1 teaspoon vanilla
¼ teaspoon salt

*C*ombine ingredients in top of double broiler. Beat well. Place over simmering water. Cook, beating constantly at high speed with an electric hand mixer about 7 minutes or until it is triple in volume and holds firm peaks. Remove from heat and ice cake.

This wonderful recipe was contributed by my wife, Nancy Harris Calhoun, vice president of Pelican Publishing Company in Gretna, Louisiana.

Easy Lemon Pie

A silky, lemony treat

4 eggs
1 cup sugar
1 whole lemon, seeded and
   cut into quarters

¾ stick margarine
Unbaked pie shell

*I*n blender, combine eggs, sugar, lemon quarters, and margarine. Blend until smooth. Pour into pie shell. Bake in a 350-degree oven for 30 minutes or until done.

★
Larry E. Beeson
Stokes County Troops
Camp #1540
King, North Carolina
★
Great-great-grandson
Cpl. John Frazier
Co. D, 57th
North Carolina Troops

Raw Apple Cake

Don't ask for seconds, 'cause there won't be any!

1½ cups Crisco oil
2 cups sugar
4 eggs
3 cups plain flour
1 teaspoon salt
1 teaspoon soda
1 teaspoon cinnamon
1 teaspoon nutmeg

1 teaspoon vanilla
3 cups raw apples, diced (after dicing, pour lemon juice on to keep from darkening)
1 tablespoon lemon juice
1 cup nuts, chopped (pecans preferred)
1 cup raisins

*C*ream oil and sugar. Add eggs. Add all dry ingredients and vanilla until well blended (batter will be very thick). Add apples, nuts, and raisins. Bake in greased and floured tube pan at 350 degrees for 1 hour or until done. Serves 8.

This recipe was made often by my Aunt Madge,
even after she was confined to a wheel chair.
It is enjoyed frequently in our home.

★
Elwood L. Long
Strasburg Guards
Camp #1587
Strasburg, Virginia
★
Great-grandson
Pvt. Joseph Milton Manry
Co. B, 9th Virginia Infantry

After the war, Joseph Manry returned to farming. He died in 1912 and is buried on his homeplace in Perquimans County, North Carolina. He leaves many descendants.

Persimmon Pudding

A tasty fall dessert

2 cups persimmons (pressed through a screen and free of seeds)

2 cups sugar

1½ sticks butter

2 eggs

2 cups self-rising flour

*M*ix all ingredients and place in a baking dish. Cook 1 hour at 325 degrees. Best eaten cool.

The Carolina Purity Law of 1751 states, "Persimmon Pudding cannot contain any ingredients except for persimmons, sugar, butter, flour, and eggs." It is a favorite of native North Carolinians, and is always the most sought after dessert at family reunions.

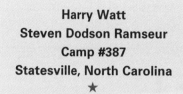

★

Harry Watt
Steven Dodson Ramseur
Camp #387
Statesville, North Carolina

★

Great-grandson
Pvt. William Thomas Watt
Co. E, 49th Regiment, North Carolina Troops

William Watt was a farmer from Iredell County, North Carolina. He was wounded in the attack on Fort Steadman at Petersburg, Virginia.

Old-Fashioned Peppermint Ice Cream

Nothing tastes like homemade ice cream

3 cups peppermint candy
   (crushed into bite-size or
   smaller chunks)

4½ cups sweet milk
³/₁₆ teaspoon salt
4½ cups liquid coffee cream

Dissolve candy in milk over a low fire or on low simmer on an electric range. Stir constantly while dissolving to avoid sticking. Add salt and coffee cream and pour into freezer churn. Freeze. Makes about a gallon.

★
Wade Hampton Harbin
Lt. James Thomas Woodward
Camp #1399
Warner Robins, Georgia
★
Grand-nephew
Cpl. John Asbury Harbin
Co. L, South Carolina Palmetto
Sharpshooters

While rounding up Federal wounded, stragglers, and deserters after the Battle of Chickamauga, John Hardin was wounded in the leg by a sneaky Yankee soldier with a boot gun! After being captured, he was treated for his wound and sent to the prison at Camp Chase in Columbus, Ohio, for the duration of the war. He died in Seneca, South Carolina, and is buried on land he donated to Shiloh Baptist Church.

Peach Fried Pies

An excellent "traveling snack" for reenactments

8-12 dried peach halves
Water
2 cups sugar

1-2 tablespoons cornstarch (if needed)
Basic pie crust recipe

Cut up or dice dried peach halves. Soak dried peaches overnight in just enough water to cover the peaches (no more than 2-3 inches). The next day, simmer or cook the peaches on the stove until tender. Add sugar and let simmer until consistency is thick. Cook on low or they will burn. If they are runny, add cornstarch for thickening. For each fried pie, roll out a basic pie crust recipe (your choice) into a 4-5-inch round crust. Put 1-2 tablespoons of peach mixture into each crust. Fold over and seal crust—a "pinched" seal is preferable.

Place into a stainless steel electric skillet with 1 tablespoon of shortening. Set at about 375 degrees. Cook about 10 minutes on each side or until really brown. You may need to experiment with your skillet.

For those of us who are into "War 'Twixt the States" reenacting, I have been told that these pies are "period correct" as they were considered a delicacy in some parts of the South.

★
Darrell Rhea
Dunn-Holt-Midkiff Camp #1441
Midland, Texas

★
Great-great-grandson
1st Lt. Daniel M. Beard
Co. I, 4th Arkansas Volunteer Infantry

Daniel was a farmer, metal worker, and land developer. He was born in 1832 in Tennessee, but later moved to Arkansas, where he married and reared a family. He was given a special mission on detached duty as a recruiter in Arkansas. In 1864, he attempted to rejoin his regiment, but the Mississippi River had been closed off by Federal forces. His name was still on the rolls when the war ended. He died in 1892 and is buried in Polk County, Arkansas.

Cold Oven Pound Cake

A moist, rich cake

2 sticks butter
3 cups sugar
½ cup oil
6 eggs
3 cups flour

1 cup milk
½ teaspoon baking powder
2 tablespoons lemon extract
1 tablespoon almond extract

---

*C*ream butter with sugar and oil. Add eggs 1 at a time. Alternate flour and milk. Add baking powder. Finally, add the extracts. Place in a cold oven and bake at 325 degrees for 1½ hours. Test to see if done—some ovens need extra time.

★

Stuart Hoffman
Father A. J. Ryan Camp #302
San Diego, California

★

Great-great-grandson
Pvt. James Henry Bartlett
Co. B, 13th North Carolina
Troops

James Bartlett was a farmer who enlisted in the Confederate army in 1862. He was wounded in the shoulder at the Battle of South Mountain (Maryland). After he recuperated, he rejoined his unit and was wounded a second time at Petersburg. He was captured and sent to Point Lookout, Maryland, where he spent the rest of the war. After his release, he married and had a large family. He died in 1913 and is buried at Mint Hill, North Carolina.

Southern Power Cookies

A combination of all the best cookies: oatmeal, chocolate chip, coconut, sugar!

2 cups dark brown sugar
2 cups white granulated sugar
³/₄ cup butter, softened
1 cup Crisco
4 eggs
2 teaspoons vanilla
3 cups all-purpose flour
2 teaspoons salt

2 teaspoons baking soda
3 cups uncooked oats (oatmeal)
2 cups coconut, shredded
1 (12-ounce) package chocolate chips
1 cup pecans, chopped
2 cups raisins (optional)

Phil E. Johnson
Gen. de Polignac Camp #1648
Arlington, Texas
★
Great-great-grandson
Pvt. William Thomas Dunn
Co. B, 19th Texas Cavalry

Cream together sugars, butter, and Crisco very well. Beat in the eggs and vanilla. In a separate bowl, combine flour, salt, and soda. Mix with first mixture. In a very large bowl, combine oats, coconut, chocolate chips, pecans, and raisins (if desired). Add sugar-flour mixture and mix with sturdy wooden spoon or hands. Dough will be stiff. Dough can be shaped into rolls, wrapped and chilled several hours, or immediately dropped by heaping teaspoons on lightly greased cookie sheets, 2 inches apart. If dough is chilled, slice and place like dropped dough. Bake in preheated 350-degree oven for 8-9 minutes until golden brown. Allow to cool several minutes before removing to rack to cool. Store in airtight container. Makes 7-8 dozen irresistible cookies.

These cookies have come to be expected as Christmas gifts by neighbors, friends, and family. A cherished elderly gentleman friend of our family would eat these when he would not eat anything else. Best if eaten warm with a cold glass of milk on a cold, rainy night . . . or any other time!

Tipsy Custard

A beautiful dessert that you can make the day before

1½ dozen Lady Fingers
½ pint sherry
1 quart boiled custard (recipe below)
1 coconut, grated
½ pound raisins
1 pineapple, grated
6 oranges (divided or cut into small pieces)
Sugar
½ pound walnut halves
½ pound almond slivers

Crumble a few of the Lady Fingers in the bottom of a crystal bowl and sprinkle a little sherry over them. Pour a layer of boiled custard over this, top with coconut, raisins, and a layer of pineapple and orange pieces. Sprinkle a little sugar on top before beginning the next layer. Top with coconut and a circle of nuts. Refrigerate until serving. Serves 10.

Boiled Custard
1 quart milk
5 egg yolks
5 egg whites
6 tablespoons sugar
2 teaspoons vanilla

Heat the milk (medium-high temperature) almost to the boiling point. Beat the egg yolks lightly and stir in sugar. Remove the milk from the stove and carefully pour a spoonful or 2 into the egg yolk mixture, beating all the while, adding more milk slowly until there is no danger of curdling. Stir this into the thoroughly beaten egg whites and return to the stove, stirring constantly until it is thickened, then add vanilla.

continued on next page

★
Stephen Lawrence Jenkins
Albert Sidney Johnston
Camp #67
Houston, Texas
★
Great-grandson
Pvt. Lawson Jenkins
Co. B, 12th Regiment, South Carolina Volunteers

Lawson Jenkins served along with his son, William Walker Jenkins. Both survived the conflict. As he walked home after the surrender, William stopped off at a plantation and was fed and kindly treated by a young lady there. He continued on home, but returned soon after and made her his bride.

This recipe has been passed down for generations in my wife's family. Her great-great-grandparents, Mr. And Mrs. William F. Phifer of Charlotte, North Carolina, hosted the last full meeting of the Confederate cabinet at their plantation in late April 1865 as Jefferson Davis and the cabinet members retreated from Richmond during the final days of the war. Secretary of the Treasury G. A. Trehold stayed at the Phifer home while he was in Charlotte. He was extremely ill during the exodus, and the cabinet met by his bedside for a final meeting. Tipsy Custard, sometimes called Cabinet Pudding because of that last full meeting of the Confederate cabinet, is served with pride in our heritage as we frequently extend Southern hospitality to our family and friends.

Mama's Old-Fashioned Tea Cakes

A classic cookie that's good anytime

1 cup butter
1 cup sugar
1 egg, lightly beaten
1 teaspoon baking powder
½ teaspoon baking soda

½ teaspoon salt
½ cup milk
3 cups flour
1 teaspoon vanilla

★
Wm. Darrell Glover
Lt. W.W. Pettus Camp #1762
Lexington, Alabama
★

Great-grandson
Pvt. Daniel McDougal Killen
Co. E, 27th Alabama Infantry

*C*ream butter. Add sugar and lightly beaten egg. Sift dry ingredients together. Add milk and vanilla alternately with enough flour to make a stiff dough. Roll out on a floured board. Cut with cookie cutter and bake 8-10 minutes at 375 degrees.

Bonton's Bread Pudding

Melts in your mouth

1 loaf French bread, broken
    into small pieces
4 cups milk
2 cups sugar
3 eggs, beaten

1 tablespoon vanilla
1 cup raisins (optional)
1-2 ounces liquor
3 tablespoons margarine

*S*oak bread in milk until soft. Set aside. Mix sugar, eggs, vanilla, and raisins (if desired) in a separate bowl. Combine with bread mixture. Add 1-2 ounces liquor of your choice for flavor. Melt margarine in bottom of 9-inch by 13-inch pan. Pour mixture into pan and cook for 45 minutes to 1 hour in a preheated 325-degree oven until puffy and a knife comes out clean. Serve warm with topping below.

Topping
1 cup sugar
1 stick margarine

1 egg, beaten
1-2 ounces liquor

*H*eat sugar and margarine together until melted (do not boil). Pour in egg and heat until thick. Flavor with liquor. Pour over individual servings of bread pudding. Delicious!

★
Willard T. Bangle
James M. Keller Camp #648
Hot Springs, Arkansas
★
Nephew
Pvt. Ephraim Gibson Bangle
Capt. Smith's Company, 19th
Mississippi Infantry

Ephraim Bangle was only 17 years old when he was killed in battle in Petersburg, Virginia. He was one of 26 children.

Gingerbread Boys

This recipe won the Arkansas State Gingerbread House competition

½ cup brown sugar
½ cup shortening
¾ cup molasses
1 egg
2 teaspoons vinegar
1 teaspoon baking soda

1 teaspoon cinnamon
1 teaspoon salt
1 teaspoon cloves
1 teaspoon ginger
3-3½ cups all-purpose flour

*C*ream sugar and shortening. Add molasses, egg, and vinegar. Sift together dry ingredients and mix well. Dough will be stiff. Refrigerate for 3 hours or overnight before using. Let dough stand at room temperature a while so it is easier to roll. Roll thick, about ¼-inch. Sprinkle a little cinnamon into the flour on your rolling board to give the dough a prettier color. Cut into gingerbread boys with a cutter. Use red hots (candy) for the eyes, nose, and buttons. Bake 8-10 minutes at 325 degrees.

Four generations of our family (so far) have enjoyed these boys at Christmas time.

★
**Mason Sickel
Col. Robert G. Shaver
Camp #1655
Jonesboro, Arkansas**
★
**Great-great-grandson
Pvt. Daniel E. (J. D.) Ellis
Co. K, Freeman's Missouri
Cavalry**

Matt's Easy SCV Dessert

You don't have to be much of a cook to make this tasty dessert

Family-size brownie mix
Large size (5-ounce)
   instant chocolate
   pudding
1 can cherry pie filling

1 (8-ounce) package frozen
   whipped topping (Cool
   Whip), thawed
1-2 toffee candy bars (Heath
   bars)

*P*repare brownies according to directions on package.
While brownies are cooling, prepare pudding according to package directions. Crumble up brownies as a base on the bottom of a serving dish (a clear trifle dish shows off the layers of the dessert well). Layer the pudding over the brownies, followed by the cherry pie filling, and finally the whipped topping. Crumble toffee candy over the top. Refrigerate. Brownies and pudding may be made ahead of time, but do not layer dessert until shortly before serving. Serves 12-15.

Like many men, I'm not much of a cook, but whenever I'm called upon for a dessert, this one never fails! My fellow SCV compatriots love it and so do my kids.

★
**Richard L. Flournoy
J. M. ("Matt") Barton
Camp #441
Sulphur Springs, Texas**
★
**Great-great-grandson
Pvt. Welcome Wright Flournoy
53rd Alabama Partisan
Rangers**

Welcome Flournoy rode with Forrest at Brentwood and Franklin, Tennessee, and with Hood during the Atlanta Campaign. After the war, he settled in West Texas, where he became a justice of the peace. He is buried in East Texas.

Chocolate Gravy

An unusual breakfast treat

½ cup sugar

3 tablespoons flour

1 tablespoon cocoa

1 cup milk

*M*ix these ingredients together in a quart saucepan. Add milk and put over low heat, stirring until it thickens. Do not let it get as thick as pie filling. Serve over biscuits. Serves 4.

This recipe is easy to double or triple. It is also good as a leftover. My wife's grandmother made this unusual breakfast for her six children over eighty years ago in the valley of the three forks of the Wolf River.

★

Tom Humphrey
Longstreet-Zollicoffer
Camp #87
Knoxville, Tennessee

★

Great-great-grandson
Pvt. Cullen M. Humphrey
Co. K, Forsyth County
Mounted Grays,
Georgia Militia

Cullen Humphrey was a blacksmith by trade who made arms for the Confederacy. He lived a long life and had six children. His brother, Thomas, was killed in action.

Beverly's Strawberry Jell-O Pie

A cool summer treat

1 deep-dish, unbaked pie shell	3 tablespoons white Karo
1 (3½-ounce) box strawberry	syrup
Jell-O	1 pint fresh strawberries
1 cup sugar	Cool Whip
1 cup water	

*B*ake the pie crust according to the package directions. In a saucepan, pour the water, sugar, Jell-O, and Karo syrup. Bring to a boil and cook 5 minutes. Slice strawberries into the pie shell and pour Jell-O over them. Place pie in the refrigerator until Jell-O sets (usually about 3-4 hours). Slice the pie and dollop with Cool Whip right before serving. Serves 8.

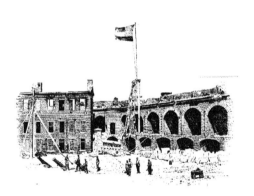

★

**David Moncus
Brig. Gen. John C. Carter
Camp #207
Waynesboro, Georgia**

★

**Great-great-grandson
Pvt. Richard Warnock
Co. B, 57th Georgia Infantry**

Richard Warnock was born in Laurens County, Georgia, in 1833. He enlisted in the Confederate army and was wounded at Baker's Creek, Mississippi, in 1863. Later that year, he was captured at Vicksburg and exchanged. He was wounded again at Missionary Ridge during the Chattanooga Campaign, but survived the war and returned home to finish rearing his family.

THE CONFEDERATE COOKBOOK

So Good Peach Cobbler

The name says it all

1 quart peaches
½ cup butter or margarine
1 cup self-rising flour

1 cup granulated sugar
1 cup buttermilk

*W*arm peaches and melt butter into peaches. Pour peach and butter mixture into a baking dish. Mix flour, sugar, and buttermilk well and pour over peach and butter mixture. Bake in a 350-degree oven for 1 hour.

★
Dan Coleman
Chattahoochee Guards
Camp #1639
Mableton, Georgia
★
Great-grandson
Pvt. William Kelley
Co. F, 45th Georgia Infantry

Yankee Cannon Balls

Mouth-watering cookies too good to throw at them Yankees!

1 cup nuts, chopped
1 cup coconut, flaked
1 cup Rice Krispies cereal
1 stick butter, melted

1 cup brown sugar
1 cup dates, chopped
Confectionary sugar

*M*ix nuts, coconut, and cereal in a bowl. Add melted butter, sugar, and dates. Stir while boiling for 7 minutes at low heat and pour over dry ingredients. Mix very rapidly and shape spoonfuls into about 50 little balls. Roll in confectionary sugar.

★
Buddy Kirtland
Col. Jacob B. Biffle
Camp #1603
Lawrenceburg, Tennessee
★
Descendant of
Cpl. John A. McGill
Co. K, 17th Tennessee Infantry

Chocolate Oatmeal Cookies

Kids can make these by themselves

½ cup butter or margarine
2 cups granulated sugar
½ cup powdered cocoa
½ cup milk (soy milk can be substituted)

3 cups oatmeal (quick or slow cook)
½ cup peanut butter (smooth or crunchy)

**Elijah Coleman
Chattahoochee Guards
Camp #1639
Mableton, Georgia**

★

**Great-great-grandson
Pvt. Merick Coleman
Co. D, 36th Georgia Infantry**

*M*elt butter in a 2-quart saucepan over medium heat. Remove from heat and add sugar and cocoa and stir. Return to heat and add milk. Stir until mixture comes to a rolling boil. Count to 60 (this step is very important). Remove from heat and add oatmeal and peanut butter. Mix thoroughly and quickly drop onto wax paper or aluminum foil. Let cool. Makes about 30 cookies.

If you counted to 60, the cookies will harden. If not, they will have to be eaten with a spoon, but they are still delicious!

Apple–Lokshen Kugel

Can be eaten hot or cold

1 (8-ounce) package medium
   egg noodles
$1/4$ cup margarine, melted
4 eggs, beaten
3 medium apples
$1/4$ cup dark seedless raisins
   (optional)

$1/4$ cup sugar (optional)
$1/2$ teaspoon salt
2 teaspoons cinnamon
$1/2$ teaspoon vanilla

Preheat oven to 350 degrees. Cook and drain noodles and put in large bowl. Stir in margarine and eggs. Peel and chop apples, add seasoning and raisins (if desired), and mix well. Pour kugel mixture into a greased 9-inch by 13-inch baking pan (glass is best). Bake 40 minutes to 1 hour or until lightly browned. Makes 12 pieces. For extra softness, add another 2 eggs. To vary this recipe, you can also layer the noodles in the bottom of the pan, then layer other ingredients, alternating layers of noodles and other ingredients.

★
Larry Irion
Capt. William McKinney Irion
Camp #1799
Salem, Oregon
★
Great-grandnephew
Capt. William McKinney Irion
Co. G, 32nd Mississippi
Infantry

Butter Roll Pie

Perfect with your afternoon coffee

2 cups flour
3 teaspoons baking powder
Pinch of salt
³⁄₄ cup water
¹⁄₂ cup oleo or butter, softened

2 teaspoons cinnamon
3 cups milk
1 teaspoon vanilla
1¹⁄₂ cups sugar

*M*ix flour, baking powder, water, and salt. Roll dough out on a floured board to ¹⁄₄-inch thickness. Dot top of dough with butter. Mix sugar and cinnamon. Sprinkle dough with 6 tablespoons of the sugar mixture. Lift edge of dough and roll it into a 2-inch diameter (roll up like a jelly roll). Coat bottom of baking dish with butter. Cut rolled dough into 3-inch lengths (until it looks like a cinnamon roll) and place in baking dish. Blend milk, vanilla, and 4 tablespoons sugar and cinnamon mixture and bring it to a brisk boil. Sprinkle remaining sugar mixture over the top. Dot with remaining butter. Pour boiling milk mixture over dough. The rolled dough will rise to top. Bake at 350 degrees for 30-40 minutes and serve hot. Serves 4.

★
**Skip Barnard
Gen. Richard Taylor
Camp #1308
Shreveport, Louisiana**
★
**Descendant of
Pvt. David Thomas Driver
Co. H, 31st Regiment,
Mississippi Infantry**

Tomato Soup Cake

An unusual cake with a distinctive taste

1 cup sugar
½ cup shortening
2 cups flour
1 teaspoon cinnamon
1 teaspoon cloves
½ teaspoon salt

½ cup raisins
½ cup chopped nuts
1 teaspoon baking soda
1 can tomato soup
1 teaspoon water

Cream the sugar and the shortening. Sift flour with spices and salt, then slowly add this mixture to the shortening. Put the raisins and nuts in with the last of the flour. Mix soda with soup and add to batter. Rinse soup can with 1 teaspoon water, add to batter, and mix well. Bake at 375 degrees for about 30 minutes in a greased 9-inch cake tin.

★

Wm. Darrell Glover
Lt. W. W. Pettus Camp #1762
Lexington, Alabama

★

Great-grandson
Pvt. Daniel McDougal Killen
Co. E, 27th Alabama Infantry

Dan Killen enlisted in the Confederate army on Christmas Eve 1861. He was one of six brothers who served the Southern cause. He and his brothers were in numerous battles and skirmishes all over the South. Once, when home on leave, he escaped capture by marauding Federal forces when his mother slit open a feather bed and hid him inside. Incredibly, all six brothers survived the war. When they returned home, Jack, an elderly servant who had belonged to their father, told them that they had all come home safely because he had prayed for them every day.

The Easiest Cheesecake

Quick, easy, and oh so good

4 small packages cream cheese, softened	2 eggs
	¾ cup sugar

---

*B*eat the above ingredients together until smooth. Pour into a prepared graham cracker pie shell. Bake at 325 degrees for 20 minutes. Allow the cheesecake to cool.

Topping	½ cup sugar
1 small carton sour cream	Vanilla extract to taste

---

*W*hip topping ingredients together and spread on cooled cheesecake. Bake at 325 degrees for 10 minutes.

★

Kenneth D. Morgan
Col. Joseph Norton Camp #45
Seneca, South Carolina

★

Great-great-grandson
2nd Lt. George Washington Campbell
Co. K, 22nd South Carolina Regiment (Evan's Brigade)

George Washington Campbell rose through the ranks to become a 2nd lieutenant. He and six of his brothers fought for the Confederacy, but only two survived. George contracted jaundice and was given a medical discharge in 1864. He died in 1891 of complications from jaundice, a belated casualty of war.

Lynda's Cookie Puddin'

A delicious homemade pudding with a rich vanilla flavor

¾ cup sugar
1 tablespoon cornstarch for
    thickening (can use 2 table-
    spoons white flour)
2 large egg yolks, beaten (keep
    the whites for meringue)

2 cups canned milk
1 tablespoon vanilla extract
1 small bag vanilla wafers

★

Shannon Walgamotte
Beauregard Camp #130
New Orleans, Louisiana

★

4th great-grandson
Thomas L. Walgamotte
Co. C, 5th Louisiana Infantry
(Bienville Guards)

*P*reheat oven to 400 degrees. In a large mixing bowl, combine sugar and cornstarch. Add egg yolks slowly and mix well. To this mixture slowly stir in milk. Pour into a large saucepan and warm slowly on low heat, stirring constantly to prevent milk from sticking and scorching. Bring to a boil (mixture should start to thicken). Remove from heat and stir in 1 tablespoon vanilla. In a 2-quart baking dish, pour a little of the resulting custard and cover with a layer of vanilla wafers (don't be stingy with the cookies!). Continue until all custard is used and set aside. Put egg whites with 1 teaspoon of cold water in a mixing bowl. Beat on high until just before it holds a "peak." Slowly sprinkle 1 tablespoon of sugar while beating, then drizzle 1 teaspoon vanilla. Place meringue on top of custard in spoonfuls until it covers top. Place in oven for approximately 10 minutes or until you see the top lightly brown. Place on rack to cool, then refrigerate.

Meringue
2 egg whites reserved from
    above

1 teaspoon cold water
1 tablespoon sugar
1 teaspoon vanilla

*This recipe comes from my mother-in-law, Paula Aydelott.
She named it for my wife, Lynda Moreau,
who loves it as much now as she did when she was a
little girl back in Winnfield, Louisiana.*

351

Sister's Scrumptious Southern Pecan Pie

As Southern as moonlight and magnolias!

3 whole eggs, well beaten
½ cup sugar
1 cup dark Karo syrup
¼ cup butter, melted

1 teaspoon vanilla
Pinch of salt
1 cup pecan halves
1 unbaked pie crust

*B*eat eggs thoroughly. Add sugar gradually, then add dark Karo syrup and melted butter, vanilla, and salt. Pour into unbaked crust, top with pecans, cover with aluminum foil, and bake at 400 degrees for 15 minutes. Uncover and bake 30 minutes longer, until the pie is congealed when you shake it.

The recipe came from my sister, the late Mineola Owen Walker, who grew up in Hope, Arkansas. It has been enjoyed for years by many of our friends and neighbors.

★
Ralph Owen
Gen. Thomas Dockery
Camp #1577
Magnolia, Arkansas
★
Great-grandson
Capt. Jackson Carroll
Coffee Moss
Co. E, 11th Arkansas Infantry

Jackson Moss was born February 26, 1815, in Christian County, Kentucky. He was captured on Island #10, Mississippi River, and sent as a prisoner of war to Johnson's Island in Ohio. After the surrender, he returned home and fathered ten children. He died in Shreveport, Louisiana, in 1904.

Opposite—Jackson Carroll Coffee Moss
Captain, Co. E, 11th Arkansas Infantry

THE CONFEDERATE COOKBOOK

Fried Apple Pies

A favorite of McDaniel-Curtis Camp #165 in Carrollton, Georgia

1 cup dried apples
2 tablespoons sugar
1 (10-count) can refrigerated
 butter-flavor biscuits

3 cups water
Peanut oil

★
John Carter Clay
McDaniel-Curtis Camp #165
Carrollton, Georgia
★
Descendant of
Pvt. David Franklin Tisinger
Co. C, 3rd Georgia Volunteers

*C*ook dried apples in water until thick and not runny. Use medium temperature and stir to prevent burning. Stir until smooth, then add sugar. Open can of biscuits and roll each biscuit into a 5-inch circle. Place 1 tablespoon of apple mixture in the center, moisten $1/4$-inch edge of circle with water, fold in half, and crimp edge with fork. Heat 1-inch deep peanut oil in skillet, drop individual pies into hot oil, and fry until golden on the bottom. Turn to brown other side. Remove from oil and place on paper towels to absorb excess fat.

For generations, family and friends of my mother, Gwyn Chesnut, have enjoyed her special brand of Southern cooking. After college, she worked for the Martha White Flour Company doing cooking classes. She also was one of the last "old stove" ladies for the Atlanta Gas Light Company.

Gingersnaps

An old folk remedy for upset stomach

⅔ cup shortening
½ cup sugar
1 egg
1 cup molasses or syrup
1 tablespoon vinegar

2 tablespoons cold water
4½ cups flour
1 tablespoon baking soda
1 tablespoon ginger

Cream shortening with sugar. Add beaten egg, then molasses, vinegar, and cold water. Sift flour, soda, and ginger and add to first mixture. Stir in as much of the flour as you can, then knead in the remainder. Roll out and cut into desired shapes (may be rolled thin or thick). Bake 10-12 minutes in moderate oven (350-375 degrees). Makes about 3 dozen cookies.

★
Donald D. Smart
Dick Dowling Camp #1295
Beaumont, Texas
★
Descendant of
Pvt. Francis M. Drake
Co. D, 21st Regiment, Texas
Infantry

Lemonade Pie

Nothing tastes better on a hot day in Dixie!

2 graham cracker pie crusts
1 (12-ounce) container frozen
   lemonade concentrate,
   thawed

2 cans Eagle Brand sweetened
   condensed milk
1 (8-ounce) container of Cool
   Whip

Prepare 2 pie shells made from graham cracker crumbs. Thaw the frozen lemonade concentrate. Blend the condensed milk, lemonade concentrate, and Cool Whip and pour into the pie shells. Freeze for at least 8 hours.

★
Thomas C. Harrill III
Chief Black Dog Camp #1829
Coffeyville, Kansas
★
Descendant of
1st Lt. William Henry Harrill
Co. B, 34th North Carolina
Regiment

Fruit Cocktail Cake

An old-fashioned Southern delicacy

1³/₄ cups sugar
2 cups flour
2 teaspoons baking soda

1 #2 can of fruit cocktail
¹/₄ cup brown sugar
¹/₂ cup coconut

*M*ix sugar, flour, baking soda, and fruit cocktail. Pour into an 8-inch by 14-inch greased and floured pan. Sprinkle brown sugar and coconut on top. Bake at 350 degrees until done.

Icing
1 stick butter
1 can Eagle Brand milk

¹/₂ cup pecans, chopped
¹/₂ cup coconut

*M*ix icing ingredients and cook in a saucepan until slightly thick. Remove from heat. Add pecans and coconut. Spread on cake while still warm.

★
Thomas G. Jones
Gen. Patrick R. Cleburne
Camp #436
Cleburne, Texas
★
Descendant of
Cpl. Emory Duncan Fisher
Co. K, 16th Louisiana Infantry

THE CONFEDERATE COOKBOOK

Microwave Pralines

A simple way to prepare this delicious candy

1 small container whipping
   cream
1 (1-pound) box light brown
   sugar

2 tablespoons margarine
2 cups pecans

★
Doug Peveto
Dick Dowling Camp #1295
Orange, Texas
★
Descendant of
Pvt. Samuel Peveto
Co. I, 13th Texas Cavalry

*M*ix whipping cream and sugar in large (8-cup) bowl. Put in microwave on full power for 2 minutes. Do not stir. (Depending on your microwave, cooking time may vary.) Take out and add margarine and pecans. Stir. Drop by tablespoons on aluminum foil. Makes about 4 dozen pralines.

Aunt Faye's Chocolate Pie

A family favorite at reunions, summer picnics, and holiday gatherings

1 cup sugar
⅓ cup cocoa
3 tablespoons butter, melted
2 eggs

½ cup evaporated milk
1 teaspoon vanilla
1 unbaked pie crust

★
Gregg Clemmer
Col. William Norris
Camp #1398
Germantown, Maryland
★
Descendant of
Matthew Bolling Clay
Co. C, 9th Virginia Infantry

*M*ix sugar and cocoa. Stir in melted butter and sugar. Add eggs and beat well. Add milk and vanilla. Pour into an unbaked pie crust and bake at 400 degrees for 12 minutes. Reduce heat to 350 degrees and bake for 10-15 minutes more. Watch baking time. Serves 6-8.

Old-Fashioned Coconut Cake

This version is a real winner!

½ cup real butter, softened
1½ cups sugar
2 eggs
2 eggs, separated

1 cup whole milk
2½ cups Southern biscuit self-
rising flour
1 teaspoon lemon flavoring

---

*C*ream butter and sugar. Add eggs 1 at a time. Add 2 egg yolks and beat well. Add milk and flour (alternate with flour last). Mix well. Add flavoring and mix well. Take 1-1½ cups batter to greased and floured 10-inch cake pan to make thin layers. Bake at 350 degrees on next to bottom rack for 10 minutes. Turn on rack to cool.

Frosting
2½ cups sugar
1 cup whole milk

1 (8-ounce) package of
coconut flakes
2 egg whites, beaten stiff

---

*M*ix sugar, milk, and coconut and bring to a boil for 5 minutes. Remove from heat and then add beaten egg whites. Stir well. Frost between layers and on top and sides of cake. If possible, let cake sit a couple of days before serving.

★
**Lamar B. Pender
Poplar Spring Grays
Camp #1700
Springhope, North Carolina**
★
**Great-great-grandson
Corp. David Crockett Young
Co. E, 24th Regiment, North
Carolina State Troops**

David C. Young lost his two younger brothers and his right arm in the Battle of Plymouth, North Carolina. He remained in the service until the end and never took the Oath of Allegiance. Mr. Young returned to farming and is buried outside of Meadow, North Carolina.

Zucchini Pineapple Cake

Just try it!

3 eggs
2 cups sugar
2 teaspoons vanilla
1 cup cooking oil
2 cups zucchini, peeled and
   grated
3 cups flour

1 teaspoon baking powder
¹/₂ cup raisins
1 teaspoon salt
1 teaspoon nuts
1 cup crushed pineapple,
   drained

*B*eat eggs until fluffy. Add sugar, vanilla, oil, and zucchini. Blend well. Add dry ingredients and mix well. Stir in pineapple, raisins, and nuts. Bake in a large greased and floured loaf pan or 2 small loaf pans. Bake in 325-degree oven for 1 hour. Cool in pan on wire rack. When cool, wrap in foil to store.

★
Peter M. Griffin
Col. William Norris
Camp #1398
Darnestown, Maryland
★
Great-great-grandson
Pvt. James Andrew
Jackson Coker
Co. H, 39th Georgia Infantry

Blueberry Cream Pie

A yummy way to enjoy fresh blueberries

1 cup sour cream
2 tablespoons all-purpose
    flour
¾ cup sugar
1 teaspoon vanilla extract
¼ teaspoon salt
1 egg, beaten
2½ cups fresh blueberries
1 unbaked 9-inch pastry shell

---

*C*ombine first 6 ingredients. Beat 5 minutes at medium speed with an electric mixer. Fold in blueberries. Pour filling into pastry shell. Bake at 400 degrees for 25 minutes.

Topping
3 tablespoons flour
3 tablespoons butter or
    margarine
3 tablespoons pecans or walnuts, chopped

---

*C*ombine topping ingredients, mixing well. Sprinkle over top of pie. Bake 10 additional minutes. Chill before serving.

★
George E. Linthicum III
Maj. Gen. I. Ridgeway Trimble
Camp #1836
Ellicott City, Maryland
★
1st cousin, twice removed
Capt. Charles Frederick
Linthicum
Adjutant, 8th Virgina Infantry

Capt. Linthicum was killed at Second Cold Harbor on June 5, 1864.

Opposite—Charles Frederick Linthicum
Adjutant, 8th Virginia Infantry

Seven-Up Pound Cake

Has a nice lemon-lime flavor

3 cups all-purpose flour, sifted
1/4 teaspoon salt
5 large eggs
3 cups sugar
1 cup butter, softened (no substitutions)

1/2 cup vegetable shortening
1 1/2 teaspoons vanilla extract
1/2 teaspoon lemon extract
1 cup 7-Up or other lemon-lime soda

Conwill Randolph Casey
Old Free State Camp #1746
Victoria, Virginia

Great-grandson
Pvt. Barzilla Harris Mixson
Co. H, 53rd Alabama Mounted Infantry

*P*reheat oven to 325 degrees. Grease a 12-cup bundt pan. Combine flour and salt in bowl. Combine remaining ingredients except soda in large mixing bowl. Beat at medium speed until light and fluffy, scrapping sides occasionally (about 5 minutes). Reducing speed to low, add the dry ingredients and soda, beginning and ending with dry ingredients. Bake for 1 1/2 hours or until toothpick inserted in center comes out clean. Cool in pan 15 minutes. Invert onto wire rack. Remove pan and cool completely. Serves 16.

Crème Brulee

Heaven in a custard cup

3 cups heavy cream
6 tablespoons sugar
6 egg yolks

2 teaspoons vanilla extract
½ cup light brown sugar

*P*reheat oven to 300 degrees. Heat the cream over boiling water and stir in the sugar. Beat the egg yolks until light and pour the hot cream over them gradually, stirring vigorously. Stir in the vanilla and strain the mixture into a baking dish. Place the dish in a pan containing 1 inch of hot water and bake until a silver knife inserted in the center comes out clean (about 35 minutes). Do not overbake—the custard will continue to cook from retained heat when it is removed from the oven. Chill thoroughly. Before serving, cover the surface with the brown sugar. Set the dish on a bed of cracked ice and put the crème under the broiler until the sugar is brown and melted. Serve immediately or chill again and serve cold.

★
Michael J. Glenn, Jr.
Eli Scott Dance Camp #1751
Street, Maryland
★
Descendant of
Cpl. James M. Newlon
Co. B, 8th Virginia Infantry

Missouri Confederate Cake

A very rich cake that freezes well

¹/₄ cup butter
1 cup sugar
1 egg
1¹/₄ cups flour, sifted
1 teaspoon baking powder
1 teaspoon baking soda

1 teaspoon salt
1 teaspoon cinnamon
2 cups apples, peeled and
    finely chopped
¹/₂ cup black walnuts, chopped

Cream butter and sugar. Beat in egg. Sift together flour, baking powder, baking soda, salt, and cinnamon. Blend into egg mixture. Fold in apples and nuts. Pour into a well-greased 8-inch square pan. Bake at 350 degrees for 35 minutes. Serve warm or cold with whipped cream. Serves 6-8.

★

Col. Robert Lewis Hawkins, Jr., (Ret.) U.S.A.
Brig. Gen. Mosby Monroe Parsons Camp #718
Jefferson City, Missouri

★

Great-grandson
Maj. William Alexander Marshall
1st Co, NE Missouri Regiment, 4th Missouri Cavalry

Maj. Marshall was an 1849 graduate of the St. Louis Medical School and served his regiment as a surgeon. Like many other doctors who served the Confederacy, he had his medical license revoked by the Federal government during Reconstruction. It was not restored until 1874. He died four years later and is buried in Newark, Missouri.

Sweet Potato Loaf Cake

Makes two cakes—one to give and one to enjoy

1½ cups sugar
½ cup vegetable oil
2 eggs
⅓ cup water
1 ¾ cups all-purpose flour
1½ teaspoons cinnamon
1 teaspoon ground nutmeg

1 teaspoon baking soda
½ teaspoon salt
1 cup sweet potatoes, cooked
   and mashed
½ cup pecans, chopped
½ cup raisins

Mix all ingredients well. Spoon batter into 2 greased and floured 1-pound empty coffee cans or loaf pans. Bake at 350 degrees for 1 hour. Cool in pans for 10 minutes. Remove from pans and allow to cool.

★
**Michael R. Bradley
SCV Camp #72
Tullahoma, Tennessee**
★
**Descendant of
Pvt. Andrew Jackson Bradley
Co. G, 1st Tennessee Infantry**

Andrew J. Bradley enlisted in Lincoln County, Tennessee, and was with the regiment at Appomattox. His first male child born after the war was named Andrew Lee Bradley, and that name is still used in the family.

Persimmon Cookies

A real Southern delight!

1 egg
1 cup sugar
1 cup fresh, ripe persimmon
   pulp
¹/₂ cup shortening
2 cups flour
¹/₂ teaspoon cinnamon

¹/₂ teaspoon cloves
¹/₂ teaspoon nutmeg
¹/₂ teaspoon baking soda
¹/₂ teaspoon salt
1 cup pecans, chopped (can
   use walnuts or pecans)
1 cup raisins

*P*reheat oven to 350 degrees. Cream the egg and sugar with a mixer. Stir in the persimmon pulp by hand. Sift the dry ingredients together. Slowly mix the dry mixture into the creamed egg and shortening. Stir in the nuts and raisins. Drop the batter by rounded teaspoon onto a greased cookie sheet. Bake at 350 degrees for 8-11 minutes. Makes about 24-30 mouth-watering cookies.

★
Larry Irion
Capt. William McKinney Irion
Camp #1799
Salem, Oregon
★
Descendant of
Capt. William McKinney Irion
Co. G, 32nd Mississippi
Infantry

Capt. Irion was wounded on October 8, 1862, while leading a charge at Perryville, Kentucky. He was captured and died a few weeks later in the prison at Harrodsburg, Kentucky.

No Bake Peanut Butter Pie

Cool and delicious

¹/₂ cup peanut butter
4 ounces cream cheese
¹/₂ cup milk
1 cup powdered sugar

1 (8-ounce) package Cool
   Whip
1 prepared graham cracker
   crust

*B*lend first 4 ingredients until smooth and fold in Cool Whip. Pour into crust. Freeze and enjoy.

★
Joseph W. Halsey
Col. Harry W. Gilmore
Camp #1388
Baltimore, Maryland
★
Great-grandson
Cpl. William Halsey
Co. I, 51st Virginia Infantry

THE CONFEDERATE COOKBOOK

Tea Cakes

A classic cookie

1 cup shortening	1 cup sugar
2½ cups flour	2 tablespoons milk
2 eggs	1 teaspoon baking powder
1 teaspoon vanilla	

*M*ix all ingredients. Roll out thin and cut with cutters into desired shapes. Place on greased cookie sheet and sprinkle with sugar. Bake at 350 degrees until light brown.

★
Scott Bell
James P. Douglas Camp #124
Tyler, Texas
★
Great-great-grandson
Pvt. John K. Bell
Co. H, 43rd Mississippi
Infantry

Pvt. Bell served faithfully until the end of the war. He migrated to Texas in 1868 and returned to farming. He died in 1879.

No Crust Coconut Pie

A new twist on an old favorite

4 eggs, beaten	¾ cup all-purpose flour
1¾ cups sugar	1 tablespoon vanilla
2 cups whole milk	2 cups coconut, shredded
¾ stick of butter, melted	

*C*ombine all ingredients in a large bowl and mix well with a spoon. Grease two 9-inch pie plates. Divide the mixture evenly. Bake at 350 degrees for 35 minutes. Yields two 9-inch pies.

★
James Ronald Moore
Camden Mounted Rifles
Camp #747
Camden County, Georgia

Index

Index

THE CONFEDERATE COOKBOOK

THE CONFEDERATE COOKBOOK

G

H

I

J

K

L

N

O

THE CONFEDERATE COOKBOOK

S